THE CRYPTOPEDIA

BY JONATHAN MABERRY

Ghost Road Blues

Dead Man's Song

Vampire Universe

Cryptopedia (with David F. Kramer)

THE CRYPTOPEDIA

A Dictionary of the Weird, Strange & Downright Bizarre

JONATHAN MABERRY

AND

DAVID F. KRAMER

CITADEL PRESS
Kensington Publishing Corp.
www.kensington.com

CITADEL PRESS BOOKS are published by

Kensington Publishing Corp.
850 Third Avenue
New York, NY 10022

All Kensington titles, imprints, and distributed lines are available at special quantity
discounts for bulk purchases for sales promotions, premiums, fund-raising, educational, or institutional use. Special book excerpts or customized printings can also be
created to fit specific needs. For details, write or phone the office of the Kensington
special sales manager: Kensington Publishing Corp., 850 Third Avenue, New York,
NY 10022, attn: Special Sales Department; phone 1-800-221-2647.

CITADEL PRESS and the Citadel logo are Reg. U.S. Pat. & TM Off.

First printing: September 2007

10 9 8 7 6 5 4 3 2 1

Printed in the United States of America

Library of Congress Control Number: 2007928704

ISBN-13: 978-0-8065-2819-9
ISBN-10: 0-8065-2819-2

From Jonathan: This is for Sara and Sam, my wife and son.

Contents

Acknowledgments   ix

Authors' Note   xi

INTRODUCTION: xv
The Larger World

CHAPTER ONE: 1
Astrology

CHAPTER TWO: 17
Cryptozoology

CHAPTER THREE: 36
Demons and Angels

CHAPTER FOUR: 82
Divination

CHAPTER FIVE: 97
Elves and Faeries

CHAPTER SIX: 120
ESP, Hauntings, and the Science of Parapsychology

CHAPTER SEVEN: 157
Herbs and Stones

CHAPTER EIGHT: 188
Mythology

CHAPTER NINE: 234
New Age

CHAPTER TEN: 290
Superstitions

CHAPTER ELEVEN: 317
UFOs and Alien Encounters

CHAPTER TWELVE: 361
Vodoun

CHAPTER THIRTEEN: 375
Wicca (Witchcraft, Olde and New)

Artist Index   389

— Acknowledgments —

The authors wish to express their heartfelt thanks to those wonderful folks who have helped us along the way with this project:

- Sara Crowe, the world's best literary agent.

- Michaela Hamilton, our editor at Citadel, who shared in the fun of this project.

- Kim Zagoren, editor of the late (and much missed) *Forever Underground*, the magazine that gave *The Cryptopedia* its start.

- The members of the HWA (Horror Writers Association), and the HWA-PA/NJ Chapter, in particular those members who helped with the research: Al Sirois, Kevin James Breaux, Daniel Choquette, Gregory Frost, Joe Augustyn, Kelly Jameson, Don Lafferty, Jon Jones, Kathy Ptacek, Wendy Zazo-Phillips, Tom Costello, Peter Lukacs, and Rich Newman.

- The members of the MWA (Mystery Writers Association) and the ITW (International Thriller Writers).

- Our amazing artists: Alan F Beck, Douglas Egolf, Lee Moyer, Jason Beam, Kathy Gold, Morbideus Goodell, Hervé Scott Flament, Jennifer Singleton, Abranda Icle Sisson, Bill Chancellor, Ken Meyer, Sam West-Mensch, Fran Kirsch, Sara Jo West, Lilian Broca, Leo Plaw, Andy Jones, Natascha Roeoesli, Michael Bateson, David Croston, Shareen Knight, Katerina Koukiotis, and Rita Isabel Sancho.

- The members of the GSHW (Garden State Horror Writers), Lunacon, the Philadelphia Science Fiction Society, and the SFWA (Science Fiction and Fantasy Writers of America).

- Our legion of friends and supporters online on the hundreds of forums and message groups that have let us reach out and share thoughts, insights, personal experiences, and much more.

•And to every person who opens this book . . . drawn by an open mind, a full spirit, and a sense of delight at the grandeur and complexity of the universe.

Thanks from David: *Research and Development:* Carol Haughey (The Good Witch of the Northeast), Trish Sanchez, and Josh Shaffer.

For Astral Travel: Cousins Deb and Chuck McCoy and Lifsha Zamalin.

Friends: Jeff Hauser, Ed Stradling, Vince D., Kelly Green, and to family living, dead, and undead.

Thanks from both: To Matthew Passarella, keep smiling, big guy! To all of our readers, please go to www.matthewsmiles.org and consider making a generous donation for research into cures for brain tumors and other forms of cancer.

— Authors' Note —

Visit the Web site www.vampireuniverse.com, home of *The Cryptopedia* and the other volumes in this series. There you'll find more information, artwork, profiles, and personal accounts of encounters with the Larger World. And visit www.cryptopediamagazine.com for the best in supernatural fiction and nonfiction.

THE CRYPTOPEDIA

━ *Introduction* ━
THE LARGER WORLD

THERE IS A LARGER WORLD than the one we can reach out and touch. The four dimensions—width, depth, height, and time—are even being called into question by new sciences like quantum physics. As we learn more about the ordinary mechanics of the so-called "real world," we are constantly discovering that everything we *know*, everything we thought was based on immutable physical laws, is almost certainly not what it seems. It turns out that things can travel faster than the speed of light. Alternate dimensions may soon be provable. Space folds and warps. Time is not a constant.

To the scientific mind of the early twenty-first century this is all new and jarring; it's disturbing because it isn't what we thought, or believed; to the scientific mind, this is world shaking. But to the spiritual community, in all its many and varied forms, this is neither novel nor particularly surprising. We've believed it all along.

To people studying ESP, remote viewing, astral projection, materialization, quantum physics and its potential is just another step toward the verification of what has been suspected, and even *believed*, since man was first capable of rational and abstract thought. Spiritual and psychic mediums, who channel nonphysical entities, don't bat at eye at the news that extra-dimensional space and even separate universes exist—it's not exactly news to them. To the millions who believe in precognition and divination, the scientific theory that all time is simultaneously occurring is old hat.

There are more people alive at any given point in history who believe in the supernatural than those who don't. Quite a lot more. Of course these beliefs vary, both subtly and dramatically. For some the belief in this "larger world" is part of their standard religious practices. Believers in the various world religions outnumber atheists and agnostics by a half million to one. For others, faith takes the form of a belief in luck—and luck is not scientific (that's chance). If folks only believed in chance, they would buy lottery cards whose numbers were randomly picked by machine. If divine intervention was only a myth, then no one would light a candle in church, pray in a foxhole, or silently plead for protection when a loved one is wheeled into surgery. Yet this happens every day, all over the world.

From a big picture perspective, the Larger World is both logical and orderly. There are clearly many things we cannot explain, even with the most subtle tests or the most sophisticated machines. If only a handful of people felt an unseen presence or saw a light in the sky, which clearly wasn't a puff of swamp gas, then the simple law of averages would be enough to discount them. But ghostly happenings have been seen by millions and studied by skeptics, many of whom could not adequately explain away the occurrences. As far as UFOs go . . . presidents, astronauts, heads of states, and hundreds of thousands of credible witnesses have seen them. Some governments even admit they exist. The most respected universities around the world regularly conduct studies regarding the nature of psi powers (such as clairvoyance, telekinesis, remote viewing, and materialization).

It's not a matter of "I want to believe." *We* do believe—the great, countless, global *we*. It's in our nature to do so.

The Cryptopedia collects many of these beliefs in thirteen chapters: Astrology; Cryptozoology; Demons and Angels; Divination; Elves, Fairies, and their Kin; ESP and the Science of Parapsychology; Herbs and Stones; Mythology;

New Age; Superstitions; UFOs, Vodoun; and Wicca. Does this cover the complete range of worldwide beliefs? Of course not, but it presents more of them in one place than you'll find anywhere else. Each of these themes includes a short essay, which will give you a broad view of that aspect of the Larger World, and then an extensive dictionary of the area's key terms, people, places, events, and phenomena. Peppered throughout each chapter are sidebars on a range of topics, some serious, some fun.

The Cryptopedia never takes a stand against any beliefs, even those not shared by the authors. After all, no one can ever make the statement that someone else's view of the spiritual workings of the world is false. Not even doctors of quantum physics can do that. So, join us as we explore the many pathways through the Larger World. This is going to be fun, because we, like you, believe.

— Chapter One —
ASTROLOGY

FEW DESIRES ARE AS FERVENT as the one to know the future. In our modern and "enlightened" age, some might blanch at the prospect of rifling through an animal's entrails to divine the future or scoff at looking for signs in tea remnants. But to face the day without the benefit of checking a daily horoscope—*that* would be unthinkable!

According to a 1996 Gallup Poll, 25 percent of those surveyed believed that the positions of the stars and planets affected their lives. However, similar studies reveal that 9 out of 10 Americans know their astrological sign and that a staggering 70 percent of them would occasionally consult their horoscope for advice and direction.

So what does this all mean? Well, if those numbers are accurate, then more people believe in the tenets of astrology than in any single religious belief worldwide. Let that thought simmer for a moment. Indeed, when it comes to the contents of your average daily newspaper, the inclusion of a horoscope is equally as important as local news, sports scores, or the Sunday comics.

The term astrology comes from the Greek *astron,* or star. *Logos,* is the basis for the familiar suffix "logy," meaning discipline or study. People have been looking to the heavens for inspiration and information since the days of ancient Babylon and, quite likely, many years before that.

The basic tenet of astrology is simple: The positions of celestial bodies somehow play a role in people's lives, personalities, attributes, and destinies.

The idea of "horoscopic astrology"—or the plotting of charts to gain information and insight—developed in Egypt in the second century B.C.E.[1] It was spawned from an even earlier Greek tradition and writings. These charts were plotted from a specific moment in time called the *ascendant*. The ancient Greek word for ascendant was *horoskopos*—from which we get "horoscope." Other terms for horoscopes include: vitasphere; sky-map; birth chart; celestial map; radix; and soulprint.

Almost every culture of the world has its own version of astrology, and one could devote an entire life to the study of just one of them. For the purposes of this chapter, we'll focus on four main types. *Natal Astrology,* which plots charts from the moment of birth; *Katarchic* or *Electional Astrology,* where a particular moment in someone's life acts as the beginning of the analysis; *Horary Astrology,* which seeks to answer questions posed for specific times; and *Mundane Astrology,* which applies charts to historical events, the weather, for example, or almost anything else.

As the sun travels across the heavens each year it traces a path called the *ecliptic*—the movements of the sun and nearby planets are called the *zodiac.*

In western astrology the zodiac is divided into twelve sections called houses. The most familiar form of this practice—sun-sign astrology—is a simplified version that focuses only on the position of the sun within the twelve signs of the zodiac, which are as follows:

•**Aries, the Ram (March 21–April 19):** Fire sign; ruled by the planet Mars. Those born under Aries tend to be creative and adaptive, but like its namesake animal, can be too headstrong and determined for their own good. They are often quick to anger, but also quick to calm. They often possess a quick wit and a good sense of humor. Sometimes their energy and eagerness cause them to begin projects that are never finished.

1. B.C.E.: Before Christian Era—a modern version of B.C.

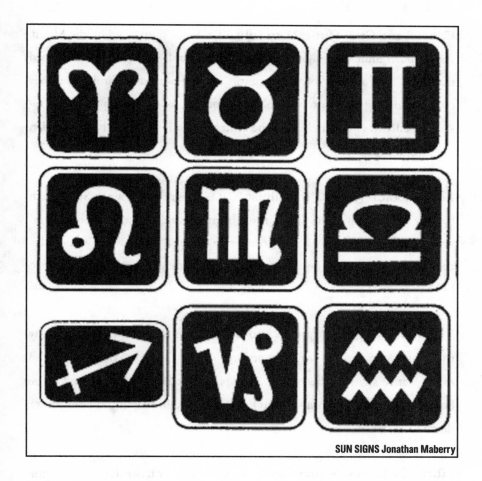

SUN SIGNS Jonathan Maberry

•**Taurus, the Bull (April 20 to May 20):** Earth sign; ruled by the planet Venus. Also like their namesake animal, Taurians can be strong, stubborn, and difficult to talk out of their opinions and views. When dealing with a difficult Taurian, it is sometimes better to appeal to their emotions rather than reason. They also tend to be practical and generous.

•**Gemini, the Twins (May 21 to June 20):** Air sign; ruled by the planet Mercury. The key to the personality of the Gemini is duality. They're versatile, but in extremes this can be seen as erratic and impulsive. Overall, this is a sign of contradictions.

- **Cancer, the Crab (June 21 to July 22):** Water sign; ruled by the Moon. People born under this sign tend to be "old school" and rely on established tradition. They are fond of the domestic life, love home and family, and they embrace history (almost to the point of choosing to live in the past). They respond badly to criticism, but can be selfless when it comes to humanitarian pursuits and causes.

- **Leo, the Lion (July 23 to August 22):** Fire sign; ruled by the Sun. Much like the famed king of the jungle, those born under the sign of Leo make natural leaders. However, with this great pride comes a price—when a lion falls, they tend to fall hard. They often possess magnetic personalities and love to be the center of attention.

- **Virgo, the Virgin (August 23 to September 22):** Earth sign; ruled by the planet Mercury. The virgin is perhaps one of the most complicated and introspective signs of the zodiac. They possess keen minds and tend to be both persuasive speakers and good listeners—though they could bore you to death with the details.

- **Libra, the Scales (September 23 to October 22):** Air sign; ruled by the planet Venus. This sign is associated with the tenets of balance and justice, though they can be a little heavy-handed in getting their message of goodwill across. They possess great empathy and are always ready to help out a friend or loved one. Fiery proponents of the underdog, even when such support might not be a wise course of action.

- **Scorpio, the Scorpion (October 23 to November 21):** Water sign; ruled by the planet Pluto (although in August 2006, Pluto was demoted from planetary status at a meeting of the International Astronomical Union in Prague). Those born under the sign of the scorpion are often fearless and are quickly spurred into action. However, this zeal can often lead to arrogance and a refusal to entertain different points of view.

•**Sagittarius, the Archer (November 22 to December 21):** Fire sign; ruled by the planet Jupiter. Those born under the sign of Sagittarius are generally cheerful and full of energy, which can be of great help in finishing projects. Sagittarians need to be careful in the application of these energies, though, as they might wear themselves out in the process. They are known for their happy and cheerful dispositions.

•**Capricorn, the Goat (December 22 to January 19):** Earth sign; ruled by the planet Saturn. The sign of many philosophers and great thinkers, Capricorns are also organized. They actively pursue knowledge on a broad range of topics, but their enthusiasm can often be viewed as extreme. Often preferring to be alone, they sometimes possess psychic abilities.

•**Aquarius, the Water Bearer (January 20 to February 18):** Air sign; ruled by the planet Uranus. Those born under the sign of Aquarius might also prefer to be alone when it comes to thinking deeply and making important decisions. They often dedicate themselves to humanitarian causes and topics. Aquarians actively seek out knowledge about all things and do not hesitate to share it with others.

•**Pisces, the Fish (February 19 to March 20):** Water sign; ruled by the planet Neptune. The sign of the fish is perhaps the most grounded and humble in the zodiac. Pisces is unusually generous and trusting, sometimes to the point of being easily taken advantage of by others.

While astrology is often similar throughout the world, there are some practices that seem to be polar opposites (to coin a phrase). Such is the case with Western and Chinese astrology.

THE EYE OF THE ASTRAL PLANE Alan F. Beck

The difference between the two is simply a matter of perception and measurement. Western astrology is based on the imaginary path traveled by the sun through the heavens. The Chinese plot the movements of the stars and planets in relation to the North Pole and the Equator—leading to a lunar zodiac that changes from year to year (rather than a solar one that changes month to month). As in the Western conception, the Chinese zodiac names each house after animals—and it is believed that those born during like years share similar attributes.

The legends surrounding the choice of namesake animals are many. In some stories, the Jade Emperor invited all of the animals of the world to a New Year's celebration, of which only 12 arrived. In other versions, it was the job of the crafty rat to spread the word about the celebration. He tricked the cat (who was once his friend) into thinking the banquet was the following day and the cat consequently slept through it. It is said that after that, the cat swore revenge, and this explains why the two are mortal enemies to this day.

Attributes of the signs of the Chinese zodiac (*shengxiao*):

•**Rat:** Despite the negative connotation of the Rat here in the West, the Chinese (as well as other Eastern cultures) view the humble rodent as quick of wit and wily in both escape and gaining material objects. It is viewed as an all around good-luck charm. It is said that those born in the year of the Rat possess charm, taste, and good humor and make for excellent and devoted friends. However, behind that charming façade, the Rat won't hesitate to use his or her wiles to get what they want and promote their own personal agendas. While Rats show extreme loyalty and devotion to those they view as friends, they can be seen as temperamental and argumentative by others. Nevertheless, the Rat enjoys trading verbal barbs and comments with others, whether or not such things are asked of him or her. When it comes to a search for a companion, the Rat should seek out a Dragon or a Monkey.

•**Pig:** Another animal overlooked in Western culture, the Pig is one of the most honest and generous signs in the Chinese zodiac. Pigs are said to possess impeccable manners and neatness, which also belies their conception here. Often, those who don't know them well view the Pig's desire for perfection as snobbery, but it's merely part of the animal's lavish nature. Those born under the sign of the Pig are intensely devoted to their friends and family, and will do almost anything to ensure their happiness. If any fault can be drawn, it would be that sometimes the Pig is so giving that he or she might be taken advantage of by others. The sign is known for having a positive outlook seemingly possessing a pair of rose-colored contact lenses. In this respect, the Pig makes a great friend and companion as he or she is loathe to dwell on the negative. The best love match for a Pig would be a Rabbit or Goat.

•**Ox:** If you're looking for someone who is a born leader, dependable to a fault, and has the potential for greatness, then look no further than the Ox. Not known for speed in thought or action, the Ox tends to move from point to point with great deliberation, forethought, and care. This behavior might make others view the Ox as overly serious or stuffy, and indeed, in social situations, he or she can hardly be considered the life of the party. However, a fierce dedication to friends, family, and ideals are the earmarks of this stately sign. If you're looking for a thoughtful and unbiased opinion, just ask an Ox. Those of the sign should look for love and companionship in the Snake or Rooster.

•**Dog:** Yet another example of how the East differs from the West is the sign of the Dog. While dogs might be man's best friend in the English speaking world, the canine can sometimes be untrusting of strangers and others according to the Chinese zodiac. Once you've brought a Dog into your fold of friends, however, you will have a loyal compatriot with a keen sense of right and wrong. He or she will also be a great and valued listener to you. The Dog possesses a sharp head for business, though they can be temperamental, somewhat narrow-minded and prone to mood swings. The restless Dog is also ever in search of a task to occupy his or her mind, and can begin to obsess over small things when not otherwise engaged. While a Dog might have trouble finding love, the best matches for one are a Tiger or Horse.

•**Tiger:** Yet another born leader of the Chinese zodiac, the Tiger seems to possess an air of authority and power, and others seem to follow his or her lead. Tigers are generally ambitious and crave control in all situations. Tigers are also highly sexual and are generally considered charismatic and attractive—seduction is their idea of the hunt. However, these emotionally driven folks are prone to mood swings and outright temper tantrums when things don't go as they plan. Tigers can also be overly sensitive and not respond well to stress. However, once a Tiger learns to roll with the punches, they can live happy and fulfilled lives. In love, the best match for a Tiger is the Horse or Dog.

•**Rooster:** The Rooster is quite a bit like its Western counterpart—always ready to puff out its chest and crow loud and long. Roosters are quick with their wits, and are resourceful and practical. It is said that Roosters are psychic because they view the world so keenly. A Rooster would make a great chemist, doctor, accountant, or attorney. The Rooster strives for perfection, but might spend an inordinate amount of time on personal grooming. Being the center of attention is the drug of choice of the sign, and they adore parties and enjoyable social situations. Watch that they don't hold others up to their own impossibly high standards. When it comes to love, the proud Rooster should seek out an Ox or a Snake.

•**Rabbit:** Rabbits are protective of and devoted to a wide circle of family and friends (sometimes to the point of depriving themselves so that others might benefit). Despite these good qualities, the rabbit is still a timid creature, and tends to shy away from confrontation—and some might consider the humble bunny to be something of a pushover. Rabbits are also domestic creatures, and their "dens" tend to be welcome places that are well decorated. When it comes to love and romance, the Rabbit is best matched with a Goat or Pig.

•**Monkey:** Like their animal namesakes, those born in the year of the Monkey can be real swingers—both figuratively and literally. They'll often vacillate between groups of friends to keep themselves entertained. They also love nothing more than having a good time and being the center of attention. Monkeys often possess a sharp wit and make for good listeners. They have a natural curiosity and love to collect information on a myriad of topics so that the can regale their peers with all they know. However, Monkeys seem to lack high morals and tend to be deficient in self-control—sometimes leading to addictions associated with food, drugs, alcohol, and other activities that are best enjoyed in moderation. When it comes to love, a Monkey is best paired with the Rat or Dragon.

•**Dragon:** The sign of the Dragon is the luckiest in the Chinese zodiac. They possess enough charm, charisma, and energy to influence others and get what they want. The Dragon is lucky when it comes to romance, and their friends are always quick to seek them out for advice on love and other matters. The Dragon also has the highest potential for greatness, but their egos can sometimes get in the way. When it comes to defeat, the word "grace" is simply not in the Dragon's lexicon. They make for powerful and potent leaders, and woe to the person who would cross them or question their opinions or judgments. When it comes to love, the best match for a Dragon is a Monkey or a Rat.

•**Horse:** Just like in an old cowboy song, Horses need land, lots of land, so they can roam free. Those born under the sign of the Horse are good with matters related to money and love to travel and see new places. They are true spiritual nomads, often drifting from place to place to seek out new people and experiences. The Horse is just as untamed when it comes to matters of love and can be aggressive in seeking out companionship. While some Horses might seem standoffish, they actually have a sincere desire to fit in with the crowd. When it comes to romance, the best match for a Horse is a Dog or Tiger.

•**Snake:** These charismatic creatures seem to be as comfortable in the boardroom as they are in the bedroom. With regard to matters of the heart, the sexy serpent knows all about the art of seduction. They also have a keen head for business and are good with money. When a Snake starts on a project or undertaking, you can bet the farm that they will see it through to completion. While some might view such behavior as stingy, Snakes tend to put a little more thought into decisions before making them. They also tend to be introspective, though others might view these hours spent reflecting as signs of laziness. In matters of the heart, the best match for the Snake is a Rooster or an Ox.

•**Goat:** Those born under the sign of the Goat are creative and prone to contemplation. They make for fine craftspeople or artists, though they are notoriously disorganized and tend to bore quickly with dry and repetitive business tasks. Goats tend to be hypersensitive in all matters, and are very susceptible to feelings of anxiety or worry. They are also said to make very attentive lovers and spare no emotional expense when it comes to lavishing affection on their partners. Once a Goat learns to relax, they can live a very fulfilling life. The best romantic match for a Goat would be a Pig or a Rabbit.

The following is a glossary of common astrology terms:

Air Signs   Gemini, Libra, and Aquarius are generally associated with the element of Air and are purported to foster communication and the powers of the mind.

Arc   When plotting the path of celestial objects, the arc is the representation of the curved path the object travels.

Ascendant   Celestial activity that occurs over the eastern horizon of one's birthplace at the moment of birth. The ascendant figures prominently in the plotting of one's horoscope as well as in his or her personal and professional lives.

Aspect   The angular relationship between two celestial bodies, this can refer to two planets, or a planet and some other point, such as a star, a comet, etc.

Astral Twins   Unlike biological twins, this relationship refers to two persons whose horoscopes are alike, but are otherwise unrelated.

Astrolabe   This predecessor to the sextant was used by both astronomers and astrologers, as well as for navigation at sea. After the invention of the greatly improved sextant in the eighteenth century, they have mainly been employed in the plotting of horoscopes.

Astrologer   Someone who practices astrology.

Astrologian   A teacher of astrology.

Astrologist   This term pertains to those who believe in the science of astrology, but do not practice it.

Barren Signs   The signs of Gemini, Leo, and Virgo are sometimes associated with the concept of infertility. The signs of Aries, Sagittarius, and Aquarius are somewhat related to this idea, and are often termed "semi-barren."

Benefic   This term describes planets and aspects of astrology that are positive and helpful. Jupiter and Venus are considered to be highly beneficial, while Mercury, the moon and the sun are purported to be only moderately so.

Bestial Signs   This term applies to signs of the zodiac that are associated with animals, such as Aries (the Ram), Taurus (the Bull), and Capricorn (the Ram).

Bicorporeal Signs   This term applies to signs of the zodiac that are either double-bodied, or associated with duality or dual experiences, such as Gemini, Sagittarius, and Pisces.

Birthtime   In astrology, this represents the beginning of life, when an infant draws its first breath outside of the womb.

Cardinal Signs   These signs of the zodiac are associated with the cardinal points on a compass: Aries (east); Cancer (north); Libra (west); and Capricorn (south).

Chart   The generic term for a plotted horoscope.

Composite Chart   A plotted horoscope composed of two or more separate charts. A composite offers more information and advice than a single chart.

Constellation   The term for a fixed group of stars.

Copernicus   A sixteenth century Polish astronomer who was among the first in the Western world to hypothesize that the earth revolved around the sun (rather than the opposite). The more enlightened Eastern world came to the same conclusion in India in about the ninth century BCE.

Cusp   The term for the "line" that divides the houses of the zodiac.

Diurnal   This term refers to the Southern Hemispheres of a horoscope and celestial activity that takes place during the day.

Diurnal Signs   Signs of the zodiac such as Aquarius, Capricorn, Libra, Pisces, and Sagittarius that are associated with the Southern Hemispheres of a horoscope.

Earth Signs   Signs of the zodiac such as Capricorn, Taurus, and Virgo that are associated with the element of Earth.

Eclipse   From the Greek *ekleipô,* meaning to vanish or conceal, this term describes an astronomical event where one object moves directly into the shadow of another—as in the case of lunar or solar eclipse.

Electional Astrology   An aspect of astrology where the person plotting the chart determines the best possible time to take action (regarding, for example, travel, relationships, job changes). This process is most often achieved by plotting into the future and working one's way back to this crucial period.

Elements   The four aspects of the universe (Air, Earth, Fire, and Water) that compose all things. Various signs and symbols of the zodiac are often associated with one of these elements.

Equator   The imaginary line that divides the earth into Northern and Southern Hemispheres.

Equinox   From the Latin *aequi nox,* or "equal night," an event that occurs twice each year during which there are equal periods of daylight and darkness. These periods are commonly referred to as the Vernal, or Spring, Equinox and the Autumnal Equinox, which not surprisingly occurs in the fall.

Event Chart   A horoscope that is plotted according to a particular date and time in the hope of gaining insight into a specific event.

Fertility Signs   An aspect of astrology pertaining to agriculture. Periods when the moon occupies Cancer, Scorpio, and Pisces are said to be good times to plant crops.

Fire Signs   The signs Leo, Aries, and Sagittarius, which are associated with fire.

Fruitful Signs   Pisces, Scorpio, and Cancer, which are associated with water and fertility.

Gregorian Calendar   The term for the current conception of our calendar—created in 1582 by Italian physician Aloysius Lilius (1510–1576) and instated by Pope Gregory XIII (1502–1585), who, consequently, grabbed all of the namesake glory. This new conception replaced the Julian calendar, begun by Julius Caesar in 46 B.C.E. and its predecessor, the Roman calendar. When referencing dates, the term OS, meaning "old style" is used for the Julian conception and NS or "new style" for the Gregorian.

Heliocentric   A term describing celestial measurement that uses the sun as a central point of reference, as well as other issues that relate to the sun.

Heliocentrism   The astronomical belief and concept that the sun is the center of the solar system (or universe).

House   Any one of the twelve separate sections of a horoscope. Each represents a particular period in the life of the person for whom it's plotted.

Horary   This term comes from the Latin *hora* or hour, and is a branch of astrology in which charts are plotted for an exact time period (often an hour, hence the name). By this method, an astrologer can offer advice and guidance for actions concerning very specific events.

Julian Calendar   The predecessor to the modern Gregorian Calendar, this conception was enacted by Julius Caesar in 46 B.C.E. It replaced the previous Roman calendar, which had many technical hitches in relation to leap years and other celestial activity.

Locational Astrology   The plotting of a horoscope in relation to the place a person lives or might wish to move to someday.

Lunar   Concepts and objects related to the moon.

Medical Astrology   A branch of astrology that studies the human body and the diseases affecting it using a horoscope as a model—probably best for ailments of the easily curable variety.

Meteorological Astrology   The practice of predicting the weather (and potentially dangerous weather conditions) through the use of astrology.

Mute Signs   Signs of the zodiac that are associated with mute creatures—such as Pisces, Scorpio, and Cancer. This is most likely a metaphorical concept, as the majority of the signs have the inability to speak.

Natal Astrology   A branch of astrology that plots horoscopes from the time of birth, and predicts the outcome of someone's life.

Occidental   While this term means "Western," in astrology it pertains to a celestial body that sets and rises after the sun.

Orbit   The path a celestial object follows as it travels around another.

Planet   From the Greek *planetes,* or "wanderers," a blanket term that describes a celestial body in orbit around a star. From an astrological standpoint, this would describe any celestial body visible from the earth that moves, as opposed to stars, which tend to remain in fixed positions in the sky.

Polarity   Any aspect of the relationship between two opposite signs of the zodiac.

Solar   From the Latin, *sol,* this term pertains to things relating to the sun.

Solar Chart   A horoscope that is plotted based on the position of the sun. It is often used when someone's date of birth is unknown.

Solstice   From the Latin *sol stitium,* or "sun standstill," one of the two periods when the sun reaches its farthest point either north or south of the equator. During the Summer Solstice, which occurs in June, the sun travels at its slowest pace, the result being the longest day of the year. Conversely, during the Winter Solstice in December, the sun travels at its fastest, creating the shortest day of the year.

Terrestrial   Matters and concepts related to the earth.

Vernal   From the Latin *vernus,* matters and concepts relating to the spring.

Vocational Astrology   A branch of astrology that offers spiritual guidance in the choice of careers. A vocational astrologer might plot a chart for a client to see if a job change might yield positive or negative results.

Waning   The aspect of the lunar cycle that begins with the full moon and ends with the new moon—in essence, the moon growing smaller.

Waxing   The aspect of the lunar cycle that begins with the new moon and ends with the full moon—in essence, the moon growing larger.

— Chapter Two —
CRYPTOZOOLOGY

FIRST, LET'S MAKE IT CLEAR that cryptozoology is a real science. The name, coined in 1959 by Bernard Heuvelmans (1916–2001),[2] refers to the scientific search for unknown animals. Not monsters or supernatural beings, but animals that are believed to exist. However, they have not yet been included in the official fossil record of known creatures. Known as *cryptids,* these "hidden" animals are the focus of serious scientific investigation by legitimate scientists in every country around the world. Sure, there are also guys out there who fake evidence (such as Roger Patterson and Robert Gimlin who fudged the legendary Bigfoot film footage in 1967, or Christian Spurling, who fooled the world with his 1934 photo of the Loch Ness Monster). Nevertheless, there are plenty of scientists and researchers in the field using sound scientific methods to prove—and in many cases disprove—the existence of cryptids.

Consider how few of the world's many animals were known to science even a century ago. Just two hundred years ago, the duck-billed platypus was considered a myth (at best) or an outright lie (at worst). It turns out a web-footed, egg laying aquatic mammal with a poisonous sting *did* and *does* exist. Similarly, other species that were once widely accepted as fakes or myths, such as the giant squid, mountain gorilla, and Komodo dragon have all been proven to be very real. Our world is vast, despite advancements in travel, deforesta-

2. *On the Track of Unknown Animals,* originally published 1955, republished in English by Kegan Paul, 1995

tion, and communication. Tools of scientific verification have also made huge inroads into mapping and cataloging. Nevertheless, there is a long way to go before anyone can say, with total accuracy, that something does not exist.

In May of 2005, a new species of medium-sized, long-tailed tree dwelling monkey, dubbed highland mangabey *(Lophocebus kipunji)* was discovered in Tanzania, East Africa. In February of 2006, a section of untouched Indonesian forest was explored in which dozens of new animal and plant species were discovered,[3] including butterflies, frogs, giant rhododendron, and a type of honeyeater bird previously unknown to science. The following month *National Geographic News* broke the story of a new shark species (dubbed *Mustelus hacat)* discovered in Mexico's Gulf of California. And in June of 2006, scientists at Hebrew University in Jerusalem excavated a cave in which they discovered eight previously unrecorded species of animal: four seawater and freshwater crustaceans and four terrestrial species of invertebrates.

It happens all the time.

Given all of this, why is it so difficult to accept the possibility of even stranger creatures out there? After all, a Coelacanth, a fish believed to have been extinct for 70 million years was caught alive in 1939 off the coast of Madagascar. Dinosaurs were supposed to have died out five million years ago. Yet science has *proven* that one species still exists. And then there is the Graptolites, a marine species believed to have become extinct 300 million years ago. It was reliably reported living as recently as 1882. Who knows—the Loch Ness monster, or Champ from Lake Champlain could be other ancient species that somehow dodged the evolutionary bullet. To say this is impossible is both arrogant and silly.

The following is an extensive glossary of terms, cryptids, people, and events that form a need-to-know body of knowledge for anyone interested in the science of unknown creatures.

3. Reported by BBC News on February 7, 2006.

Abu Gogo   A race of tiny humans, approximately 3.5 feet tall, descended from *Homo Erectus,* who have recently been moved out of mythology into hard science. Nicknamed "Hobbits," scientists found their remains on the island of Flores, in Indonesia.

Agogwe   A Tanzanian (East Africa) hominid that stands only 4-feet tall. It has a densely muscled upper torso, a gorilloid head, and is covered in rust-colored hair.

Ahool   A night-hunting giant bat creature reported for centuries by the Sudanese Muslims of Java.

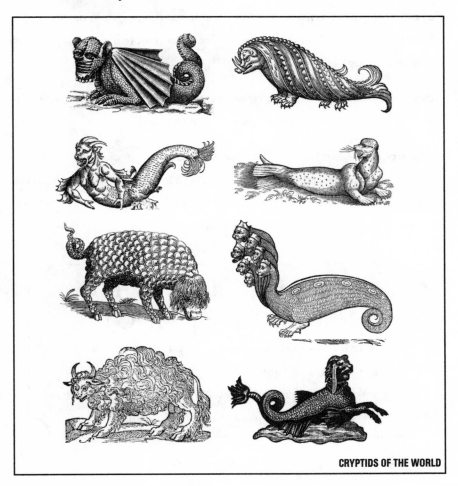

CRYPTIDS OF THE WORLD

Almas   A species of hominid sighted in the wastelands of Siberia. They are approximately the same height and build as humans, though covered in coarse reddish-gray hair.

Altamaha-ha   A 30-foot sea monster frequently sighted around the scattered islands of South Georgia and the South Sandwich Islands. Cryptozoologists have theorized that it is either a new species of freshwater dolphin,[4] or one showing mutative changes. Altamaha-ha may holdover from an earlier era, perhaps a Basilosaurus, a type of cetacean believed to have become extinct in the Eocene Age, forty million years ago.

Barmanou (also Barmanu)   The Barmanous (literally "big hairy one") is a large, hairy hominid believed to live in the most remote mountain passes of Pakistan and Afghanistan.

Beast of Bodmin Moor   A gigantic hunting cat of unknown species believed to hunt in the region of Bodmin Moor, Cornwall.

Beast of Gevaudan (Also Le Bête de Gevaudan)   A murderous (and extremely well-documented) monster resembling a large wolf that terrorized the Auvergne and South Dordogne regions of France between 1764 and 1767. It is believed to have killed nearly 100 people, mostly women and children.

⊣ BAD EYESIGHT OR ⊢ POOR REPORTING?

The serious cryptozoologist has to put up with a lot of flak, pretty much from all sides. Since this is a relatively new science there is always resistance from the older and more established scientific community. This is some-

---

4. Long-snouted freshwater dolphins include the Ganges River Dolphin *(Platanista gangetica gangetica)* and Indus River Dolphin *(Platanista gangetica minor)*.

what unfair: Many of the world's more exotic species have been added to the known fossil record in the last century, and new species are discovered every day. The popular press also takes potshots at cryptozoologists, accusing many of them of being crackpots who see monsters that aren't there. Sadly, hoaxes like the infamous Bigfoot film footage and the classic "Nessie" photograph don't do much to help this image. Also serious ongoing cryptozoologic studies in Loch Ness—and other places around the world—seldom yield huge or immediate results. Another hurdle is the fact that the vast majority of cryptid sightings fall into the same class as most UFO sightings; they really aren't what witnesses claim them to be. Mermaid stories are almost certainly sightings of manatees by sailors who had way too much rum and not enough contact with actual females of their own species. Tourists have reported encountering "Sea Monsters" like the Giant sturgeon or a big gar fish. The first person to describe a giraffe was almost certainly not believed (and there is documentation about a Chinese traveler who came back from Africa with stories of a towering "monster"). Yet if you eliminate the 99 percent of the hoaxes, incidents of misreporting, poor eyesight, and encounters with known species (but which are unknown to the witness), there is still 1 percent that can't be explained away or dismissed. It is here, in this narrow range between the known and the possible that cryptozoologists work.

Bergman's Bear A gigantic bear called the "God Bear" by the natives of the Kamatchka Peninsula in Russia was first believed to be a myth. Later it was proven to be a new, but extinct, species now known as *Ursus arctos piscator.*

Bessie (also **South Bay Bessie)** Bessie is a lake cryptid that has been spotted off and on since 1817 in and around Lake Erie, Pennsylvania.

Big Bird A giant batlike bird spotted in the Rio Grande Valley. It is reported to stand five feet tall, with great leathery wings, and a face like a night ape.

Black Tiger A pseudo-melanistic[5] tiger of unknown species bagged by a hunter in South Delhi that measured 8.5 feet long.

Blobs (also **Globster)** The nickname given to any of the several masses of unknown tissue washed up on beaches around the world (particularly in Bermuda, New Zealand, and Tasmania).

Blue Tiger (also **Maltese Tiger)** Great hunting cats frequently sighted throughout the Fujian Province of China in the early twentieth century.

Brosnie A lake monster living in Lake Brosno frequently reported by residents of Benyok (a few hundred miles from Moscow, Russia).

Bunyip A creature of Aboriginal myth with some of the qualities of a hell-hound. It is often described as being as big as a moderate-sized calf. The name comes from the Aboriginal word for "spirit."

Buru A Cryptid infrequently spotted in the valleys between the Sub-Himalayas in India that sounds remarkably like a sauropod, possessing vestigial forelegs, a large tail that acts both as support when standing and a counterbalance when running, and a large head with a big mouth filled with rows of sharp teeth.

---

5. Melanism is a genetic condition resulting in increased amounts of black or nearly black pigmentation on skin, hair, or feathers. Pseudo-melanism in tigers is a defect in their natural marking: Stripes are darker and broader, so that they partially or totally obscure the yellow body hairs.

Caddy (also **the Sea Hag)**   A large serpentine sea creature, 40–50 feet in length, with a ridged or knobbed spine and flippers shaped like those of a humpback whale. Caddy has been spotted in the waters of Cadboro Bay, near Vancouver Island, B.C.

Canvey Island Monster   A possible bipedal dinosaur species whose badly decomposed remains were found on the beach of Canvey Island in 1954.

Centre for Fortean Zoology   A professional organization of Cryptozoologists founded in 1992 by Jon Downes.

Champ   A water monster reminiscent of a plesiosaur, frequently seen (and even photographed) in Lake Champlain, which borders New York, Vermont, and Quebec.

Chupacabra   *El Chupacabra,* which translates as "sucker of goats," is a bizarre being that has three powerful claws on each hand, a ruff of tall spines running from skull to tailbone, mottled skin, and a voracious appetite. It has been spotted throughout Latin America and even into the American Southwest.

Coleman, Loren   (b.1947) A noted contemporary cryptozoologist and author of seventeen books (and more than three hundred articles on the subject). Coleman is frequently seen on cryptozoology-based shows on A&E, the Discovery Channel, the History Channel, and others.

Con Rit   A Vietnamese monster centipede reported to be 60-feet long, with a chitinous, segmented body. It has leglike filaments sprouting from each segment that measure over 2-feet long.

Cryptid   Cryptids are creatures that are believed to exist (or to have once existed) but for which there are no existing physical records or evidence. The science of cryptozoology is built around discovering proof of these creatures so that they can be moved from the long list of "unknown" animals to proven additions to the ever-growing fossil record.

Devil Bird (also **Ulama, Maha Bakamuna)**   A species of owl (*bubo nipalensis*) only recently discovered and classified. It lingered for centuries as a mythic monster bird in folklore among the natives of Sri Lanka and India. The devil bird now joins the ranks of a small but growing number of animals, including the mountain gorilla, okapi, platypus, and the coelacanth, that have crossed out of myth and into reality.

Dobhar-Chu (also **Dobhar-chú, Dobarcu, Doyarchu, Dhuragoo)**   A doglike, Gaelic monster (literally, "waterhound") that measures about 8 feet from tooth to tail. It has a centuries-old reputation in Cornwall as a man-killer.

Dragon of the Ishtar Gate (also **Sirrush)**   A saurian creature depicted on the walls of Babylon (built circa 575 B.C.E.) that is cited in the Apocrypha[6] as a dragon kept in the Temple of Be by King Nebuchadnezzar.

⊰ DRAGONS AND ⊱ DINOSAURS

Dragons are one of the most common monsters in world myth. Many of them share similar physical qualities, even in cultures whose legends developed long before there was any contact with other dragon-believing peoples. Cryptozoologists, along with archeologists, anthropologists, zoologists, and paleontologists have speculated for years about this. The most commonly

6. The collection of stories which are claimed by some to be excised sections of the Bible. Most major religions, such as the Catholic Church, and many biblical scholars dispute the authenticity of these stories.

advanced theory is that various cultures, in the course of agriculture, building, or exploration have actually unearthed the bones of dinosaurs. The age of the earth and the ages of the dinosaurs, was an unknown concept to them. It was, therefore, understandable that these peoples would have assumed that the bones were of something that had only recently died. It's only a short step from the finding of weird bones to the creation of a myth; and myths sometimes endure as stubbornly as fossils. Another, albeit more radical theory, is that some species of dinosaurs either escaped the mass extinction 65,000,000 years ago, and were only killed off by errant dragon-hunters over the last few thousand years. Neither theory is currently provable, and there is both good argument and heated debate on both sides.

Emela-ntouka   A cryptid, known as "killer of elephants," from the Likouala swamp regions in the Republic of the Congo. It is described as being as large as an elephant, but with an armored tail more reminiscent of a Nile crocodile.

Ferla Mohr (also **Brenin Llwyd, Big Gray Man, Grey King)**   A 20-foot tall gray-furred gorilla reported in the Scottish Highlands, and elsewhere in Great Britain.

Fort, Charles Hoy (1874–1932)   An American researcher and writer who had a great fascination with anomalous phenomena. His extensive writings delved into a variety of areas, including cryptozoology. Fort's worldwide influence on the study of the unknown gave rise to the term "Fortean"; ergo a Fortean search was one for something not currently classified by science.

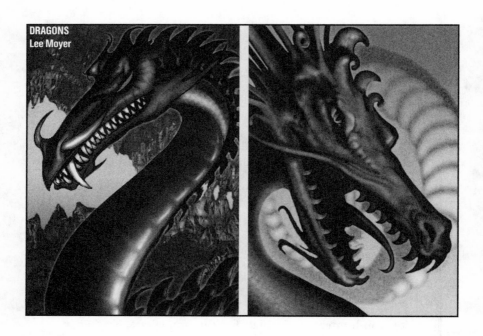

DRAGONS
Lee Moyer

Fouke Monster (also **Boggy Creek Monster)** A 9-foot tall vicious and predatory hominid of the Texarkana region of Arkansas. It has been sighted extensively since 1997.

Giglioli's Whale The Giglioli whale is an as yet unconfirmed species of whale first reported by Italian anthropologist and zoologist Enrico Hillyer Giglioli (1845–1909). He spotted it 1,200 miles off the coast of Chile in 1870.

Goatman A cryptid, which has been spotted from Washington, D.C., to west Texas. Goatman is described (by some) as a great brute of a man with a huge black goat head set on muscular shoulders. Others claim that the head and upper torso are that of a man, but that he walks around on a gnarled pair of hairy goat legs.

Greenwell, J. Richard (1942–2005) A globe-traveling cryptozoologist who served as Secretary of the International Society of Cryptozoology since its founding in 1982.

Heuvelmans, Dr. Bernard (1916–2001)   A native of Belgium, and a doctor of zoology, Heuvelmans was a scientist dedicated to the discovery and classification of hitherto unknown species of animals. His seminal book, *Sur la piste des betes ignorees*[7] *(On the Track of Unknown Animals)* was published in 1955 and has become the bible of cryptozoology, a term he coined in 1959. Heuvelmans was a true scientist and would debunk an artifact if he could, as he did with the so-called "yeti skullcap," an object also debunked by Sir Edmund Hillary (Heuvelmans disproved it first). Even so, he believed that there are many species of creatures alive in the world that are unknown to science, including sea serpents, hominids, and perhaps even stranger beings.

Hibagon (also **Hinagon)**   An apelike hominid that has been sighted in Japan with increasing frequency since the early 1970s.

Incanyamba (also **Howie)**   A South African lake monster, revered by the Zulu. Incanyamba is described as being strikingly similar to a plesiosaur—the group of aquatic dinosaurs that generally have long necks and flippers.

Jersey Devil   A commonly sighted cryptid from the Pine Barrens of New Jersey whose legends date back to Colonial times. Origin stories of the Jersey Devil vary wildly, but usually contain the common theme of the beleaguered mother of a dozen children. On giving birth to a thirteenth child, it transformed into a monster and flew off to haunt the forest.

Kasai Rex   One of Africa's man-reptilian cryptids. Unlike the more docile lake monsters, this beast is a bipedal predator built along the lines of a tyrannosaur. It has a reputation for hunting and killing rhinos and hippos.

Kingstie   A 30-foot water cryptid that has been spotted in Lake Ontario since 1917. Since many of the sightings have been near Kingston, Ontario, the creature has been dubbed "Kingstie."

---

7. Heuvelmans, Bernard, *On the Track of Unknown Animals,* 3rd ed. (London: Kegan Paul International Limited, 1995).

Kongamato   A flying creature, whose name even means "overwhelmer of boats." Kongamato has been described as looking like a pterosaur, and it has been seen throughout the sub-Saharan region of Africa.

Lake Van Monster   The most frequently sighted sea monster in the world, first spotted in 1995 in Lake Van, Turkey. It was caught on film in 1997.[8]

Ley, Willie (1906–1969)   A German-born scientist and science writer who took his own love of paleontology and used it as a springboard to explore the possibilities of supposedly extinct animals surviving into modern times. His most relevant book is *Exotic Zoology* (p. 1959), in which he discusses sea serpents, Yeti, and more.

The Loch Ness Monster (also **Nessie, Niseag)**   The world's most famous lake monster and one that has been spotted as far back as 565 C.E. in a sighting reported by Saint Columba.

The Loveland Frog (also **Loveland Lizard)**   A bizarre 4-foot batrachian[9] cryptid spotted in the vicinity of Loveland, OH since 1955.

⊰ STRANGE MAIL ⊱

In the 1947 holiday classic film *A Miracle on 34th Street*, a lawyer proved the existence of Santa Claus by showing that the U.S. Post Office delivered letters addressed to the jolly old elf—and who wants to doubt the postal department? Now it seems that post offices worldwide are subtly making an argument for the existence of cryptids. More and more often as-yet-unproven creatures are appearing on stamps issued by different countries. Canada,

---

8. The footage was shown on CNN and is still available on their Web site.
9. Any of the vertebrate amphibians without tails, such as frogs and toads.

for example has stamps for Bigfoot, the Kraken, and Ogopogo; both the Tasmania tiger *(Thylacine)* and the Bunyip appear on Australian stamps; Bhutan has a yeti stamp; Nicaragua has a sea serpent stamp; Scotland has its Loch Ness monster stamp; and Germany has a stamp with the Dragon of the Ishtar Gate. Perhaps soon we'll be able to pay our bills using a Jersey Devil stamp, or perhaps one for everyone's favorite goat-sucking alien monster, El Chupacabra.

Mackal, Dr. Roy P. (b.1925)   An engineer and biologist from the University of Chicago who is known for his fascination with cryptozoology. He is the author of *The Monsters of Loch Ness* and *Searching for Hidden Animals,* though his most well-known work is *A Living Dinosaur? In Search of Mokele-Mbembe.*

Mahambo   A giant crocodile featured in legends of the Congo reported to be at least 50-feet from tooth to tail that may be a surviving member of a line of giant prehistoric crocodiles called the *Sarchosuchus Imperator.*

Mamlambo   A murderous and unknown species of water snake whose name means "brain sucker." Mamlambo is believed to haunt the Xhosa people of the Bisho region of South Africa. The government there was sufficiently convinced of its existence to send troops out to hunt it down; this was not successful, however.

Mapinguari   A hairy Brazilian cryptid believed by many cryptozoologists to be a surviving Megatherium, or giant ground sloth, a species believed to have become extinct more than 8,000 years ago.

Marked Hominids   Any of the class of shorter hairy wildmen spotted in various places around the world. See: OLD YELLOW TOP and MOMO.

Megalania Prisca (also Mungoongalli)   A saurian cryptid spotted occasionally in Australia and New Guinea. It resembles a modern Komodo dragon, but Megalania Prisca is considerably larger, weighing an estimated half ton and stretching 25–30 feet from snout to tail.

Mermaid   A staple of folklore, mermaids, with the upper torsos of women and whose bottom halves are fish, can be any of a number of aquatic creatures. They typically are said to lure sailors to their deaths.

Minhocão   A gigantic 70-foot long tentacled worm first spotted in mid-nineteenth century Portugal. Its burrowing tunnels are believed to cause the collapse of roadways and bridges.

Mngwa (also Nunda)   A feline calico-colored cryptid the size of a donkey spotted in Tanzania and East Africa. Its name implies its nature: Mngwa means "strange one."

Moehau (also Maeroero, Maero)   A species of hominid spotted in New Zealand with a unique hunting method: They have long, bony fingers used to stab their victims.

Mokele-Mbeme (also N'yamala, Guanérou, Diba)   A massive elephant-sized lake monster from the Likouala swamps and Lake Tele in the Republic of the Congo[10] whose name translates as "one who stops the flow of rivers."

Momo   A homind, about 5-feet tall, which has occasionally been spotted in Missouri since 1972.

Mòrag   A saurian water creature, roughly 30 feet from head to tail, believed to live in Scotland's deepest lake, Loch Mòrag.

Mothman   A tall, vaguely humanoid creature with fiery red eyes and large wings seen in and around Point Pleasant, West Virginia.

10. Not to be confused with the Democratic Republic of the Congo, which is a separate nation.

WHAT LIVES BELOW Douglas Egolf

Ogopogo (also N'ha-a-itk, the Lake Demon) A plesiosaur-like creature believed to live in and around Lake Okanagan in British Columbia, and is similar in many ways to CADDY of Cadboro Bay.

Old Yellow Top A stunted version of Bigfoot first sighted in 1906 near the town of Cobalt, in Ontario, Canada, and last seen in the mid-1970s.

Olitiau The Olitiau is an as-yet unclassified species of giant bat sighted and documented by noted cryptozoologist Ivan Sanderson in West Africa. It is likely the same species as the Ahool.

Onza (also **Cutlamiztli**)   A giant cryptid hunting cat from the Sierra Madres of Mexico that appears to be a longer, leaner species of jaguar.

Orang-bati   A huge batlike predatory cryptid from the Indonesian island of Seram that has been blamed for the abductions and murders of a number of small children.

Pua Tu Tahi   A shape-shifting and vicious sea monster from Tahitian legend.

Queensland Tiger   A predatory marsupial, properly known as a Thylacine. It is believed to have become extinct eighty years ago but continues to be spotted in rural New Zealand.

Ropen   A batlike carrion-eating cryptid from Papua, New Guinea. Ropen has a long tail with a delta-shaped tip and a beak filled with needle-sharp teeth.

Sasquatch (also **Bigfoot**)   The most famous of the North American hominids is the mighty Sasquatch who gets his name from the word Sésquac, which means "wild man" in the Stó:lõ dialect of the Halkomelem language used by the Salish Indians of the Fraser Valley and parts of Vancouver Island, BC. Nicknamed "Bigfoot" by journalists in the mid-twentieth century following a number of sightings in Northern California, the Sasquatch has been reported by more than 3000 eyewitnesses. The Sasquatch legend got its biggest media boost in 1967 when former rodeo rider Roger Patterson (1933–1972) took 16mm film of the big hairy fellow walking through the forest. Though astounding to see, Patterson's Bigfoot film has been largely discredited; however, the sightings of this American wildman continue. Anthropologist Dr. Grover S. Krantz (1931–2002) collected Sasquatch artifacts including castings from footprints, and raised the theory that Sasquatch was a surviving member of a species of prehistoric ape called *Gigantopithecus Blacki*, which crossed over the ice bridge during the ice age 10,000 years ago.

Shuker, Dr. Karl P. N. (b.1959)   A zoologist recognized worldwide as a top expert in cryptozoology. Dr. Shukar has written extensively on the subject, including *Mystery Cats of the World* and *The Unexplained: An Illustrated Guide to the World's Natural and Paranormal Mysteries.*

Shunka Warak'in   A wolflike creature—known to attack humans as well as animals—spoken of in the ancient legends of the Ioway native peoples.[11] The creature was spotted frequently on the Great Plains by Native Americans and settlers as well during the late eighteenth and nineteenth centuries.

Tatzelworm   A monstrous wormlike creature about 4–5 feet in length. It has a distinctly feline head and many short legs. Tatzelworm has been reported in the Bavarian Alps, Austria, and Switzerland.

Trunko   A white-furred sea monster that, in 1922, was seen by a ship's crew off the coast of Margate, South Africa. It lost a murderous sea battle with two whales, and its corpse washed up on the beach, where it was measured at 47 feet and presented a number of anatomical anomalies.

Veo   A cryptid from the region of Rintja in Indonesia, believed to be a night-hunting insect-eater similar to an anteater, though scaly and as large as a horse.

Waheela   A wolflike cryptid seen in the Nahanni Valley of Canada's Northwest Territories. It has a body similar to a hyena, but with short hind legs, overdeveloped forelegs, a burly chest, and thick snow-white fur.

Wendigo (also **Witigo, Windigo, Witiko,** and **Wee-Tee-Go)**   A fierce predatory monster from the legends of the native American peoples (primarily from those in Ontario and Minnesota). Wendigo surfaces whenever humans resort to cannibalism.

---

11. A Sioux tribe who live in, and have given their name to, the state of Iowa.

Wildmen   Also known as "Hominids," this is the biggest subgroup of cryptids, ranging from the shy Bigfoot of the American Northwest to the murderous Yeren of the Himalayas. The science of searching for and studying these creatures is called Hominology, a term coined in 1973 by Russian researcher Dmitri Bayanov. *Hominids*, in the strict scientific sense, refers to humans; *Hominidae* includes humans and apes, and is included in the superfamily of all apes, the *Hominoidea*. Not all scientists use this broad a description, however, and there is some heated debate on the point ongoing in scientific circles. For our purposes, however, the term *hominid* will be used to describe the shaggy beastmen in all their variety, mainly because they have not yet been properly and scientifically classified. If they exist, they will probably prove to be cousins, however distant, of *homosapiens*.

Since the wildmen are usually predatory in nature, and are not truly human—or anything else represented in the fossil record—they are included here among other potentially supernatural monsters.

Yardley yeti   A nickname[12] given to a strange doglike cryptid frequently spotted in and around Bucks County, Pennsylvania. Two versions[13] of the creature have been spotted, a small brownish one weighing an estimated 30 pounds and a much larger gray that appears to be the size of an adult German shepherd.

Yeren   A more savage and ferocious version of the Yeti, found in the rocky northern territories of China.

Yeti (also **the Abominable Snowman**)   A race of towering hominids believed to dwell in the snowy heights of the Himalayas.

Yowie   An Australian hominid comparable to the North American Bigfoot.

---

12. Coined by Bucks County newspaper columnist J. D. Mullane.
13. For more on the Yardley Yeti—including photos and eyewitness accounts, go to www.vampireuniverse.com/yeti.htm

YARDLEY YETI Sara Jo West

— *Chapter Three* —

DEMONS AND ANGELS

WHICH CAME FIRST, THE SINNER OR THE SIN?

Man is thrust into the world naked, bloody and screaming—and for much of the world's history, recorded or otherwise, things don't get much better from there. The life of prehistoric man hinged on a bizarre passion play of brute force, dumb luck, and the chaotic will of the elements.

It's not difficult to imagine that life itself at the time was regarded as little more than a temporary state of being—the very unspiritual matter of being plunked down in one place in the world and making one's way to another. With hunger, thirst, the need for shelter, and the will to procreate ever clawing away at humankind, there wasn't much time for religious contemplation.

But the story is pretty much the same throughout time. Man evolves. The seeds of civilization are sown. With his opposable thumb and a new attitude, Man rises up to build his fires, make his tools and create shelters that keep out the rest of the world.

And from that spark of humanity came the *real* seed that was either the beginning of all doing, or perhaps, all undoing—a literal Pandora's box called spare time.

With this gift, there wasn't a continuous need to fret about hunger, thirst, and sex. Man could think. Man could plan. Man could lie in wait with the patience to act at the right time.

Perhaps it was on that day that consequence and conscience were born.

Perhaps concepts of crime and punishment formed from whirling ether, and perhaps, for the first time, there was a place called hell.

The word hell comes from the Germanic *hel* meaning to cover, hide, or conceal. The demon-filled netherworld of fire and brimstone seems to spawn from the Greek tradition of the afterlife, but the origins of hell are nearly benign in comparison.

After death, the ancient Greeks envisioned themselves in a true netherworld just beneath the surface of the earth, the Elysian Fields. For the wicked, there was Tartarus, ruled by its overlord Hades—Tartarus was a pit of suffering and endless torment.

In the Greek tradition, the bodies of the privileged dead were buried with a coin beneath their tongues as payment for the ferryman Charon. He would take their spirits across the river Acheron. Those who died without friends and wealth were said to gather on the far shore, ever denied entrance into Hades. Three other rivers were also said to flow there—Cocytus, Phlegethon, and that most familiar waterway, the river Styx.

In the Jewish tradition, the afterlife was *Sheol*—a shadow world inhabited by the spirits of the dead. As the Hebrew term itself also translates as "grave," the idea could likely be a metaphor for death—a fate that awaits the poor as well as the rich, the oppressor as well as the oppressed.

Rather than a place of actual tortures and punishment, Sheol seems to be a Purgatory-like spiritual waiting room where even the most wicked souls will spend no more than a year before being cleansed and released to the cosmos.

Hell also hearkens back to the Greek *Gehenna*—from the Hebrew *Gehinnom,* most likely a nod to the valley of Gehinnom, an area southwest of Jerusalem where the Phoenicians made sacrifices to dark and bizarre gods.

In later days, this location served as a landfill where trash and refuse were burned, and the bodies of executed criminals were disposed of without ceremony. This perpetual cycle of rotting and immolation most likely served as a model for what hell was to become, but the Jewish conception of hell was *not* a place of brimstone and torment, nor is the threat of eternal damnation an aspect of Jewish dogma.

In Muslim conception, hell is a place called *Jahanam*—which also springs from the Hebrew Gehinnom—and is much closer to Christian and later ideas of hell as a place of fire and pain. It is of interest to note that while there are seven levels of hell in Islam, only two of these sections are devoted to its followers—the remaining five are said to be the eventual dwellings of infidels who do not accept Allah and his teachings.

Jaheem, the shallowest level of hell, is dedicated to followers of Islam, but those who have transgressed from its teachings. *Jahanam* is the eventual destination for idolaters after the end of the world. Those who worship the power of fire are resigned to *Sa'ir,* while those who do not accept Allah will languish in *Saqar.* The Jews will be relegated to *Ladha,* and Christians will spend eternity in *Hawiyah.* The deepest pit of Hell is *Hutama*—the dwelling place of that rare breed—the religious hypocrite.

The plains of hell got the administrative kick in the pants they needed from the Catholic Church. The concept was now four-fold: hell as a place of torment for damned souls; *limbus parvulorum,* the limbo of infants, where those who died with the "original sin" of birth itself are confined and punished; *limbus partum,* the spiritual double-whammy of limbo for the multitudes who lived and died before Christ, but are still denied entry into heaven because of the sin of Adam; and Purgatory, where those who commit lesser (venial) sins are cleansed by punishment and finally ascend to Heaven.

Catholic hell is eternal, and even the suffering itself is relegated to two categories: *poena damni,* the pain of loss that comes from being separate from God, coupled with the loss of faith; and *poena sensus,* the more familiar and visceral torment of fire, a very real concept of Catholic dogma.

The fires of hell are generally perceived as a new torment, as they are unlike anything man has ever experienced in his time on earth—they burn at their perpetual hottest without need of fuel or kindling.

To followers of Taoism and Buddhism, the punishment for living a frivolous and evil life is an eighteen-level smorgasbord of hideous tortures. Sinners might be pulled asunder by torrential winds; ground into powder; consumed by flames; frozen by ice; boiled in mammoth cauldrons of oil; dismembered by saw or by being pulled apart by chariots; made to eternally scale a mountain of knives; detongued; pounded into smithereens by massive hammers; severed in two; impaled by hooks and hung like so much meat in a butcher's window; gouged in the eyes; pierced by having their hearts pulled through their chests; disemboweled; skinned alive; devoured by maggots; or placed on a platform atop a perpetual inferno.

With all the sin and wickedness in the world, it's easy to imagine that any and all conceptions of hell are clerical nightmares from the get-go.

❧ DEMONS AND OTHER ☙ SERVANTS OF DEVILTRY

Aamon   Assistant to the demon Astaroth. He possesses knowledge of the future as well as the past, and those willing to make a deal with Satan are given access to it. When time comes to settle that infernal tab, however, they pay a terrible price. Demonologists differ as to his appearance, because he can have the head of an owl or wolf, often with a snake's tail. Aamon's origins are associated with the Egyptian god Amun or Ba'al Hammon, a deity of the people of Carthage, which is now the North African country of Tunisia.

Abbaddon   The book of Revelation calls him "the Destroyer" or "King of the Grasshoppers." He is chief of all demons in the seventh hierarchy. His presence was felt so profoundly that throughout history, the term Abbaddon has been used interchangably for any number of demonic figures, the Devil itself, or a pit in the deepest recesses of hell. In the epic poem *Paradise Regained*, Milton perceived it as a place, and the Dead Sea Scrolls refer to the "Sheol of Abbadon" and speak of the "torrents of Belial [that] burst into Abbaddon." In

DEMONS IN ALL THEIR GUISES

Hebrew, Abbaddon translates as "place of destruction" and, indeed, its greatest role is mentioned in the biblical apocalypse. As written in Revelations:

"The locusts looked like horses prepared for battle. On their heads they wore something like crowns of gold, and their faces resembled

human faces. Their hair was like women's hair, and their teeth
were like lions' teeth. They had breastplates like breastplates of
iron, and the sound of their wings was like the thundering of many
horses and chariots rushing into battle. They had tails and stings
like scorpions, and in their tails they had power to torment people
for five months. They had as king over them the angel of the Abyss,
whose name in Hebrew is Abbaddon, and in Greek, Apollyon.
(Rev. 7–11)

The Bible, like any text, is open to human interpretation. It would be re-
miss not to mention that the passage above was also crucial to the philosophy
of Charles Manson, the cult figure behind the "Helter Skelter" killings of 1969.
Manson saw the coming of the Antichrist in a more innocuous form—The
Beatles. The lads from Liverpool and their shaggy manes certainly were feminine, and an electric guitar isn't so far removed from a breastplate.

Abdiel His name comes from the Hebrew for "servant of God." Abdiel figures most prominently in Milton's *Paradise Lost,* where he is said to reject Satan after hearing of his plans to overthrow heaven.

Adad To the ancient Babylonians, he was the god of storms. He is viewed as
a demonic figure mainly because of the dual nature of the weather—the rain
can bring a bounty of crops, but an excess of rain can just as easily bring blight
and starvation.

Adramelech Originally an Assyrian god to whom children were offered up
as burning sacrifices. Adramelech later became a Judeo-Christian demonic figure. He is perceived by the Medievel Catholic Church as the President of the
Senate of Demons and has the dubious honor of being overseer of Satan's
wardrobe. Adramelech is depicted as being similar to a centaur, with a human
torso and the body of a mule, capped off with the ornate feathers of a peacock.
He is the counterpart to ANAMELECH.

Agaliarept   A general of hell who was said to command the dark forces that amassed in Europe and Asia Minor. Agaliarept's consorts were Buer, Gusoyn, and Botis. He is depicted as an older human male with a moustache, and he can relate the magical qualities of metal to mankind. Also known as Agalierap, and Agalierept.

Agares   A dark prince, Agares is said to rule the eastern provinces of hell and is served by thirty legions of devoted demon consorts. He can cause earthquakes and reveal languages to man. Agares revels in teaching "immoral expressions" (read: dirty jokes) and is described as being relatively benevolent as far as demons are concerned. Agares is often depicted riding a crocodile, carrying a sparrow hawk, a bird of prey similar to a falcon.

⊰ HELLISH QUOTES: ⊱ A DIABOLIC TOP 20

1. "War is hell."—General George Smith Patton, Jr., army general, United States (1885–1945)

2. "If you are going through hell, keep going."—Sir Winston Leonard Spencer-Churchill, Prime Minister, England (1874–1965)

3. "Maybe this world is another planet's hell."—Aldous Huxley, author, philosopher, England (1894–1963)

4. "Hell is a half-filled auditorium."—Robert Frost, poet, United States (1874–1963)

5. "Hell is other people."—Jean-Paul Sartre, existentialist philosopher, France (1905–1980)

6. "Heav'n hath no rage like love to hatred turn'd, Nor Hell a fury, like a woman scorn'd."—William Congreve, playwright, England (1670–1729)

7. "The safest road to hell is the gradual one—the gentle slope, soft underfoot, without sudden turnings, without milestones, without signposts."—C. S. Lewis, author, Ireland (1898–1964)

8. "Hell is an idea first born on an undigested apple-dumpling; and since then perpetuated through the hereditary dyspepsias nurtured by Ramadans."—Herman Melville, author, United States (1819–1891)

9. "We are praying now for the repose of his soul. Hoping you're well and not in hell. Nice change of air. Out of the frying pan of life into the fire of purgatory."—James Augustine Aloysius Joyce, author, Ireland (1882–1941)

10. "The mind is its own place, and in it self Can make a Heaven of Hell, a Hell of Heaven."—John Milton, poet, England (1608–1674)

11. "One cannot walk through an assembly factory and not feel that one is in hell."—W. H. Auden, poet and critic, England (1907–1973)

12. "I cannot help thinking that the menace of hell makes as many devils as the severe penal codes of inhuman humanity make villains."—George Gordon (Noel) Byron, poet, England (1788–1824)

13. "The hell of these days is the fear of not getting along, especially of not making money."—Thomas Carlyle, essayist, Scotland (1795–1881)

14. "Hell is oneself, hell is alone, the other figures in it merely projections. There is nothing to escape from and

(continued)

nothing to escape to. One is always alone."—T. S. Eliot, poet, dramatist, critic, United States (1888–1965)

15. "The hottest place in hell is reserved for those who remain neutral in times of great moral conflict."—Martin Luther King, Jr., Baptist minister and activist, United States (1929–1968)

16. "A perpetual holiday is a good working definition of hell." George Bernard Shaw, playwright, Ireland (1856–1950)

17. On the perfect cup of coffee: "Black as the devil, hot as hell, pure as an angel, sweet as love."—Charles Maurice de Talleyrand, diplomat, France (1754–1838)

18. "Man is the cruelest animal. At tragedies, bullfights, and crucifixions he has so far felt best on earth; and when he invented hell for himself, behold, that was his very heaven." Friedrich Wilhelm Nietzsche, philosopher, Germany (1844–1900)

19. "It is better to conquer yourself than to win a thousand battles. Then the victory is yours. It cannot be taken from you, not by angels or by demons, heaven or hell."—Attributed to Buddha

20. "It is good to have friends, even in hell."—Spanish proverb

Agathodemon   The ancient Egyptians worshipped this unusually benevolent demonic figure often depicted as a serpent with the head of a man. Also called the "bold serpent" or "serene dragon." His "evil" spiritual counterpart is Kakodemon.

AGRAT BAT MAHLAHT
Jason Beam

Agrat bat Mahlat Also called "the angel of prostitution," she was one of the four mates of the rebel angel Samael, along with Lilith, Naamah, and Eiseth Zenunim. She is considered one of the mothers of all demons, and was purported to cause children to be afflicted with epilepsy.

Ahpuch The Mayan name for the Aztec god of the dead, Mictlantecuhtli and the king of Mitnal, the Mayan Underworld. Also called Hunhau or Hunahau.

Ahriman The eternal enemy of the followers of Zoroastrianism, an off-shoot of a religion practiced in ancient Persia. It can be said that Ahmiran is the Zoroastrian "devil" ever at odds with Ahura Mazda. In the beginning of time, these two forces were separated by a void, Mazda, associated with the light half, and, Ahriman, of the dark.

Aim A great duke of Hell in command of twenty-six legions, Aim is the bringer of fire and destruction, setting great cities alight. He can bestow wit and reveal the truth in personal matters. Depicted as a handsome man, Aim has three heads—a serpent's, a man's (with two stars on his forehead), and a calf's. He is also referred to as Aym or Harborym and is depicted as riding a large venomous snake and carrying a firebrand, which he uses to wreak his fiery havoc.

Alastor In Greek mythology he is "the avenger" and the diabolic personification of deadly feuds between families—and of sins passed down through generations. Men under Alastor's influence are easily moved to murder. Born mortal, the son of Neleus, king of Pylos, he became a demonic figure after he and his brothers were slain by Heracles—Hercules to both the Romans and fans of Ray Harryhausen films. Christendom sees Alastor as hell's chief executioner.

Aldinach A demon of ancient Egypt. He is said to be the cause of natural disasters, such as floods and famine, as well as accidents at sea. Aldinach is often depicted in the form of a human female.

Allocer Another great duke of hell, Allocer has command of thirty-six legions. He can bestow immortality, knowledge of the arts, and astronomy to mankind. Allocer is depicted as human with the horned head of a lion, seated atop a horse whose legs are reptilian, like a dragon.

Alu-demon An early Jewish demon or imp-like figure who prowls the streets at night searching for victims.

Amaymon   A prince in command of the western providences of hell, he is said to possess poisonous breath. Anyone who would conjure him had best stand firmly on his feet and be polite, for the demon is easily offended. Once a conjurer has invoked the creature's ire—the intended goal of the spell, for good or for ill, is doomed to failure.

Amdukias   A grand duke of hell in command of thirty legions. His voice can be heard in the booming cacophony of great storms, and his invocation is often associated with thunder. When he appears, Amdukias is accompanied by the blare of musical instruments—one of the few demons who comes with his own soundtrack. He is sometimes depicted as a man with talons, instead of hands and feet, holding a trumpet—which is a difficult enough task in itself. Other cultures saw Amdukias as a unicorn that could transform into a man at will.

Anamelech   His name means "good king," and he is often associated with the moon. To the Assyrians, he was the bearer of troubling news, and he appeared in the form of a quail. He is counterpart to ADRAMELECH.

Andras   A great marquis of hell with thirty legions of demons in his command. Andras exists to sow discord in the hearts and minds of men. He is often depicted as an angel, but with the head of a crow or owl, sometimes riding a black wolf.

Anguta   In Inuit lore, it is the lot of Anguta to gather the dead and carry them down to the underworld. The souls must spend one year in his company.

Aningan   The Inuit personification of the moon. Aningan perpetually chases his brother, the sun, across the sky in a giant sled loaded down with seals. During the day, when not engaged in the hunt, he lives in a giant igloo in the heavens with his demon cousin Irdlirvirisissong.

Ardat-Lile   A succubus-like female spirit to the ancient Hebrews. Ardat-Lile dwells on earth, seeking to marry men and destroy their lives.

Asmodeus (also **Aeshma, Aesma**)   The origins of this demon are in ancient Persia. Later he is mentioned in the New Testament Book of Tobit, as well as the Talmud. Originally the chief all demons, eventually Asmodeus evolved into a demonic and lustful figure who aimed to arouse impure thoughts in humankind. He also took pleasure in ruining the beauty of virgins and caused their hearts to blacken.

Astaroth   While dukedom is bestowed in a fairly loose fashion in the fiery depths, Astaroth is generally regarded as the Grand Duke of Hell. He has four demon assistants: Aamon; Pruslas, a great seducer of women; Barbatos, who can speak in the tongue of any animal, knows the past and future, and can reveal things that are hidden; and Rashaverak—whose fame seems to come by association alone.

He is a demon of the first hierarchy and is depicted as a naked man wearing a crown and holding a serpent. Astaroth possesses both the scaled wings of a dragon and the feathered wings of an angel. He seduces man by inspiring laziness and sloth, but can also reveal knowledge of mathematics and the arts.

Astarte   A Greek translation of the Semitic goddess of love and life, Ishtar; she is also associated with Aphrodite. To the Jews, Astarte was a demon who inspired lustful acts. In recent history the name has been associated with the feminist New Age movement, as she represents the indomitable spirit of Woman.

Azathoth   A literary demon borne of the mind of H. P. Lovecraft as part of the Cthulu mythos. Azathoth is portrayed as all powerful, but slow witted and blind. With a legion of spirits known only as "the servitors of the outer gods," he is ever holding court at the center of the universe.

Azazel   A Hebrew term closely associated with Satan. Azazel first appears in Leviticus in the Old Testament in describing a Yom Kippur ritual where a goat is cast into the wilderness, carrying with it the sins of the people. This practice is the origin of the term "scapegoat" and Jews perform a less drastic version as part of Yom Kippur observances today—when a congregation might leave their place of worship for a nearby creek or stream. There they would cast their sins into the waters. The term has also become synonymous with the desolate valley where the goat was cast out each year.

Originally Azazel was the leader of an order of angels called Grigori (the watchers). Among those that had fallen and mated with women (to create the order or Nephilim), Azazel taught men to create weapons of war. He also showed women how to wear makeup. Both didn't sit well with God—who thought it best to wipe the slate clean with a great flood of some renown.

Baal   A Hebrew title meaning "lord," this term is generally used to describe any one of a collection of spirits and demons. See BAALBERITH. Christendom offered up a personification of the creature, and viewed him a king of hell with sixty-six legions of demons in his command.

Baalberith   Once a member of the cherubim race of angels, Baalberith was cast into hell with Satan and his coconspirators. Overseeing pacts and transactions between demons and men, his seal appears on all such hellish contracts—in a sense the notary public of fiery depths.

Babael   A high captain of the legions who guard the gates of hell, Babael is also keeper of the dead.

Baell   A king of the eastern provinces of the underworld, Baell commands sixty-six legions of devoted demons. He is alternately depicted as either a cat, toad, or human—or as a nightmarish creature with three heads in those forms.

Balaam   In the Old Testament, Balaam makes an appearance as an evil prophet or magician. The king of Moab enlists his counsel to place a curse upon the children of Israel. Though in this story the will of God intervenes—

and the Israelites are blessed instead of cursed—he is still viewed as a demonic figure.

Baraqiel Another disgraced angel of the Grigori (watcher) order, Baraqiel can bestow upon humans the knowledge of astrology.

Barbas A great president of hell who has thirty-six legions under his command. Barbas can reveal that which is hidden, both inflict and remove disease, teach the secrets of mechanics, and transform humans into otherworldly creatures. His name is a combination of the Latin *barba* (beard) and *hellebore,* a flowering plant said to have medicinal and magical properties. He is depicted as a huge lion that can transform into a man.

Barbatos A great duke of hell who can communicate with dogs and birds, reveal that which is hidden, and dissolve magical seals and enchantments on troves of treasures and sacred items. He knows the past, present, and future and is in command of thirty legions of demons. Barbatos is depicted as a horned hunter.

Bathin A great duke of hell in command of thirty legions. Bathin may appear as a man of great strength with the tail of a snake sitting upon a white horse. He can bestow upon humankind a knowledge of herbology and gemology. He is also capable of transporting men from one country to another with the aid of powerful magic.

Beelzebub (also **Belzebud, Belzaboul, Beelzeboul, Baalsebul, Baalzebubg, Beelzebuth, Beelzebus)** This Philistine god is closely associated with Baal, and the term does indeed seem to be a prefix, which translates as "Lord of the Flies" (from the Hebrew *zebub* "to fly"). Beelzebub has also become a name used interchangeably with Satan or the devil. Later theologians and demonologists suggest he was yet another fallen angel of the cherubim order, and has become associated with the deadly sins of pride and gluttony. Beelzebub also figures prominently in Milton's *Paradise Lost* where he is regarded as an equal to Satan.

Behemoth   Though the term's roots come from a common Hebrew term for "animal," it is believed that the inspiration for this beast spawned from a large, fearsome, and misunderstood animal—perhaps an elephant, hippopotamus, or water buffalo. Other more "adventurous" minds have suggested that the creature could be a product of dinosaur evidence—dragging the idea a bit too far to suggest that God created dinosaurs and man in the same period—though scads of physical evidence proves otherwise. The creature is the counterpart to the equally fearsome leviathan (which comes from the Hebrew term for "whale"). It is said that at the end of the world, both the leviathan and behemoth will be slain, and their flesh fed to the righteous.

Beleth   A powerful and terrible king of hell, Beleth is in command of eighty-five legions of demons. He rides a white stallion, and his appearance is heralded by the thunderous blare of trumpets. Those who would dare conjure him must treat him with the utmost respect, and guard themselves by wearing a ring of silver on the middle finger of the left hand.

Belial (also Belhor, Baalial, Beliar, Beliall, Beliel)   The Hebrew roots of this name are unclear, and it has been translated alternately as "worthless," "never to rise," or "yokeless"—which would suggest one with no allegiance or master. The Old Testament sees him as an all-around bad guy. Belial is a demon of the highest order who can move humankind to commit sins of lust and pride.

Belphegor   A corruption of the name Baal-Peor, a Moabite god of orgies and excess whose influence seduced the Israelites while they dwelled in the land of Moab. A sensible and enjoyable alternative to wandering the desert for endless years, the men began to engage in immoral acts with the Moabite women and made sacrifices to their gods. A plague was said to follow, which claimed 24,000 wicked, yet satisfied, souls, as recounted in Numbers 25:3.

The Belphegor of the middle ages has been variously described as a demonic man or a beautiful naked woman or hideous monster, though in written text the creature is generally referred to as "he." Kabbalistic writings call him "the disputer" whose joy was to sow discord among men. Though capable of granting the gifts of invention and discovery, he can only be invoked by repulsive rituals involving human excrement.

Legend tells that Belphegor was sent to earth by Lucifer to see if marital bliss was real. Not surprisingly, the creature didn't have to spend too much time in the earthly plain to have it confirmed a myth—ensuring the idea that human beings were never destined to live in harmony with their own kind. The word has since become a literary term that describes a licentious, immoral character.

Beherit   A great duke of hell known for his ferocity, Beherit has twenty-six legions under his command. The consummate alchemist, he knows the past and future and is able to turn all base metals into gold. Beherit is depicted as a red-skinned soldier clad in red and seated upon a red horse, with a golden crown on his head. The Jews call him Berith.

Bifrons (also Bifrovs, Bifröus)   Originally the name of the Roman god of thresholds and gates, this diabolic version is a lord of hell with six legions in his command. Bifrons can reveal the mysteries of science, the arts, herbology, and the nature of precious stones to mankind. He is depicted, as creatures that can reveal prophecy often are, with two heads, one revealing the past and the other the future. Bifrons also had the unique and dubious ability to move corpses from their graves to other locations.

Bhairava   The "terrible" aspect of the Hindu god Shiva, Bhairava can be considered a demonic figure of sorts. He is said to have severed the head of

Brahma, the Hindu god of creation, and is damned to bear it with him until the act is absolved.

Bile   The god of hell to the Celts—the ancient peoples of Ireland, Wales, Scotland, Cornwall, the Isle of Man, and Brittany.

Big Heads   Demon gods of the Iroquois Indians, depicted as giant headless bodies that fly in storms seeking to devour men.

Botis   Another president of hell in command of sixty legions of devoted demons, Botis has full knowledge of history and can predict future events. He can also transform lifelong enemies into allies. He is depicted alternately as a serpent or as a fanged human with horns.

Buer   A president of hell with fifty legions in his command, he can bestow knowledge of nature, philosophy, and herbology. Buer is capable of healing wounds and illness, and is often depicted like the zodiac sign Sagittarius—an archer with the head and trunk of a man and the body of a horse. He is alternately described as having a lion's head and a goat's body with five legs capable of moving in all possible directions.

Bune   A powerful duke of Hell with thirty legions in his command. Like Bifrons, he has the curious ability to move corpses from their graves to new locations and transform these unfortunates into demons. Bune can bestow the gifts of knowledge to humankind. He is alternately depicted as a griffin, dragon, human, or some hideous combination of all three.

Caacrinolaas (also **Caassimolar, Classyalabolas, Glassia-labolis, **and **Glasya Labolas)**   A lord of hell in command of thirty-six legions, he can bestow the knowledge of arts and sciences on humankind, as well as possess the minds of men, moving them to love, hate, or murder as willed. Caacrinolaas is often depicted as a winged canine.

Cerberus   The three-headed canine that serves as guardian to the underworld in Greek and Roman mythology.

Camio   The Gaelic pronunciation of the biblical Cain and the godfather of all acts of murder. While it is unclear from a biblical standpoint if Cain went to hell for his sins, artists and writers of later years were quick to place him as one of the underworld's most famous occupants. Camio can speak in the tongues of animals and can predict future events. Some demonologists have depicted him as a black bird that can transform into a man.

Chiang-Shih   Not a demon per se, the Chiang-Shih are the "hopping vampires" of China. Spawned from unnatural or violent deaths, or even by not closely adhering to burial customs, these fearsome creatures take great pleasure in ripping apart their victims. They also possess a diabolic lust that moves them to rape women. The Chiang-Shih are immortalized in Hong Kong horror films.

Charon   Charon is the familiar visage of the boatman who ferries souls across the river Styx into the underworld in Greek mythology. It was an ancient Greek burial custom to bury the dead with a coin beneath their tongues, so that they could pay the infernal fare. Charon became a Christian demonic figure when Dante, in the *Divine Comedy,* wrote about him as the first character he encounters in his journey to hell.

Chemosh   Another Moabite god reviled as a demon by the ancient Hebrews. He is seen as "the leveler," or "the subjugator," and his name means "five" in Hebrew.

Choronzon   A creation of the demonic lexicon of John Dee and Aleister Crowley, a creature of dispersion and chaos.

Cimejes   A lord of hell with twenty legions of demons in his command. Cimejes has been described as a knight riding a black horse who can teach grammar, logic, and critical thinking to humankind.

CERBERUS Adam Garland

Coyote   The concept of the coyote as a spirit animal and trickster of men is widely held among Native American tribes throughout the United States. The Pomos of Northern California believe the coyote gave birth to humanity and captured the sun to keep his charges warm. The Sioux of the Dakotas believe the coyote created the horse as a gift to its people.

Crocell   A duke of hell in command of forty-eight legions of demons, Crocell can teach humans the secrets of geometry and other sciences.

Dagon A deity of the Philistines demonized by the Hebrews. He is alternately portrayed as either a god of grain and agriculture or as a mammoth sea serpent.

Dagwanoenyent To the Iroquois, she was the daughter of the wind. Dagwanoenyent often took the form of tornadoes or violent storms.

Daityas To the Hindu, a race of giants or evil spirits who rebelled against the gods and succeeded in scattering them throughout the world.

Dantalion A great duke of hell in command of thirty-six legions. Dantalion is often depicted as a man with a multitude of faces, both male and female. He can reveal the secrets of science and the arts and move men and women to love, as he knows the thoughts and wills of all humankind.

Decarabia A marquis of hell with thirty legions under his command, Decarabia can appear in the form of any type of bird to those who would dare conjure him. His symbol is the pentacle (five pointed star) and he can reveal the nature of precious stones to humankind.

Eblis The main demonic figure in Islam. It was said that Eblis disobeyed the will of Allah and was expelled from heaven and cast into Jahannam, the Islamic conception of hell. Since that time, like the devils of the West, he has interfered in the lives of man, whispering words of sin into the ears of anyone who would listen and act upon them.

Eligos (also **Abigor, Eligor**) A great duke of hell in command of sixty legions. Eligos is capable of discovering the hidden, can predict the future, and, perhaps more importantly, can portend the outcome of military actions and battles. In this capacity, powerful men have coveted the demon's counsel. Eligos is often depicted in the form of a knight dressed for battle, carrying a lance and a scepter. However, Aleister Crowley envisioned him as a serpent.

Enma daiou   The judge and ruler of the Japanese conception of hell, called Jigoku. It is his task to judge wicked souls and confine them to the proper eternal punishment. Enma Daiou is often depicted as a human wearing a judge's cap.

Erinyes   In Greek mythology, these winged demonic women personified the vengeance of those wrongly killed. The Romans called them "the furies." They are depicted as hideous women with hair of writhing, deadly serpents who took great pleasure in tormenting those who would murder their own kin.

Ereshkigal   In ancient Babylon and Assyria, she was the goddess of the underworld.

Eurynome   This demonic figure was one of the "titans" of Greek mythology. Later demonologists envisioned the creature as the prince of death and an eater of carrion. Eurynome drapes himself in the skin of a wolf to hide flesh that is covered with festering sores.

Focalor   A great duke of hell in command of thirty legions of demons. Focalor has been depicted as a winged human. He holds sway over storms at sea and takes great pleasure in sinking ships and drowning sailors.

Furfur   A great ruler of hell in command of twenty-six legions of demons. Furfur can inspire men to love, create great storms, and reveal divine secrets. He is depicted alternately as a winged stag with human arms, or as an angel.

Gaap   More often known as the anagram for "Generally Accepted Accounting Principles," which is indeed a scary topic, this Gaap is a prince and great president of hell in command of sixty-six legions of demons. He is said to be the ruler of the southern provinces of the underworld. Gaap is capable of bestowing the knowledge of philosophy and science, and he can inspire love and hate in men, or cause them to become ignorant.

Grigori   One of the groups of fallen angels (called "watchers") who mated with mortal women to create a race of superhumans called the Nephilim. From Genesis 6:2, "the sons of God saw that the daughters of men were beautiful and married any of them they chose." Though the Nephilim are later described as "heroes of old, men of renown," it was soon after this period that God was said to condemn the world for its wickedness and caused the great flood.

Mentions of the demonic version of the Grigori, however, are apocryphal and appear in the Book of Enoch, purported to have been written between the Old and New Testaments (150–80 B.C.E.) and also mentioned in the text of the Dead Sea Scrolls.

It is said that they number 200, and the chiefs among them are named Samyaza, Urakabarameel, Akibeel, Tamiel, Ramuel, Danel, Azkeel, Saraknyal, Asael, Armers, Batraal, Anane, Zavebe, Samsaveel, Ertael, Turel, Yomyael, and Azazel

Hecate   To the Greeks, she was the goddess of the wilderness and childbirth. She was also regarded as a goddess of sorcery, which is most likely how she came to be viewed as a demonic figure in western theology and thought.

Incubus   A lustful demon in male form that rapes women and drains their life essence. The female version of this creature is called a succubus. However, the creatures also seem to represent the sexual repression of the Middle Ages, pregnancy out of wedlock, nocturnal emissions, sleep paralysis, and the loss of control that accompanies orgasm (which have all been "blamed" on such creatures). Whether incubi and succubi are technically male and female has been the subject of debate; many demonologists suggest that the creature is singular, and can change its sex to suit its intended victim.

Irdlirvirisissong   The Inuit cousin of the moon, perceived as a sort of demonic clown who sometimes comes down from the sky to dance and make

HECATE Jason Beam

people laugh. However, if anyone gets too close, they are in danger of being killed and having their intestines devoured.

Kappas Malevolent water-spirits of Japanese mythology, Kappas are depicted as creatures with green skin, rounded heads, and an extended proboscis. It is said that their heads are filled with water, which if poured out, cause the demon to lose its power.

Legion   The demon of Gadarenes or Gergesenes, where it is said that Jesus performed the first biblical exorcism. When asked its name, the spirit replied, "My name is Legion, for we are many."

Rather than be returned to the pit of hell, the spirits asked Jesus to cast them into a herd of 2000 pigs, where they promptly ran to a cliff's edge and threw themselves into a lake to drown. Theologians differ on the nature of the story, some calling it a parable of early anti-Roman resistance and little more than very, very old religious propaganda.

Loki (also **Veles, Volos, Weles, Voloh)**   In Norse mythology, Loki is the trickster god of mischief, and is able to shape-shift into many forms. He caused the slaying of Balder, god of beauty and the son of Odin, by forming a dart out of mistletoe and tricking Balder's blind brother Hoor into throwing it.

Lucifer   A combination of the Latin *lux* (light) and *ferre* (to carry), this name, "bearer of the light," is synonymous with the biblical devil. To the Greeks, he was the "morning star," Heosphoros, or literally "bringer of the light." In Christian theology, Lucifer was the highest-ranking archangel in heaven. His greed and lust for power, however, caused him and his fellows to rebel against God, a sin for which they were cast into perdition.

Malphas   A great prince of hell in command of forty legions of demons. Malphas can construct great buildings, or topple those of the enemies who would conjure him. He is depicted as a black bird or raven that can transform into a man.

Mammon   While this term is Aramaic for "wealth," in the Middle Ages, he became the personification of the lust for material possessions and greed.

Mantus   To the Romans and Etruscans, Mantus and his wife Mania were gods of the underworld.

Mastema A demon of the unholy union between a Grigori, watcher angel, and a mortal woman. His name is Hebrew for "hatred" or "hostility," and some theologies perceive him as the Satanic figure in the biblical story of Job.

Mephistopheles Perhaps the most famous literary demonic figure, this name is used interchangeably with Satan or the devil. However, there's no direct mention of Mephistopheles in the Bible. He appears to be yet another creation of the inventive minds of the Renaissance. According to those accounts, Mephistopheles was the first rebel angel to align with Lucifer and, consequently, the second to be cast into hell.

Mephistopheles is most closely associated with the legend of *Faust*—the classic cautionary tale of a man who sells his soul to the devil in exchange for untold riches and pleasures. The story was recorded by Christopher Marlowe in late 1500s. In 1806 it was adapted by German author Johann Wolfgang von Goethe (1749–1842) as the tragic play *Faust—der Tragödie erster Teil,* and it appears as well in scores of legends, stories, songs, plays, and operas.

Mictlantecuhtli To the Aztec Indians in what is now Mexico, this god of death was often portrayed as a skeleton. Mictlantecuhtli is the ruler of the Aztec underworld, Mictlan.

Mormo Not quite a demonic figure, Mormo is the bogeywoman of Greek mythology. A companion of Hecate, she was said to prowl the world ready to bite children who misbehave.

Murmur A grand duke of hell with twenty legions under his command. Murmur can reveal the nature of philosophy and raise the dead to answer any questions the conjurer might pose. He is depicted as a crowned soldier seated atop a vulture.

Naamah "The Angel of Prostitution" of Jewish Kabbalistic texts. Naamah is consort to the demon Samael and considered the inspiration for the practice of divination.

Oni   Supernatural creatures of Japanese folklore, the Oni have been depicted, wearing tiger skins, with horns, sharp claws, and gaping mouths. More than simply monsters, the Oni of hell are the personification of the dark nature of man and can cause disease. The red- or green-bodied Oni prowl the earth in search of sinners and deliver them by chariot to Enma Daiou, the god of hell, who judges them with the aid of two decapitated heads.

Orias   A great duke of hell with thirty legions of demons under his command. Orias can reveal the secrets of the zodiac and all types of divination to those that would conjure him. He is often depicted as a lion with a tail of snake or, alternately, as a man with a lion's visage riding a stallion and holding a serpent in each hand.

Paimon   One of the kings of hell said to be more obedient to the will of Lucifer than others. Paimon can bestow knowledge of philosophy, science, and the arts. He can also reveal the mysteries of the world. Alternately depicted as either a man with a woman's face, or a man of feminine appearance with a crown on his head and riding a camel, Paimon is preceded by a host of demons. They are in human form and play musical instruments of all types. His name means "tinkling sound," and Paimon was the arranger of public ceremonies in the underworld. Legions under his command are said to number 200.

Pan   One of the most eternal images associated with Greek mythology. Pan, god of lust, appears as a faun, a horned and bearded man with the lower half of a goat, and with his namesake "panpipes," a wind instrument, about his neck. Rituals devoted to his worship consisted mainly of orgies and the consumption of wine. Hence, his demonic status in the eyes of Western religion.

Rabbit   To many Native American tribes throughout the Southwest, the rabbit is a Luciferian type of spirit animal. It first brought the gift of fire to mankind.

Raven Native American tribes of the Pacific Northwest envisioned the spirit of the raven as a greedy trickster—forever hungry and lying in wait to deceive. However, it was the raven that stole the moon and placed it in the night sky to aid humankind.

Samyaza (also **Semjaza, Shemyaza, Samyaza, Shemhazai)** is another of the fallen angels of the Grigori (who mated with human women to create the giant race of the Nephilim). The name translates as "infamous rebellion," which most likely harks back to his original deceit and rebellion against God.

Satan Also the devil, Prince of Darkness, Beelzebub, Belial, Mephistopheles, Lucifer, or Samael. This is the name most closely associated with the devil in the Western world. In Hebrew, Greek, Latin, and Aramaic, Satan means "adversary" or "accuser," and the figure is represented dually as an angel or demon. Satan makes only a single appearance in the Old Testament as the tormentor of Job. From the New Testament onward, the term has since come to mean an enemy to God as well as to man.

Shax (also **Chax, Shan, Shass, Shaz, Scox)** A great duke of hell in command of thirty legions of demons. At will, he can strike men blind and deaf and destroy the abilities of their minds, as well as rob them of their horses and other property. Shax can also reveal that which is hidden.

Sidragasum A sort of diabolical Hugh Hefner, serving as an assistant to Satan and inspiring women to dance in a lascivious manner on the holy Sabbath.

Stola A great prince of hell with twenty-six legions of demons at his beck and call. Stolas can reveal the secrets of astronomy, herbology, and the nature of precious stones. He is often depicted as an owl with a crown or, alternately, as a man or raven.

Surgat   The locksmith of the diabolic world, Surgat can open any seal or lock for those who would dare conjure him.

South Star   To the Pawnee Indians of what is now Nebraska, South Star is the god of the underworld—and counterpart to North Star.

Tzitzimime   To the Aztec Indians, these demons were the personification of the dark in the never-ending battle against the powers of the sun and light.

Tengu   Japanese demons who dwell in the mountains and revel in the torment of hapless travelers. They are often depicted as birds with the heads of men. Artisans often left tributes to the Tengu to ensure the quality of their crafts.

Valac (also **Ualac, Valak, Valax, Valu, Volcas)**   A great president of hell with thirty-three legions under his command. Valac offers true answers to the location of buried treasure and can paralyze serpents, placing them into the hands of those that would conjure him. Valac is depicted as a young man with angel's wings riding a two-headed dragon.

Valefar (also **Malaphar, Valafar, Valefor)**   A duke of hell with ten legions under his command. Valefar tempts man to steal and protects the ideal of "honor among thieves." Unfortunately for these honorable thieves, it is also this demon's charge to bring them to the gallows for their crimes. He is depicted alternately as a lion with the head of a man or a donkey.

Vapula (also **Naphula)**   A great duke of hell in command of thirty-six legions. Vapula can reveal secrets of philosophy, complicated mechanics, and a wide array of sciences. He is depicted as a winged lion.

Vepar   A female great duke of hell in command of twenty-nine demonic legions. Vepar controls the waters and guides ships of war to their destinations. If her ire is incurred, she can raise great storms and cause sailors to hallucinate a sea full of ships. Vepar can kill men in three days by a disease that causes rotting wounds. She is depicted as a mermaid.

Xaphan Another of the original angels that rebelled with Satan against God. It is said that it was his idea to set the heavens ablaze. As such, he is damned to forever fan the flames of hell. Xaphan is depicted as carrying a great fireplace bellows, but must feed the flames with his mouth and hands instead.

Yeter'el Another of the fallen angels, and a member of the race of Nephilim. He is another demonic figure mentioned mainly in apocryphal writings of the Book of Enoch.

Vual (also **Uvall, Voval, Wal, Wall**) Another great duke of hell in command of thirty-seven legions. Vual is often depicted as a dromedary camel that can change into human form. He is capable of granting the love of women, and Vual can dissolve long-lasting friendships between men of all stations in life. He also knows all events, past, present, and future.

Zagan A great king and president of hell who commands thirty-three legions. Zagan would be the demon to invoke to ensure a great party. He is capable of inspiring wit in men, can turn water and blood into wine, blood into oil and a fool into a wise man. Zagan can also turn metal into coins. He is the protector of those who would deceive others by fraud and counterfeiting. Zagan is depicted as a winged bull that can change into human form.

Zepar A great duke of hell with twenty-six legions of demons under his command. It is said that Zepar is capable of seducing women by taking the human form of their husbands or lovers. He can also inspire women and men to love. Often Zepar is depicted as a soldier wearing red clothes or armor.

◄ ANGELS ►

One of the most longstanding and potent mantras associated with the occult are the simple words, "As above, so below." Thousands of years old, this simple phrase suggests an inextricable and important duality between man and the gods—and perhaps an even more important relationship between gods and humankind. Either, without the other, might cease to exist from a spiritual standpoint—but despite all of this, the great heavenly contraption seems to hum eternally above while the gears of humanity clack away with equal gusto down here on good old terra firma.

While the imagination of man might seem limitless, even the highest flights of fancy concerning the nature of the heavens are grounded in the human experience. Creation is a beautiful thing—but as with demonology, view it from an administrative standpoint. Even before man came onto the spiritual scene, the angels had their hands full.

So, it's not too far a stretch to envision angels and demons as the blue-collar workers of the cosmic world. In early Judaism, Islam and Christianity, these messengers of the gods kept busy trafficking arcane information, flaming retribution and the divine word to the ears and minds of man—whether or not he cared to know. However, the definition of these both helpful and/or hurtful spirits is so broad, it can be said that nearly every culture and religious belief has its angels.

The word angel comes from the Latin *angelus* by way of the Greek *angelos* or *"messenger."* In the Old Testament, angels reveal themselves to a select few to offer up an omen of some future event or are the embodiment of God's wrath, offering up good old-fashioned fire and brimstone.

Much like on earth, life in heaven has a certain degree of uncertainty to it. If various religious histories tell us anything, it is that angels are subject to the same trappings as man—jealousy, petulance, and lust. So, there are a great many entries in this section that have identical counterparts in the Demons section.

Like most of the concepts associated with "angelology," the following names and ideas were put to paper hundreds of years after the first biblical writings. These, in turn, were quite a historical distance from the events themselves.

To call some of these angelic concepts "apocryphal" is indeed being kind. However, there is also no doubt that these ideas are canon to many faiths.

There are three hierarchies of angels and nine distinct orders—each with unique purpose, characteristics, and history. The hierarchies are unceremoniously referred to as the first, second, and third—after which things get slightly more complicated.

Angels This very broad term encompassed celestial beings of all varieties and can be used for any figure that comes as a messenger of God, or bears his will or word. Once fallen, these demonic figures still act as conduits of arcane and forbidden knowledge—this time revealing them for a price rather than under divine order.

Archangels There are little to no references of this caste of high-ranking angels in the Old Testament. Even in the New Testament, there is but a single mention of an archangel (signaling the return of Christ). Later Christian writings disagree regarding the archangel order. The number of archangels for "holy ones," can be only one, as in Protestant belief, or as many as eight for those who would include the archangel Lucifer. There are even two archangels observed in Muslim belief.

Cherubim The Cherubim offer a more classic version of the angelic form— the manifestation of Cupid is perhaps the most recognizable. However, in the Old Testament, Cherubim were often depicted as human/animal hybrids rather than well-fed babies with wings. In the Book of Ezekiel, for example, they are described as having four faces (one of an ox, a lion, an eagle, and a man). They also had cloven hooves associated with demons. The artists of the Renaissance gave the Cherubim the forms used in cutesy greeting cards and garden statuary.

Dominions (also called **Dominations)** These angels are said to be so numerous as to belie any human conception of number. They are dedicated to the ideals of order and perfection and serve as leaders in the angelic community. They also regulate the duties of lower-order angels.

Powers (also called **Dynamis, Potentiates, Authorities)**   The angels of this order serve as protectors, and are always ready to combat demonic forces wherever they might try to cast their influence. They have knowledge of philosophy and theology. They are also purported to divide power and influence among all people.

Principalities   Angels of this order fall into the "guardian angel" category and are often the patrons and protectors of towns or villages. In carrying out their duties, they have no qualms about interfering in the lives of humans to carry out the will of God. They are often depicted as beams of light.

Seraphim   In the Old Testament, this highest order of angels has only one reference. In the book of Isaiah, they are depicted in classic angelic form, but with six wings rather than two. The Seraphim aren't mentioned biblically again until the Book of Revelation in the New Testament. While not mentioned directly, the depiction is nearly identical to the one offered up in Isaiah. Christian thought views the Seraphim as the highest angelic order.

Thrones (also the **Ophanim)**   These celestial beings are the most unlike conventional angelic figures. Sometimes called the "Wheels of Gallagin," they are typically depicted as just that—wheels covered with a multitude of all-seeing eyes.

Virtues   The angels of this order can control the weather and the elements. In the writings of Thomas Aquinas, Virtues hold sway over earthly miracles, and can imbue humankind with grace and valor.

⊰ ANGEL GLOSSARY ⊱

Aba   An angel of wisdom and fertility who also, according to more modern Kabbalistic practices, helps humans with their sexuality. There seems to be some debate as to whether Aba is a fallen angel, a Christian angel, or a supernatural spirit merely *called* an angel for lack of a better description.

Abbaddon   The book of Revelation calls him "the Destroyer" or "King of the Grasshoppers." Abbaddon, a fallen angel, is chief of all demons in the seventh hierarchy. His presence was felt so profoundly that throughout history, the term Abbaddon has been used interchangeably for any number of demonic figures, the devil itself, or a pit in the deepest recesses of Hell.

Abachta   In Jewish thought, he is one of the seven angels associated with confusion. The others are named Barbonah, Bigtha, Carcas, Biztha, Mehuman, and Zether.

Abalim   The Hebrew name for the Thrones order of angels.

Achaiah   In Kabbalistic writings, he is referenced as a Seraph, the patron of patience, who can reveal secrets of nature to man.

Agares   *(fallen angel)* A dark prince, Agares is said to rule the eastern provinces of Hell and is served by 30 legions of devoted demon consorts. He can cause earthquakes and reveal languages to man. He revels in teaching "immoral expressions" (read: dirty jokes) and is described as relatively benevolent as far as demons are concerned. He is often depicted riding a crocodile and carrying a sparrow hawk, a bird of prey similar to a falcon.

Agrat bat Mahlat   The angel of prostitution. She is beautiful but leads virtuous women into sin. Some Victorian Era (and later) artists have depicted her wearing a crown of thorns in mockery of the suffering of Jesus.

Aha viel   One of the angels of protection whose name was often inscribed on Hebrew charms.

Ahjma'il   A guardian angel from Arabic lore whose name in invoked when performing exorcisms.

Akriel   One of the "lost cause" angels, Akriel is appealed to by barren women. She is also the patron angel of stupidity and helps the desperate open their minds.

Akteriel (also **Akathriel)**   An angel consulted by generals and kings for insights into strategy.

Almiras   An angel of invisibility who is invoked during magic ceremonies.

Altarib   The angel of winter; his aid can be sought through prayer to avert blizzards and killer cold.

Anahita   A fertility goddess of ancient Persia. Anahita was also the patroness of women and the goddess of war. Her name means "the immaculate one," and in ancient times she was depicted as being dressed in golden robes with a crown of diamonds. However, a far earthier version of Anahita sprang up in Europe shortly after the fall of Rome, in which she appeared in paintings and other art as a nude woman of surpassing beauty and sexual appeal. The Christians of medieval Europe gave Anahita a somewhat more modest makeover, garbing her in white and giving her angel wings. Even so, she was still known as the "Angel of Fertility."

Ardousisur (also **Arduisher)**   A Zoroastrian angel who eases the pain of childbirth and helps new mothers produce sufficient breast milk. Her name means "giver of living water."

Armaita (also **Aramaiti, Armaiti)**   The ancient Persian angel of truth, wisdom, and goodness.

ANAHITA
ANGEL OF FERTILITY
Jason Beam

Aruru A Sumerian angelic being who became a messenger of the gods. Her firstborn son was the hero Gilgamesh.

Asmodai (also **Aeshma, Aesma)** Once chief of the Cherubim order, he became a demonic figure after the fall. Asmodai's origins are in ancient Persia. Later he is mentioned in the New Testament Book of Tobit as well as the Jewish Talmud. Originally the chief all demons, eventually Asmodeus evolved into

ARMAITA
ANGEL OF TRUTH
AND WISDOM
Michael Bateson

a demonic and lustful figure whose only aim was to arouse impure thoughts in humankind. He also took pleasure in ruining the beauty of virgins and caused their hearts to blacken.

Astaroth   Once an angel of the Seraphim order, Astaroth is generally regarded as the Grand Duke of Hell. He has four demon assistants, Aamon; Pruslas, a great seducer of women; Barbatos, who can speak in the tongue of any animal, knows the past and future and can reveal things that are hidden; and Rashaverak—whose fame seems to come by association alone.

Azazel   A Hebrew name closely associated with Satan. Azazel first appears in Leviticus in the Old Testament in describing a Yom Kippur ritual where a goat is cast into the wilderness, carrying with it the sins of the people. This practice is the origin of the term "scapegoat" and Jews perform a less drastic version as part of Yom Kippur observances today—when a congregation might leave their place of worship for a nearby creek or stream, where all might cast their sins into the waters. The term has also become synonymous with the desolate valley where the goat was cast out each year.

Barbatos   *(fallen angel)* Once an angel of the order of virtues, after his fall he became a great duke of Hell. He can communicate with dogs and birds, reveal that which is hidden and dissolve magical seals and enchantments on troves of treasure and sacred items. He knows the past, present and future and is in command of 30 legions of demons, and is generally depicted as a horned hunter.

Barachiel   His name means "blessings of God," and in art he is often depicted clutching a white rose. Barachiel is purported to be the chief of all of the guardian angels. He is often invoked for luck during games of chance.

Barbiel   An angel once associated with both Virtues and the Archangels, who became a demonic figure after his fall.

Beelzebub   *(fallen angel)* Also Belzebud, Belzaboul, Beelzeboul, Baalsebul, Baalzebubg, Beelzebuth, Beelzebus. This Philistine God is closely associated with Baal, and the term does indeed seem to be a prefix, which translates "Lord of the Flies" from the Hebrew zebub (to fly). Since that time, it has become yet another term used interchangeably with Satan or the Devil. Later theologians and demonologists suggest he was yet another fallen angel of the cherubim order, and has since become associated with the deadly sins of pride or gluttony.

He also figures prominently in Milton's *Paradise Lost* where he is regarded as an equal to Satan.

Beleth   *(fallen angel)* Once an angel of the order of powers, after his fall he became a powerful and terrible king of Hell in command of 85 legions of demons. He rides a white stallion and his appearance is heralded by the thunderous blare of trumpets. Those who would dare conjure him must treat him with the utmost respect, and guard themselves by wearing a ring of silver on the middle finger of the left hand.

Benad Hasche   Female angels whose name means "daughters of God," worshipped by Arabs.

Berith   Once a prince of the Cherubim order, after the fall he became a great duke of hell known for his ferocity, with twenty-six legions under his command. Berith knows the past and future and is the consummate alchemist, able to turn all base metals into gold. He is depicted as a red-skinned soldier clad in red seated upon a red horse, with a golden crown on his head.

Bodiel (also **Bodiel, Boel, Boul, Booel, Bohel**)   An angel of the Thrones order, his name means "God is in him."

Cahetel   An angel of the Seraphim order, he is the patron of agriculture. Cahetel is another of the seventy-two angels that bear the name of God. In Kabbalistic practices, his spirit is sometimes invoked to ensure a bountiful harvest.

Camio   *(fallen angel)* The Gaelic pronunciation of the biblical Cain and the Godfather of all acts of murder. While it is unclear from a biblical standpoint if Cain went to Hell for his sins, artists and writers of later years were quick to place him as one of the Underworld's most famous occupants. Camio can speak in the tongues of animals of the land and sea and can predict future events. Some demonologists have depicted him as a black bird that can transform into a man.

Camael (also Kemuel, Shemuel, Chamuel, Camiel, Camniel, Zamael, Cancel) Chief of the Order of Powers, his name means "he who sees God." Camael is ruler of the planet Mars.

Cherubiel By some, he is regarded as the chief of the Cherubim order of angels; others believe that position belongs to the archangel Gabriel.

Damabiah A being of the angel order that is the patron of shipbuilders, he is one of the 72 angelic figures bearing the name of God.

Diabolus See Astaroth.

Elijah In the Old Testament, he was an angelic figure who ushered the souls of the righteous into heaven. In Jewish belief the messiah has not yet come, and will be heralded by Elijah. His spirit is also invoked yearly during Passover. During the Seder, a cup of wine is poured for him, and the door of the home opened to allow him to enter and bless the ceremony.

Eloa According to some medieval Christian beliefs, Eloa was created from a tear that Jesus shed in the Garden of Gethsemane before his arrest. She is both the angel of sorrow (for Jesus was betrayed by a close friend) and compassion. Eloa is invoked by those who need help in starting their lives over again.

Focalor *(fallen angel)*—An angel of the order of Thrones, after his fall he became a great duke of Hell in command of 30 legions of demons, and has been depicted as a winged human. He holds sway over storms at sea and takes great pleasure in sinking ships and drowning sailors.

Forcas A duke of hell with twenty-nine legions of demons under his command. Forcas can bestow the secrets of mathematics, locate lost items, and render invisible those that would conjure him.

Forneus An angel of the order of Thrones. After his fall he became a great marquis of hell in command of 29 legions of demons. Forneus is often de-

ELOA
ANGEL OF COMPASSION
AND SORROW
Kathy Gold

picted as a mammoth sea serpent. His domain is languages and rhetoric, and he causes men to be charismatic.

Gaap *(fallen angel)*—Once an angel of the Powers order, after his fall he came to be regarded as a prince and great president of Hell in command of 66 legions of demons. He is said to be the ruler of the southern provinces of the Underworld. He is capable of bestowing knowledge of philosophy and science, and can inspire love and hate in men, or cause them to become ignorant.

Gabriel An important angelic figure in Judaism, Christianity, Islam, and the B'Hai Faith. Gabriel is alternately translated as "left hand of God" or

"God's might." He has been portrayed as the messenger of God, an oracle figure who foretold the birth of Christ, and as the vessel by which the Koran was given to man.

Gressil   A demonic figure that embraces filth and impurity. Gressil has been portrayed as a flying lizardlike creature that feeds on the dead and lives in caves and other moribund places.

Grigori   *(fallen angel)* One of the groups of fallen angels (called watchers) who mated with mortal women to create a race of "super" humans called the Nephilim. From Genesis 6:2 *"the sons of God saw that the daughters of men were beautiful and married any of them they chose."* Though the Nephilim are later described as "heroes of old, men of renown" it was soon after this period that God was said to condemn the world for its wickedness and caused the Great Flood.

Hafaza   In Muslim belief, the Hafaza are angelic figures that are purported to protect humankind from evil, as well as catalog its actions.

Hahuiah   One of the seventy-two angels that bears the name of God.

Hosts   One of the original orders of angels whose wings were clipped by Pseudo-Dionysius, the Areopagite—whose fifth century writings fashioned many accepted concepts of the hiearchy of angels.

Jegudiel   His name means "laudation of God." Jegudiel is the patron of those who toil in the fields, and of judges and kings.

Jehoel   The angel who holds the beast Leviathan at bay. Jehoel is often regarded as a potent mediator and a patron of disputes, both domestic and business related.

Jinn   In Muslim belief, these spiritual figures existed before the creation of man. Then, the same old story unfolds as these proud creatures refuse to bow down to God's creation Adam. The Jinn were thus cast out of heaven and became demons. The females are called Jinneyeh.

Lauviah   One of the angels of the order of Thrones. He became jealous of God's humankind and plotted its destruction. Along with fellow angels Berith, Salikotal, and Marou, he helped place the forbidden tree in the Garden of Eden.

Leviathan   *(fallen angel)* (which comes from the Hebrew term for "whale".) It is said that at the end of days, both the Leviathan and Behemoth will be slain, and their flesh fed to the righteous.

Lucifer   *(fallen angel)* A combination of the Latin *lux* (light) and *ferre* (to carry), this "bearer of the light" has become synonymous with the Devil itself. To the Greeks, he was the "morning star," Heosphoros, or literally "bringer of the light." In Christian theology, Lucifer was the highest-ranking archangel in heaven, but his greed and lust for power caused him and his fellows to rebel against God, a sin for which they were cast into perdition.

Marou   Once an angel of the Cherubim order, he was another of the angels who became jealous of humankind and plotted its destruction. Along with fellow angels Berith, Salikotal, and Lauviah, he helped place the forbidden apple tree in the Garden of Eden.

Michael   A prominent angelic figure in the Old and New Testaments, his name means "who is like God." Michael appears in the book of Revelation, and is regarded as a patron and protector of Israel. To the knights of yore, he became associated with chivalrous deeds of all kinds. Catholism canonized him.

Metatron   Outside of fans of Kevin Smith's controversial 1999 film *Dogma*, most people are unaware of this angelic figure, and with good reason. There is little mention of him from a biblical standpoint, though he has been referred to as a "lesser YHVH" (YHVH being the acceptable name to represent "Yahweh," the true name of God, which cannot be written). This moniker suggests that Metatron, a "messenger," could be "like" God. Despite all this, his visage seems to be more popular in anime and videogames than in theology.

Murmur *(fallen angel)*—Once an angel of the order of Thrones, after his fall he became a great duke of Hell with 30 legions of demons under his command. He can teach the secrets of philosophy or call the souls of the dead to appear for those that would conjure him. In art, he is often depicted as a soldier riding on either a griffin or vulture—or simply as a vulture.

Nathanael An angel of the Seraphim order whose name means "gift from God."

Nelchael Once an angel of the order of Thrones, he became a demonic figure. While he is one of the seventy-two angels bearing the name of God, he is regarded as fallen, and can reveal the secrets of astronomy, mathematics, and geography to those that would conjure him.

Ophanim (also **Many-Eyed Ones)** A species of eternally vigilant celestial beings mentioned in the Book of Enoch who sleeplessly watch the throne of God. Some sources suggest that the Ophanim are part of the class of angel known as Thrones.

Phenex After his fall he became a great marquis of hell with twenty legions of demons. Phenex is, not surprisingly, often depicted as a phoenix.

Purson Once an angel of the order of Virtues, after his fall he became a great king of Hell with twenty-two legions of demons under his command. Purson can tell of events of the past, present, and future. In art, he is depicted as a man with a lion's face, carrying a serpent, and riding upon a bear.

Pseudo-Dionysus the Areopagite A fairly mysterious fifth century theologian (more likely a group) whose writings, *Corpus Areopagiticum,* are the basis of of the hierarchies and angelic orders referenced in this chapter. Conceptualizations of angels could be considered to be either or pre- or post-Dionysius in scope. This is only one conception, however popular, and these writings have been condemned by religious figures from Martin Luther to the present day.

Raguel   His name means "friend of God," and his domain is said to be fair play, justice, and harmony. It is his charge to watch the actions of his own kind, and be prepared to dole out punishment to angelic transgressors at the end of days.

Raphael   Another archangel who is a prominent figure in Judaism, Christianity, and Islam. His name means "God has healed." Not surprisingly, Raphael is the patron of the healing arts. He is also closely associated with the air, the east, and the color yellow.

Raum   Once an angel of the order of Thrones, after his fall he became a great earl of hell with thirty legions of demons under his command. He is a favorite of wizards with thievish intentions and was purported to be able to steal the treasures of kings.

Raziel   A prominent figure in Judaism, specifically in the arcane lore of the Kabbalah. Raziel was purported to be something of a "secretary" to God, and penned a book of all the things he saw and heard. This fabled tome, *The Book of Raziel*, was coveted for its wealth of forbidden knowledge.

Salikotal   One of the angels who became jealous of humankind and plotted its destruction. Along with fellow angels Berith, Lauviah, and Marou, he helped place the forbidden tree in the Garden of Eden.

Samael (also the Devil, Prince of Darkness, Beelzebub, Belial, Mephistopheles, Lucifer)   In Hebrew, Greek, Latin, and Aramaic, Samael means "adversary" or "accuser," and the figure is represented dually as an angel or demon. He makes only a single appearance in the Old Testament as the tormentor of Job. From the New Testament onward, Samael came to mean an enemy of God as well as to man.

Satan   *(Fallen Angel)* See the Devil, Prince of Darkness, Beelzebub, Belial, Mephistopheles, Lucifer, Samael.

Semyazza (also Semjaza, Shemyaza, Samyaza, Shemhazai)   Another of the fallen angels of the order of the Grigori who mated with human women to create the giant race of the Nephilim. The name translates as "infamous rebellion," which most likely harks back to his original deceit and rebellion against God.

Selaphiel   An archangel whose name means, "communicant of God." Selaphiel is the patron of prayer.

Seraphiel   An angel mentioned in the apocryphal Book of Enoch.

Shamsiel   An angel of the Watcher order whose job it was to guard the gates of the Garden of Eden after the expulsion of Adam and Eve.

Sonneillon   Once an angel of the order of Thrones, after his fall he was regarded as a demon of hate, who could sow discord in the hearts of men. Sonneillon was purported to have possessed the soul of a nun in the sixteenth century.

Uriel   One of the archangels, his name means "flame of God." Uriel is associated with the earth, true north, and the color green. He is regarded as the angel of hope, and is purported to escort the souls of the righteous into heaven.

Verrine   A demon figure and fallen angel associated with death and impatience.

Watchers   Another name for the Grigori order of angels.

Zophiel   An archangel whose name means "beauty of God."

— *Chapter Four* —
DIVINATION

IT WAS NOT LONG AFTER MAN assumed dominion over the earth that the problems began. He did not understand what occurred; the world seemed full of mysteries; the unknown was too vast. Despite his perceived importance, he could not control the availability of game, the changes in weather, or guarantee fire, warmth, and shelter. It is the nature of man to either control his environment, bend it to his will, or when things are beyond his power, to at least understand why.

Many early religions were peopled with dozens, even hundreds, of gods, monsters, angels, demons, and spirits. This came about largely because the existence of such beings explained why the universe works the way it does. If a hurricane destroys a valley full of crops, it was easier to blame a spiteful storm demon than to assume that weather patterns are arbitrary. Conversely, if the harvest yields unexpected abundance, then it is a time to celebrate the beneficence of a god or patron spirit.

As time passed and humans became more familiar with many gods, the conclusion was made that they had something to say, and ways were sought to connect with the secret language of the unseen world. People sought, by various means, to *divine* hints, portents, omens, and other clues to the mysteries that surrounded them.

Divination is a method by which many cultures used to glean information from supernatural or celestial sources. The practice cuts across all cultural and historic lines, and has been in constant use since the birth of civilization. Divination is still practiced today in even the most modern of cultures. Tarot cards, palmistry, astrology, and many other methods are part of our everyday life. Whether we read horoscopes for fun, or put credence in the position of stars, many people believe that information is available not found in science or the evening news.

The vestiges of divination are with us today, though now we might see a group of girls playing jacks on the sidewalk. We might settle our differences with games of paper, rock and scissors or by flipping coins and casting lots to make fair decisions. To our more "sophisticated" mind, it is the randomness of these acts that makes them fair methods, but ancient minds beheld the same randomness and saw inside it a divine order, messages from the spiritual world written for us, requiring only that we master the precise technique and subtlety of thought to perceive them.

Following are nearly eighty different forms of divination, each ending in the suffix "mancy," which is derived from the Greek "manteia", meaning "prophesy."

Aeromancy   Divination by the study of the sky, as well as an interpretation of the shapes made by clouds and other astral phenomena.

Alectryomancy   In this practice, a cock is permitted to eat grains of corn spread over an area. The outcome of the reading depends upon which grains of corn have been consumed from what sections representing a letter, thought, or idea. In a variation of this practice, the letters of the alphabet are read aloud while listening to see if a cock crows upon the recitation of particular letters.

Alueromancy   From the Greek *aleuron,* for flour, and *manteia,* divination, an example of this practice would be the Chinese Fortune Cookie where answers to life questions are written on small scraps of paper, folded into dough, and baked. An alternative to this practice consists of the study of the patterns of flour in a bowl into which some water has been added.

Alomancy (also called **adromancy, ydromancie, idromancie, halomancy)** Divination by observing the actions of salt that has been cast into the air. Because of its rarity in ancient times, salt has always been associated with luck and wealth. This is most likely the basis for superstitions pertaining to salt, such as throwing some over a shoulder when it is spilled to ward off bad spirits.

Alphitomancy This practice is akin to trial by fire. A group of people suspected of committing a crime are all given a piece of bread to eat. Supposedly, it will cause the perpetrator of the crime to become ill, not affecting the innocent. Exactly how the bread is made unpalatable is a fact perhaps best left to posterity.

Anthropomancy (also **called splanchomancy)** The practice of divination by human sacrifice practiced by the ancient Egyptians and Romans. Afterward the entrails of a victim are studied.

Apantomancy This type of divination is two-fold. First, the diviner works him or herself into a spiritual frenzy until they see visions of various animals. The significance of what type is seen is unique to the culture. For example, it is said that the site which is now Mexico City was first founded when Aztec magicians envisioned an eagle flying from a cactus carrying a snake in its beak. This symbol can still be found on pottery, blankets and crafts, as well as on the Mexican flag.

Astraglomancy A form of divination in which dice bearing various letters and numbers are used. It is the predecessor of games of chance involving dice.

Augury A form of divination practiced in ancient Rome where the movements of animals and birds were said to portend future events. Those who practiced the technique were called augurs. This term can also be applied to reading signs or omens of any type.

Austromancy   The observation or study of the wind for purposes of divination.

Axiomancy   Divination through the interpretation of the quivering movements of an axe blade that had just been thrust into a table, block of wood, or tree.

Belomancy   Practiced by the Babylonians, Greeks, and Arabs, in this practice, arrows are marked with various occult symbols or possible outcomes to a situation. They are then fired from bows and their trajectory is studied. The arrow that travels the farthest distance, or in some cases the least distance, indicates the answer to the query. In a variation of this practice, marked arrows are mixed in a quiver and one is drawn at random, indicating the answer to a question—although this is closer to casting lots.

Bibliomancy (also **stichomancy)**   In this practice a book, usually the Bible or other sacred text, is opened and a passage is read at random. The chosen passage is then studied for possible significance.

Botanomancy   A practice in which branches and leaves are burned and the actions of the fire, smoke, and winds are studied.

Capnomancy (also called **libanomancy)**   While all of us can be entranced watching a fire, this practice concerns the observation of smoke from a cooking or sacrificial blaze.

Cartomancy   Divination through the use of cards. These may be simple playing cards or ones specifically created for this purpose, such as tarot cards.

Catoptromancy   A form of the wider practice of "crystal gazing," this method involves gazing at a reflection of the moon in a mirror. It is said that the answers to questions appear in blood on the surface of the moon.

Causimomancy   Divination by fire. In some cultures, this was as simple as placing a questionable object into a fire to see if it would burn. Items immune to the effects of fire were said to be a good omen.

Cephalomancy   Literally "head divination." This practice involves using the head of a goat or donkey to predict future events. However, cephalomancy also indicates the use of a head (human or otherwise) for purposes of divination.

Ceraunoscopy   The observation of thunder, lightning, and other features of the atmosphere to predict future events. Other practices specifically look at lightning or thunder alone for such signs.

Ceromancy   Anyone who has ever poured the contents of a burning candle into cool water is very familiar with this form of divination. The patterns yielded can be ominous and beautiful indeed. The object is to look for specific shapes of day-to-day items such as broomsticks, hats, and animals—each has special significance.

Chiromancy   Another term for palm reading.

Chirognomy   Rather than looking at the lines of the palm, this practice involves an examination of the shape, size, and appearance of the hand. Not only do a person's hands reveal much about him or her, but many diseases and conditions manifest themselves in the hands as well.

⊰ PROFESSIONAL ⊱ PSYCHICS

A great number of people make their living as professional psychics. These can range from astrologers who write newspaper columns to TV celebs who channel the dead relatives of the audience; from friends who read tarot cards at parties to carnival palm readers. Although most psychics don't overplay the role too elaborately, some do—and for most of their customers the crystals, darkened rooms with gauzy scarves hanging on the walls, incense, gypsy clothing, and the like provide a comfortable setting for a palm or card reading. Though sometimes this shtick is taken too far (theremin music playing in the background for instance), there are psychics of great quality even among the fringe crowd.

Clairaudience   Literally "clear hearing." This is the perception of voices and sounds outside of the normal spectrum of hearing, and a form of ESP, or extra sensory perception.

Clairvoyance   Literally "clear seeing." The perception of visions beyond the normal spectrum of sight, also a form of ESP.

Cleromancy (also **sortilege)**   This practice is similar to "casting lots" where objects such as seashells, stones, or pebbles are cast to the ground and examined.

Clidomancy   This practice involved taking a key and placing it within the pages of a book (usually a Bible) so it is able to move. Then, a question is proposed and the key is said to move, indicating the answer to the question. This term also describes the use of a pendulum where the direction of the swinging is analyzed.

Critomancy   The choice of divination for those with a sweet tooth. In this practice, barley cakes are examined for flour swirls and patterns that are said to indicate the future.

CARNIVAL PSYCHIC
Jennifer Singleton

Cromniomancy   Continuing with food-related divination, this practice involves predicting the future by the observation of onion sprouts.

Crystallomancy   The observations of crystals for divination. This practice is related to the well-known art of crystal-ball gazing, also referred to as scrying.

Cyclomancy   Divination through the observation of a wheel, top, or other spinning object. This practice was often used to choose a direction when travelers came to a fork in the road. Cyclomancy is also the precursor to the game of "spin the bottle."

Dactylomancy   A practice similar to clidomancy, but a ring, rather than a key, is used.

Daphnomancy   The practice of divination where one listens to the crackling sound of burning laurel branches to predict future events.

Demonomancy   When the aid of demons is used for purposes of divination.

Dowsing   The use of a "divining rod" or forked stick to find sources of water or precious minerals beneath the earth. It is said that a divining rod will quiver under its own power when held over an underground source of water.

Gastromancy   Literally "divination from the stomach." This practice is a form of ventriloquism where a voice seems to emanate from the belly of the practitioner. Indeed, the modern practice of ventriloquism seems to have been created from this exercise.

Geloscopy   Divination by examining the tones and nuances of someone's laughter.

Genethlialogy   Divination by the notation and study of the exact position of a star at the time of one's birth. This isn't too far from conventional astrology, and if you're aware of the exact time of your birth, it is said to be possible to get a more intuitive reading.

Geomancy   A system of divination that involves casting and interpreting the shapes and positions of stones, pebbles, and sand. The Chinese version of this practice is called feng-shui (meaning wind and water) and is employed by interior engineers and designers today.

Graphology   Divination through the analysis of handwriting. Rather than predicting one's future, this practice is purported to reveal hidden aspects of the writer's personality and intent.

Gyromancy One of the more amusing methods of divination, the querent may either spin in place or walk repeatedly around the circumference of a circle inscribed with various letters and symbols. Once the person becomes dizzy and falls into the circle, the symbol where he or she landed is noted.

Heptascopy (also **haruspication)** Prediction through examining the entrails of various types of animals. The prefix "hepta" denotes a more exact practice as well, the examination of the liver.

Hippomancy Divination by the study and cataloguing of the behavior of horses. This may be as simple as noting the actions of horses before a coming storm, or for matters of greater import.

Hydromancy Divination by the examination of water in a pool or basin where pebbles or small stones are dropped. Other subtleties such as the color and appearance of the water are also considered.

⊰ THE TAROT ⊱
CELTIC CROSS

Of all of the hundreds of types of tarot-card readings, the Celtic Cross is the most respected. Single-question/single-card and three-card past/present/future readings are more common (largely because they are less time consuming and easier for less-skilled readers). The ten-card Celtic Cross allows the reader to get a far more complete picture of the subject and the forces at work around them. The cards are laid out in the pattern of a cross, composed of six cards on the left side and four cards in a vertical line to the right. Each card has a different meaning and are laid out in the following order:

1. *Present position:* This identifies the major problem and sets the tone for the reading.

2. *Immediate influence:* This card identifies the challenge or crisis facing the subject.

3. *Short-term outlook:* This probes the subconscious of the subject and gives some substance to the feeling he has about the matter in question.

4. *Distant past foundation:* This shows the events that laid the groundwork for the current matter.

5. *Recent past events:* This indicates the most immediate forces at work that have brought the matter to the crisis point.

6. *Future influence:* This suggests how the current matter will be influenced by events yet to happen.

7. *The questioner:* This card ties in the attitude, mood, determination, will, and other factors that the subject brings to bear on the matter.

8. *Outside forces:* This card shows how other factors beyond the control of the subject bear on the matter.

9. *Inner emotions:* This indicates how the subject feels about the matter and its possible outcome.

10. *Final outcome:* The final card reveals how the situation will be resolved.

Ichtomancy   Examining the entrails of fish to predict future events.

Lampadomancy   The use and employment of lamps for divinatory purposes.

Libanomancy   When the behavior of incense smoke is studied to predict the outcome of future events. Divination of this type was commonly practiced by the ancient Babylonians.

Lithomancy   The practice of divination by the examination of crystals or stones of various types. In some cases, two stones of different colors might be drawn from to answer a "yes" or "no" question. Other stones might symbolize astrological signs.

Margaritomancy   A unique method of divination or "trial by fire" where a pearl is placed beneath a vase and placed near a fire. The names of supposed wrongdoers are then read aloud; upon mentioning the name of the guilty party, the pearl is purported to pierce the vase.

Metagnomy   Practitioners of this craft study visions that come to them while in a trance-like state.

Meteromancy   Divination by the notation and the study of the appearance and behavior of meteors.

Metoposcopy   The discovery and examination of a person's character by studying the lines of their forehead.

Moleosophy   Not the philosophy of moles and other earth tunneling creatures, but the study of their behavior as an indication of a person's character.

Molybdomancy   In some cultures, it is believed that prophecy can be gleaned by listening the hiss and crackle of molten metal.

Myomancy   Examining the behavior of rats and mice for purposes of divination.

Numerology   The study of numerals, dates, times and values assigned to various letters of the alphabet for purposes of divination.

⊰ EYES OF NOSTRADAMUS ⊱

Since the sixteenth century many people have searched through the writings of Michel de Nostradamus (1503–1566) to compare his predictions to current events. His writings, *Les Propheties,* were published in 1555, and were purported to reference happenings throughout history—from the rise of Napoleon to the fall of the Twin Towers, as two examples.

Ultimately, more than 900 predictions were made. Each is written in quatrains (rhymes of four lines) and arranged in sections of 100 verses each. Nostradamus wrote in an older French dialect, thus making translation a bit tricky. So much so, in fact, that any given set of verses seems to be open to a wide number of possible interpretations. Scholars of Nostradamus *interpreted* his writings and found references to such events as the Great Fire of London in 1666, the French Revolution, the rise of Hitler, World War II, the fall of the Kennedys, and more—but since these verses were neither dated nor presented in any clear chronological order, translation is very much up to the reader.

Nostradamus published his prophecies in sections. The first appeared in 1555, followed two years later by a second installment with an additional 289 verses. In 1558, 300 more were made available. An omnibus edition called *The Centuries* was published after Nostradamus's death in 1568, which contains 941 rhymed quatrains grouped into 9 sets of 100 and one of 42—this is the most commonly referred to text with the predictions.

Omphalomancy   While it is said that the eyes are the windows of the soul, those who practice omphalomancy claim they can be granted prophecy by the study of someone's eyes.

Oinomancy   While we all feel a bit more prophetic after a glass of wine or two, it is believed that wine can be used to predict the future. Thus, oinomancy.

Oneiromancy   The reliance on the interpretation of dreams to predict future events.

Onomancy   This practice looks for significance in the names of people or historic figures. The application of this practice is called onomantics.

Onychomancy   Divination by the study and examination of fingernails.

Oomantia (also **ooscopy, ovomancy)**   Divination by the study and examination of various types of eggs.

Ophiomancy   Divination by observing the behavior of snakes.

Orniscopy (also **orinithomancy, apantomancy)**   Divination by studying omens associated with birds in flight.

Pegomancy   Even when a brook is simply babbling, it's best to listen. This practice of divination concerns the examination and study of springs and naturally running sources of water.

Phrenology   The practice of "reading" the bumps and other imperfections on the human head. Its roots are in ancient Greece, but phrenology's heyday was in the late-nineteenth century. Victorians accepted it as genuine and scientific.

Phyllorhodomancy   A practice in which a rose is slapped against an open hand. The volume of the sound is said to portend the future.

Physiognomy   A picture does paint a thousand words, especially in this practice of divination by examining someone's physical features.

Rhabdomancy   A predecessor of dowsing and the use of a divining rod. It uses a stick or wand to predict future events.

Rhapsodomancy (also **stichomancy)**   A practice where a book is thrown open and a random passage is read aloud. This passage is then considered in relation to the situation in question.

Sciomancy   The employment and use of "spirit guides" to predict the outcome of future events. An appearance of such spirit guides offering aid can also fall into this category.

Spodomancy   Divination by the examination of soot and cinders from a freshly burned pyre or fireplace.

Stolisomancy   Perhaps one of the few methods of divination still practiced on the "red carpets" on a variety of award shows. It is said one can predict the future by study of the way people dress.

Sycomancy   A practice in which messages are inscribed on the leaves of trees. The more time it takes for the leaves to dry, the more fortunate the omen. A modern variation of this practice is to write possible responses on parchments, which are then rolled up and held over a boiling pot. The first answer to unroll is said to be significant.

Tarot   The most evolved form of cartomancy. Though its precise origins are unknown, there are records of tarot use as early as the fifteenth century. Originally the deck was created for card games. The earliest known published manual on tarot divination was in *The Oracles of Francesco Marcolino da Forli,* which outlined the basics of card reading. The standard tarot deck consists of 78 cards. The largest part of the deck is a group of 56 cards, known as the minor arcana, divided into four suits: wands, coins, cups, and swords. The remaining

DEATH TAROT and LOVERS TAROT Morbideus W. Goodell

22 cards comprise the higher arcana, and each card in this set is unique and relates to specific aspects of life, the world, fortune, and so on. Those cards include The Fool, The Magician, The High Priestess, The Empress, The Emperor, The Hierophant, The Lovers, The Chariot, Strength, The Hermit, Wheel of Fortune, Justice, The Hanged Man, Death, Temperance, The Devil, The Tower, The Star, The Moon, The Sun, Judgment, and The World.

Tasseography   The famous practice of "reading tea leaves." The diviner looks for various shapes in the remnants after someone has finished drinking a cup of tea (and it has been turned upside down for a short period of time).

Tephramancy   A practice in which the bark of trees is burned, and the ashes are examined for omens.

Tiromancy   Divination by the study of cheese. As is well known, Swiss is still the most holy variety.

Xylomancy   Depsite its musical sounding name, this practice of divination concerns observing the behavior of wood while it burns.

— *Chapter Five* —
ELVES AND FAERIES

WE ALL LOVE TO BELIEVE IN A LARGER WORLD, in a universe that is layered, so that dimensions and spiritual realms overlap with the mundane physical world. Religions are built on this idea, as is folklore. There are countless spiritual beings populating these worlds, and many are covered elsewhere in this book, including gods (Chapters 8 and 12); demons and angels (Chapter 3); ghosts (Chapter 6); and creatures of unknown origin (Chapter 2). Other volumes in this series discuss those supernatural creatures that possess a decidedly darker nature such as vampires,[14] hags, and werewolves. Two of the largest and most fascinating of these groups, however, are the faeries and the elves.

The term "faerie" is used—often loosely—to describe any of a variety of supernatural beings that inhabit the "otherworld," the dimension or plane between the physical world (earth) and the spiritual realm (heaven). These beings vary greatly in size, powers, disposition, appearance, and character. They are also described differently depending on the culture to which they are attached in folklore, and to the era from which their stories descend.

The root of "faerie" is "fae," a word that has traveled a long way from the Latin root word, "fata," which referred to the various personifications of destiny, or fate. The term was filtered, both in spelling and meaning, as it passed

---

14. See *Vampire Universe: The Dark World of Supernatural Beings That Haunt Us, Hunt Us, and Hunger for Us* (Citadel Books, 2006); and *Beyond Vampire Universe* (Citadel Books, 2008).

through ancient Greek and Roman cultures, medieval France and England, and, finally, to Ireland and Scotland. In the oldest stories, the fates were supernatural beings who would appear three nights following a new birth and who would then determine that child's destiny. They were described as wrinkled and unsympathetic old hags, a far cry from the charming Tinkerbelles of later stories. In Catalan and Portuguese they were the "fada" and in Spanish they were known as "hada"; these expressions having about the same essential meaning as "fairy" or "faerie" in English.

Another splintering of the definition comes from the old French word "fée," which means "enchanter." Thus, a "féerie" referred both to the state of being enchanted as well as to the being whose nature is defined through enchantment. Most folktales about faeries have the theme of enchantment about them—the faerie casts a glamour (spell), and the human is enchanted and either believes an illusion, is compelled to do something against his or her will, or is lured into a tryst (which seldom works out well).

Faerie folk, like humans, range from good to evil, smart to dumb, powerful to frail. Most, however, possess magical powers. Many are able to predict the future—in whole or, more often, in part. They are often spiteful and sometimes playful, and many stories are built around some trick they've played on a hapless human. Shakespeare's *A Midsummer Night's Dream* is one of our greatest faerie stories, detailing the power struggle between Oberon and Titania, the king and queen of the faerie folk. They are feuding over a human boy they both covet. It is largely because of Shakespeare that most folks nowadays (especially those with ancestry from the British Isles) regard faeries and elves as interchangeable names for the same kinds of creatures, which they are not. In *A Midsummer Night's Dream, elves* are as small as insects—which is far more common for faeries, even though elves are, admittedly, little people. They're just not quite *that* little. Conversely, the great poet Edmund Spenser's "elves" are the same size as humans, as he describes them in *The Faerie Queene*.

Also known as the "fair folk" in Wales, the "good neighbors," "honest folk" *(Daoine Coire)* or "good people" *(Daoine Matha)* in Ireland, the faeries have appeared in stories, histories, tales, songs, poems, and plays for many centuries.

Elves are also supernatural creatures that appear in folklore around the world, but most notably in Germany, Scandinavia, and the United Kingdom. To the Norse they were a race of minor gods who oversaw the mundane aspects of the natural world: water, trees, forests, and so on; but over time their own mythology grew so that they were a race apart from the gods of Valhalla.

In German folklore, elves are distinctly evil. Known as *Albtraum,* which means "elf dream," the same word is used for "nightmares," which speaks to their natures in that country. The *Albtraum* are similar to the succubi and incubi, who come at night and perch on a person's chest while leeching sexual or vital energy from them.

British elves are far more amiable and have kindly natures when appeased, though admittedly they can be very cranky when offended. Appearing often in folktales, songs, and ballads throughout England and Scotland, elves are generally seen as magical but not hostile. In these tales, such as *Thomas the Rhymer*[15] and others, the elves interact with humans, sometimes as captors, sometimes as lovers. There is usually a bit of clever trickery on the part of the human that sets him or her free. In these tales the elves are honorable and the tales are quite often wrapped around a bargain or debt of honor to which the elf will adhere.

On the other hand, some tales are more sinister and speak of imprisonment, murder, rape, and other crimes perpetrated by elves, as in *Lady Isabel and the Elf-Knight,*[16] in which abduction and murder are the motives of the elf.

Over the years, the English elf has gotten a bit of a makeover and has become more detached from the affairs of humans, appearing only now and then to do a quick spot of mischief. In many of these more modern tales, the

15. An anonymous piece of balladry based very loosely on the life of Thomas Learmonth of Erceldoune, a thirteenth-century Scottish soothsayer.
16. Anonymous English children's round.

GREEN SPIRITS Lee Moyer

elves are invisible and even take on some of the kinetic traits of the classic poltergeist.

J.R.R. Tolkien gave them a complete redefinition with the wise and noble elves who brought culture and beauty to Middle Earth. Since those books were published, fictional elves more often follow Tolkien's model; the folkloric qualities of the elves of older myths are now ascribed to creatures like Brownies, Kobolds, and others.

Though there is enough folklore of elves and faeries to fit a hundred volumes, gathered here are the most significant creatures and terms you'll need to know if you plan to wander into the enchanted lands of the *fey*.

Álfar Norse for "elf." There are two basic types of elves in Norse mythology, dark elves (Dökkálfar) and light elves (Ljósálfar).

Álfatofrar In Norse mythology Álfatofrar is the catch-all term for all forms of magic used by elves.

Álfheim The Old Norse name for "elf home," the place where the light elves (Ljósálfar) live. Known is England as elfland or elfenland.

Arkan Sonney   Known as "Lucky Piggy" on the Isle of Man, the Arkan Sonney is a strange faerie piglet that will bring good luck to anyone who can capture it. The good luck is conditional, though. Once the Lucky Piggy has made
its promise, it must be released, otherwise bad fortune will ensue.

Asrais   The asrais are diminutive and very fragile female creatures that dwell
in shadows, very similar to faeries. They will sicken and die if exposed to direct
sunlight; and captivity is also fatal to them. When they die, the asrais dissolve
into water.

**Ballybogs (also Bogles, Bolliwogs, Peat Faeries, Mudbogs, Bor-a-
boos, Boggies)**   The ballybog is an earth elemental who favors marshy
ground (as the name suggests), and is usually seen slathered in mud. They
have round, bulbous bodies, no visible necks, and limbs as thin as sticks. Despite their frail appearance, the ballybog is nimble and quick—also quick-
tempered and easily offended by oafish humans who try to capture them.
When annoyed they can be very spiteful and will lead the human into a boggy
pool or quicksand pit. One of the golden rules of the faerie kingdom is: Don't
annoy the little people.

**Bean-Fionn (also Greentooth Woman, Jenny Greentooth, Green
Mother)**   Bean-Fionn is an Irish water faerie who has a kind heart for human children and acts to protect them from harm. A child kissed by Bean-
Fionn becomes immune to all sickness and physical harm. Should she
encounter a human who has hurt or abused children, the benevolent Bean-
Fionn will show her less genial side, and will drag the abuser down into the water to drown.

Bean-nighe (Banshee)   The banshee is a "death omen," a creature of the
night that appears to herald the coming of death. Though not a predator herself, the banshee is always around when death—usually violent death—is imminent. A more accurate name for the banshee is the bean-nighe, which means

"little washer by the ford." As told in legend, the name refers to the banshee as a tortured soul who died while giving birth. As a result her mind and soul went mad with grief, and she is often seen washing bloody clothes by the banks of small remote streams, ostensibly washing away the bloody proof of her own demise.

The banshee's cry is plaintive and both sad and frightening; but one thing the banshee does not do is wail. The "wail of the banshee" is a literary device bearing no relation to the centuries of folklore.

The banshee is seldom seen. When she is, observers either see a spectral figure floating on the night winds, or a strange hag with glaring eyes, a sharp single front tooth, a single large nostril, pendulous breasts, and great webbed feet. She is horrible to behold and yet some intrepid adventurers have tried to find her. This is due to a legend that says if someone suckles the breast of a banshee, they will be granted a single wish and, thereafter, be protected by the creature.

Beltane   May Day (May 1) as celebrated by elves and faeries.

Bendith Y Mamau   These are the benevolent faeries of the Welsh region of Carmarthenshire. Just saying their name is a charm against harm, particularly harm to small children.

Brownie (also **Bodach, Bwca, Fenodaree**)   Like the bluecap, the brownie is a benign creature who delights in helping humans, though brownies are inclined more toward domestic chores than mining. Brownies become attached to a certain family and will work tirelessly at household tasks.

They stand about three-feet tall and are usually dressed in drab rags. Though they love their work, they often look sad because, as legend has it, they were created to ease Adam's burden after his eviction from Eden, and it is by God's will that they serve without thought or want of payment.

In the Harry Potter novels by J. K. Rowling,[17] the "house elves" fit the basic

---

17. Beginning with *Harry Potter and the Sorcerer's Stone.*

description and character of brownies. However there is also a violent side to them. In some Welsh tales, where the brownies are called bwca, they turn on their masters if they suspect that anyone in the household has become a servant of the devil. Since bwca, like English brownies and the Cornish pixie, are descendants of creatures appointed by heaven to serve man, they have a strong religious sense of right and wrong. Old tales tell of bwca slaughtering whole families after learning that the family had become dedicated to evil.

Brownies appear in the folklore of other lands as well, such as the *Tomte* of Scandinavia, the *Domovoi* of Russia, and the *Heinzelmännchen* of Germany. Though the legends vary from place to place, these creatures all appear to be of the same essential species.

Changeling   These are the offspring of faeries, elves, or other similar supernatural creatures. Once born, they are secretly swapped for human children. The reason for this is uncertain, but the tales suggest that the faeries want to have human slaves, servants, and, in some cases, lovers. Therefore, they make the swap in order to steal the child without raising alarm. Some human parents see through the glamour, however, and once a changeling has been identified as such, its supernatural parent is compelled to take it back and return the human child.

In Ireland a left-handed person was once thought to be a changeling; and in Wales changelings are said to start out looking like normal children, but as they mature they become ugly and deformed.

Clurichaun   A subspecies or cousin to the leprechaun. They are solitary and extremely surly, and are often depicted as drunkards. The clurichaun can be bribed into serving as a very effective guardian for a person's wine cellar, but if they are in any way mistreated they will spoil the wine and wreck the whole house. The clurichaun use dogs and sheep like horses and are occasionally seen riding over the hills by moonlight.

CHANGELING
Hervé Scott Flament

Coblynau (also **Koblernigh**)   The coblynau are mineshaft faeries from Welsh folklore who are very similar to kobolds and knockers. They stand about a foot-and-a-half high, dress in miner's clothes, and are ugly. Despite their appearance, the coblynau are good natured and helpful. If given a bit of beer and some bread, they'll knock on the walls of a mine to let their benefactors know where the lodes can be found.

Dark Elves   Throughout the folklore of Europe, there are both dark and light elves, creatures who embrace one side of the energetic spectrum or the other. Among the Celts the dark elves are known as the Daoi-Sith (or Daoine Sidhe). A variation of this is Du-Sith (or Erdluitle), which means "black elves."

In Norse culture the dark elves are called *Svartálfar* (black elves) or *Dökkálfar* (dark elves). In that mythology their nature and appearance tend to overlap with the folklore of mountain dwarves. Different from their Celtic cousins their dark skin is the result of soot from endless hours working at their forges; their natures are dark or light depending on the individual personality.

The *Trow* of the Orkney Isles of Great Britain are the dark elves of that region. Though they are also black from working at forges, they tend to be more ill-natured than not. Their close cousins, the *Drow* of the Shetland Isle are completely evil.

Dwarves (also **Dwarfs**)   Dwarves of the folkloric kind are short, stocky, and very powerful creatures who mature fast (they are adults by age three). Generally bearded (they have full beards by age seven), they are clever at digging, tool-making, and mixing potions. Dwarves live in caves and holes and cannot abide sunlight, unless they use magic to protect themselves from the sun's blinding light. To be touched by sunlight without magical protection will cause a dwarf to turn instantly to stone. In some stories trolls share this same vulnerability to light.

Dwarves are fabulous miners, and they burrow deep into the rock in order to make their homes. Once established, they seek out treasure and bring it back to fill their halls.

The legends of the dwarves comes from Norse mythology, but they appear frequently in the legends of the faeries of Great Britain, and, in some tales, it is suggested that they are of similar nature.

◄ TOLKIEN'S ELVES OF ► MIDDLE EARTH

In the creation of the Lord of the Rings trilogy, and other books of Middle Earth, J.R.R. Tolkien clearly drew upon folklore. However, he built a much grander and more extensive history of his elves than anything we see in folktales and myth. Tolkien's elves are also known as the "Firstborn" or "Elder Kindred," and were the first sentient race brought into being by Eru Ilúvatar, the creator of the universe. Since the elves were the first beings that possessed the power of speech, they took the name "Quendi" (the Speakers).

Tolkien's elves are a wise and ancient race who bear superficial resemblance to humans. They are far more beautiful (male and female) than humans, a bit taller, and possessed of perfect grace and poise.

Like folkloric elves, the Firstborn are devoted to music, but these elves go much further. They weave magic into each note and syllable, so that their music—be it tragic, epic, or simple air—is transcendent.

The Middle Earth elves can sleep while walking or doing other ordinary things, suggesting that their physical bodies exist on one plane and their spiritual selves on another. Each of their senses is far superior to those of humans, and even the legendary Aragorn is no perceptual match for his elvish companion, Legolas.

Despite their grace, the elves are hardy. They can survive wounds that would kill a mortal; however, they are not invulnerable. Should an elf die, his soul (known as a fëar) travels to the Halls of Mandos in Valinor where it dwells while undergoing a process of purification (ridding itself of earthly ties). After this, elves are reborn in bodies (called hröar) identical to those that they've left behind. In his larger body of writing, Tolkien tells of how an elf, Lord Glorfindel, made such a return.

Tolkien also provides an amazingly detailed history of the elves in his book *The Silmarillion.*

Erlkönig (also **Erlking)**   A sprite from German and Scandinavian folklore who preys on children by using illusions to lure them into dangerous situations (such as into ponds or over cliffs). Unlike most elves in folklore, the Erlkönig is the only one of its kind (thank goodness) and has been linked by some eighteenth and nineteenth century storytellers and clerics to the devil.

Franz Schubert composed a Romantic lieder for *Der Erlkönig,*[18] a poem by Johann Wolfgang von Goethe. It tells of a sick child who sees the evil Erlkönig pursuing him to try and take his soul. Recently the Erlkönig has been featured in a short story, "The Erlking"[19] by thriller writer John Connolly.

Fairy Cross   A traditional name for the mineral staurolite, which is believed to possess various metaphysical and healing properties. Fairy cross is also believed to provide a connection between whomever holds it and the spirit world. It has been used both as a protective charm against evil and as a method of attracting the aid of sympathetic faeries.

Fir Darrig (also **Fear Deang)**   A particularly nasty elf species. Fir Darrig are known for playing tricks that often lead to injury or death for hapless hu-

18. *Lieder* is the plural form of the German word *lied,* which means "song." The function of lieder is to set fine poetry to beautiful piano music.
19. The story appears in *Nocturnes,* Atria Publishing, 2005.

mans. They're theriomorphs (shapeshifters), and Fir Darrig often use this shapeshifting ability as part of their deadly trickery.

Forest Faeries   Forest faeries are a frequent subject of songs and tales, and include subspecies such as dryads (Greek myth), sidhe draoi (Ireland), oakmen (Celtic Europe), adhene (Isle of Man), alux (Mayan), curupira (Philippines), duende (Spain), and paristan (Persia and the Middle East).

Gaen-canach (also **Ganconer, Gean-cannah)**   A faerie of Irish folklore whose name means "love talker," and who are real supernatural Don Juans. Gaen-canach is always alone and often smoking a dudeen (a clay pipe). If a maiden meets him, she falls immediately under his spell, but the gaen-canach is a lecher. Should the woman escape, she is nevertheless cursed to pine for him and will eventually waste away. If a man meets him on the road, that fellow's luck will turn bad instantly.

Ghillie Dhu (also **Ghillie Yu)**   A Scottish tree spirit that, like the greenman, appears to be composed entirely of leaves and twigs. Ghillie Dhu's color changes from brown to green according to the season. His name means "dark shoe," and he certainly has a dark temperament—disliking all humans and occasionally doing harm to those who cut down trees. It is very likely that Tolkien based his Treebeard character on the Ghillie Dhu. Offend a Ghillie Dhu and he'll reach out with long, strong, green arms and drag you into a crushing embrace. Later the body will become compost for the trees Ghillie Dhu protects.

Gnomes   Gnomes are small creatures who generally live underground. Much like the larger dwarves, they are skilled miners and metalsmiths. Like dwarves they cannot abide sunlight and will be turned to stone if exposed to it. The fifteenth century alchemist Paracelsus averred that gnomes were vital elemental spirits who, in essence, formed part of the spiritual matrix of the earth. Gnomes are able to move through earth and rock as easily as humans move through air, and in some tales they are shapeshifters who become toads or frogs by day (as a protection against the sun's rays).

They are known by a variety of names throughout Europe (with some regional differences): in Prussia they are the *Kaukis;* in Switzerland they are the *Barbegazi;* in Iceland they are the *Vættir.* Gnomes are sometimes mischievous but, generally, not as outright mean-spirited as some faerie folk. Appearing most often in German folktales, they were central figures in a number of stories by the Brothers Grimm. In many of these folktales the gnomes were very industrious and very greedy. They sought precious things—gold, silver, and jewels—which they hoarded in their rocky lairs. In some of these same tales, gnomes were said to gather and store secret knowledge. This belief is hinted at in their name, since the word "gnome" is derived from *gnomus,* a New Latin term itself derived from the Greek *gnosis,* meaning "knowledge."

Goblin Goblins are wandering spirits of evil. They haunt the rural French countryside and invade country homes, either to prey on the children or to set up camp in the wine cellar. Though small in size, they often possess vast malicious intent and supernatural power. When not lurking around a chateau, they are most often found in deserted grottos or swamps.

In olden times families often welcomed goblins into the household because they promised to do chores around the house, and they generally lived up to their claims. There are plenty of stories of families that had long and harmonious associations with them; but there are even more about goblins who turned on the families that had taken them in. Sadly, it is not in the nature of a goblin to be well-behaved. When the goblin's impish side emerges, the creature will act out in much the same way as a poltergeist—banging pots and making noises in the night, disturbing sleep, hiding things, and moving furniture.

Sometimes goblins become violent. They nip and bite members of a family as they sleep. If evicted the goblin's spite sometimes becomes so great that it will leave in the middle of the night, taking with it the most beautiful child of the family! Fleeing to its former grotto, the goblin will enslave the child, forcing it to serve until death.

In a few quaint folktales, one odd method of eviction is purported to be very effective: Flaxseed is thrown on the kitchen floor every night. After a few days, the goblin will tire of picking up all the seeds and will just leave of its own accord. But this seems like a charming fairy-tale resolution and not one that would work against a creature with the intelligence, diligence, and spite of a real goblin.

Hobgoblin   A mischievous magical creature frequently found in Western European folklore, the hobgoblin is an abbreviation of "Robin Goodfellow," better known as "Puck", a pre-Christian pagan trickster. In many of the older tales the hobgoblin is neither good nor bad but acts simply as a trickster, with the moral consequences of his actions often falling in one way or another on the human it tricks. Over the centuries the name has been slurred to Robin Goblin and hobgoblin; however as the name changed the nature of the creature seems to have changed as well and over the last few centuries the word "hobgoblin" has come to refer to a malicious spirit rather than a prankish one. In modern times the name is fairly interchangeable with "bogeyman," "bugaboo," and "bugbear," among others.

Household Faeries   This group often overlaps with other kinds of diminutive supernatural beings, such as the kobolds, korrigans, brownies, pixies, redcaps, and others.

Korrigans (also **Corrigan)**   In the legends of Brittany there is a race of faeries known as the korrigans. Korrs are tiny women, smaller than dwarves, who have magnificent hair and flashing red eyes. These creatures are druidic and violently opposed to Christianity, which they regard as a false faith evangelized by invaders.

The korrigans have great powers of seduction and few men can escape their charms. Falling under the love spell of a korr, however, is a death sentence. Korrigans kill their victims, and, in some cases, their legends overlap with those of the vampires in that these faeries sometimes feed on the blood or the life essence of the humans they slaughter.

Leprechauns   The diminutive leprechauns of Irish folklore are a kind of elf (some will argue that they are faeries) who inhabited Ireland long before the coming of humans. They are tricksters who are often mildly prankish and occasionally vicious, depending on who is telling the tale. Their name comes from *leipreachán,* a Celtic word meaning "small-bodied"; some scholars contend that the name is drawn from *leath bhrógan,* which means "shoemaker."

Leprechauns are solitary creatures who amass and horde great fortunes. They covet gold and other precious metals, devising clever places to hide their wealth. However, should a person capture a leprechaun (far easier said than done), and question the little fellow, the leprechaun is bound by some extraordinary spiritual pact to reveal the location of his treasure.

Light Elves   Known as the *Ljósálfar* in Norse mythology, these elves possess more evolved, and less overtly nasty, natures than their dark elf cousins. They are also more common—light elves is the more general term to describe all elves.

Nippel   In German and Czech folklore the nippel is a guardian spirit of the forest. He particularly dislikes poachers and will kill them in the same way animals were killed during the hunt. A singular creature rather than the name of a race of beings, the nippel is likely a kind of dwarf. He is a shapeshifter, and, in vengeance mode, he is in his dwarf form. In a more benevolent mood, he sometimes takes the form of a lordly human. Legends have it that the nippel lives on Niklasberg Hill, a hill between Bělá nad Radbuzou and Tremesna, two Czech towns near the German border. The nippel is not always violent, and he has sometimes deigned to help lost travelers by giving them food, directions, and even some money.

Nuberu   There is a wind elemental in northern Spain who goes by the name of El Nuberu. If appeased, or properly invoked, he will send rains to farmers and prevent storms from doing too much damage. The rains that El Nuberu sends possess an extraordinary power, which makes the crops grow to wondrous ripeness. Like most elementals, though, insulting or ignoring him tends to make him angry, at which point he'll send ice storms, floods, torrential rains, and heavy winds. If someone deeply offends him, El Nuberu will send a rain of frogs or biting insects.

Nymphs   Nymphs are female supernatural spirits who range from being completely passive to murderous. In poetry and art, particularly in the works of the pre-Raphaelite artists of the late nineteenth and early twentieth centuries, nymphs were generally portrayed as gorgeous and sexually available young women who existed, apparently, for no other reason than to pleasure a passing young knight. In folklore the nymphs were, despite their appearance, not human at all. They often enchanted a young fellow to his death. The ancient Greek story of Hylas relates such a fate, and the pre-Raphaelite master John William Waterhouse rendered a magnificent painting of the tale (he focused more on the obvious charms of the nymphs).

The two primary categories of nymphs in Greek mythology are based on where they lived:

• *Land nymphs* include alseids (groves), auloniads (pastures), dryads (woods), hamadryads (trees), ieimakids (meadows), meliae (manna ash trees), napaeae (mountain valleys), and oreads (mountains).

• *Water nymphs* include crinaeae (fountains), eleionomae (marshes), limnades or limnatides (lakes), naiads (rivers, brooks, streams), nereids (the Mediterranean Sea), oceanids (salt water), pegaeae (springs), potameides (rivers), and sirens (shores and rocky coastlines).

Otherworld   The realm of the faerie folk and other magical beings. The otherworld exists apart from the human world, though it overlaps it in many ways. At times it is connected on certain days of the year (St. John's Eve, Samhain, and Beltane).

Perilous realm   Another name for the otherworld.

Pixies   A very mischievous subspecies of faerie that enjoy playing pranks on both humans and fey folk alike. Most Pixie pranks are harmless (though annoying), but there are some accounts of Pixies causing great harm and grief with their jokes.

Portunes   The portunes are fairylike creatures—with wrinkled faces, hooked noses, and jowly chins—about the size of a man's thumb. They are remarkably industrious and will often appear, seemingly at random, and do extensive and excellent fieldwork on rural farms. They ask no payment but seldom say no to a little fruit and beer left outside for them. Once they've had a wee bit of ale, they become prankish and will amuse themselves by seizing the reins of a horse and, against all efforts by the rider, lead it into a swamp or pond.

Their name is drawn from the Roman deity Portunus (also Portunes, Portumnes), the god of locks and keys (and the root of the word opportune). The path by which this Roman god became a farm imp in England is a mystery of folklore.

Samhain   The Celtic name for Halloween, the point where the veil between the human world and the otherworld of the faerie are thin and can be traversed.

Seelies   In Scotland faeries are divided into two "courts," the "seelie" and the "unseelie." The former is composed of faeries who display either a beneficial or benign nature toward humans, and who occasionally intercede for

FAERIE Hervé Scott Flament

good. The seelies ("blessed") are, therefore, thought to be the more civilized—even aristocratic—of the faerie folk.

The unseelies, or unblessed, are the more pernicious faeries. They either deliberately cause harm or turn fun and mischief into cruelty and malice.

The two courts of faeries occasionally go to war with one another, and if humans get caught in the middle, the result is generally tragic.

⊰ THE OTHERKIN ⊱

Within our own human, real-world society there are many subcultures of people who have come forward to state with all seriousness that they are not human. Generally known as "the otherkin," these nonhumans are many and varied. Some are avowed vampires, others are theriomorphs (shapeshifters), some claim to have come from other worlds or other dimensions, and some con-sider themselves to be animals in human form.

The otherkin are not necessarily a unified commu-nity, and more often congregate with others of their own kind—elf to elf, vampire to vampire. Some share online sites as a way of showing strength in numbers. This makes it clear that they are not part of a role-playing game, and are not pretenders or wannabes.

Many claim that, although they are currently in hu-man form, the physical is merely a temporary vehicle for them; at the essential level, they're nonhuman. Some oth-erkin say that they were different beings (aliens, animals, or faery folk) in previous incarnations. Others claim that they are not biologically human at all (they only have the appearance of humanity in order to blend in). Many say they have supernatural powers.

The otherkin community as a whole is growing rap-idly, adding diversity to an already amazing and wonder-fully strange world.

Sidhe   The sidhe (pronounced "shee") are the last of Ireland's ancient race of faerie folk, the *Tuatha de Danann*. Most fled to the magical land of *Tir Nan Og* after their defeat by the Milesians—humans who invaded the isles from His-pania (now Spain) and later settled the lands and became the first Irish. The *Tuatha de Danann* were not true faeries, but their descendants, the ones who stayed in Ireland, somehow did become fair folk. The process of transforma-tion is not clearly described in folklore, and fragments of it exist in thousands of overlapping tales. The upshot is that these beings, descending from an elder race of demigods—and no longer the lords of the land—faded into the gap between the real world and the heavenly one. From this shadowy limbo, they occasionally venture out to confront man. Like the seelies, the sidhe (the name means "people of the hills") can be both very good and very, very bad. Dialectically, sidhe originally referred just to the mounds in which the refugee *Tuatha* lived, but over the centuries the term has become synonymous with the beings themselves.

To this day the sidhe are ruled by the great immortal king, Finvarra, who is a wise ruler as well as a skillful warrior. His queen is Donagh, one of the most compellingly beautiful women of either the natural or supernatural world. Typical of many kings, however, Finvarra has a roving eye and is on a par with Zeus for using any magical means necessary to sow his preternaturally wild oats.

Sprites   A term loosely given to a large number of different beings, including elves, faeries, gnomes, imps, dwarves, and other diminutive supernatural beings. The word derives from the Latin "spiritus," meaning "spirit."

St. John's Eve   Also known as Midsummer's Eve, this is the evening before the summer solstice when the fairyfolk hold their midyear celebrations. As the solstice typically falls on June 22, St. John's Eve is June 21.

Tiddy Mun   A water elemental from Lincolnshire, England, who has power over the movement of water. When there have been heavy rains the people of that region often call on the Tiddy Mun to either prevent flooding or to cause floodwaters to recede. He's temperamental, and when offended or (worse) injured, Tiddy Mun will spread disease, blight, and pestilence throughout the herds of the region and even spread sickness among children.

Venusleute   The Venusleute are tiny elemental creatures from the folklore of Germany and surrounding countries who lived inside rocks. The Venusleute, though small enough to sit in a person's palm, are quite lovely and generous of spirit; they'll aid children who have become lost or are hungry.

QUEEN OF THE SIDHE
Abranda Icle Sisson

Water Faeries   This group is comprised mostly of female faeries and similar beings. Included are the well-known Greek nymphs, naiads (or nyads), and water sprites, as well as vilas (Slavic), gwyllion (Scotland), nixie (Scandinavia), nûññě'hǐ (Cherokee), ponaturi (New Zealand), encantado (Brazil), geow-lud-mo-sis-eg (New Brunswick, Canada), and others.

Wight   A general term for a dwarfish being of unpleasant disposition, a term derived from the German "wicht," meaning "small person." In folklore wights are sometimes rather ghostly creatures who haunt ancient burial grounds and other remote areas. In some tales, however, they are similar to redcaps and other more predatory creatures.

The Wild Hunt   In Britain there are ancient legends of a raucous band of faerie folk roving abroad with mischief in mind. Known as the "Wild Hunt," this legend has its roots in even older folktales of Northern Scandinavia and Germany. In all of the stories a group of supernatural hunters go out as a band, racing across the landscape, and sometimes across the sky itself, ostensibly hunting for game but more often hunting for human women.

Seeing the hunt was believed to be very bad luck—it foretold plague, war, or famine. Being in its path was a ticket to the boneyard for anyone except the very bravest or cleverest of warriors.

In some of the many hundreds of variations of the tale, the wild hunt is composed of the very worst faerie folk; and yet in other tales the hunt has an aspect of nobility. There is little consistency. When looking at the roster of the hunt as it stretches across history and national lines, its members have included everyone from King Arthur to Satan. Even gods like Odin occasionally rode out with the faerie horde.

Will o' the Wisp   Strange lights dancing in the woods have lured many a traveler off their path and into trouble. It is a phenomenon written about in nearly every country around the world and back through history. Ghost lights, faery lights, corpse candles, dead lights, demon-eyes, and jack-o'-lanterns are just a handful of the many names given to these strange lights. No one really knows what they are. Everything from swamp gasses to mirages has been blamed, but no one really knows for sure.

In the folklore of the supernatural, however, there are plenty of explanations. They are ghosts, spirits, demons, and vampires; and sometimes all of the above. Legends around the world speak of monsters that travel as balls of glowing light, dancing in the darkness, luring the unwary into deadfalls, lakes, or down wells.

Will o' the wisp is the most common name given to these beings. Here it is used as a general category, though many of the creatures that fall into it bear little resemblance to one another.

Examples of supernatural predators that occasionally take on the appearance of a ball of light include the obayifo of the Gold Coast, the loogaroo of Haiti, the asema of Surinam, the bluecap of England, the zmeu of Romania, the lidérc nadaly of Hungary, the trazgos of Spain, the soucouyan of Dominica, and the vjestitiza of Montenegro. Predators all.

The Latin for this phenomenon is *Ignis Fatuus,* which means "foolish fire," and it is a wry comment on the judgment of those persons who follow dancing lights into the unknown darkness.

Great Britain certainly has the largest number of Will o' the Wisp variations, and each region has its own nickname for the creatures: hobby lantern (Hertfordshire and East Anglia), peg-a-lantern (Lancashire), joan the wad (Cornwall and Somerset), the lantern man (East Anglia), hinky punk (Somerset and Devon), will the smith (Shropshire), pinket (Worcestershire), jacky lantern, jack a lantern (West Country), spunkies (Lowland Scotland), pwca and the ellylldan (Wales), will o' the wikes (Norfolk), hobbedy's lantern (Warwickshire Gloucestershire), and jenny with the lantern (North Yorkshire, Northumberland).

Xindhi   The Xindhi are Albanian creatures, similar to elves, who have the common characteristic of being helpful at times and viciously unkind at others. The Xindhi are capable of becoming invisible and sometimes the only clue to their presence is the unexpected creaking of a floorboard.

Yumboes (also **Bakhna Rakhna)**   A rare faerie species from the Jaloff people of Goree Island in Senegal, West Africa. The Yumboes are only two- or three-feet tall, their skin is a luminous white, their eyes are very dark, and they have flowing silvery hair.

They are very good-natured and fun-loving (not always a trait in faeries) and often invite humans to partake in their elaborate feasts, which are only held when the moonlight is bright. Though generous, they sometimes steal the food they then serve to guests.

Chapter Six

ESP, HAUNTINGS, AND THE SCIENCE OF PARAPSYCHOLOGY

THERE ARE MANY MYSTERIES that are tied into the spiritual world. Some, like elves, vampires, and werewolves tend toward the supernatural; others like gods and demons belong to the world of religion; UFOs are part of science; but as for the rest—ghosts, hauntings, psychic abilities, extranormal powers—these fall under the broad umbrella term called "paranormal."

"Para" means "beyond," so by strict definition paranormal experiences are those events that are past the boundaries of what is part of ordinary human experience. This covers a lot of ground; there are many tens of thousands of anomalous phenomena in human history.

For many centuries the paranormal was considered to either be part of theology or part of pagan beliefs. Then in the late nineteenth century, a spiritualist named E. Dawson Rogers led a movement to have the study of all things paranormal fall under the purview of science. This brought about the founding of The Society for Psychical Research (SPR), founded in England in 1882. Within five years Rogers and his colleagues made such a compelling case for the scientific study of the paranormal that members of the very conservative British Royal Society joined its council. Over the years the SPR conducted regulated and monitored tests to establish hard scientific data (*repeatable* data, which is the only kind the scientific community truly respects). Similar groups began springing up all over the world. By the 1920s, as the new field of electronics was being expanded, men like R. A. Fisher began developing instruments that could more precisely monitor and record statistical information. As the twentieth century moved forward, the old terms, "spiritualism" and "psychic research" fell into disuse and were replaced by the name of a brand new science: parapsychology.

The new wave of parapsychologists was led by J. B. Rhine, who developed most of the key ideas and methods for testing psychic ability, many of which are still used. He established the respected *Journal of Parapsychology* in 1937, and he formed both the Parapsychological Association and the Foundation for Research on the Nature of Man (FRNM).[20]

Rhine, who also coined the term "extra sensory perceptions," or ESP, had a three-pronged approach to his studies:

1. To establish programs for systematic study of psychic (psi) abilities in ways that would allow scientists to identify and characterize the different aspects of psi talent.

2. To have parapsychology recognized as a legitimate field of study, which would gain academic recognition (a goal he accomplished by basing his research at Duke University).

3. To establish that psi abilities are latent in all people rather than in a select few.

Of course, despite the overwhelming body of evidence collected by Rhine and his followers there are still plenty of folks in the scientific community who scoff at parapsychology as junk or pseudoscience. Since much of what is known about psi abilities comes from anecdotal evidence rather than measurable lab work, the skeptics consider themselves to be on firm ground. But the evidence—scientific evidence—in support of true psychic abilities is mounting day by day and year by year. Governments all over the world have been experimenting with ESP since before World War II, and during the Cold War psi abilities were actively sought by all governments for use in espionage.

---

20. Now known as The Rhine Research Center, located in Durham, North Carolina. A visit to their Web site, www.rhine.org, is quite fascinating.

Parapsychology overlaps with some faith-based aspects of spiritualism, such as belief in ghosts, as well as areas where no clear classification has yet seemed to fit. Following are key terms, names, and events in the vast world of the paranormal.

Absent Healing   Healing accomplished when the healer is not in direct contact with the patient, even to the point of being in another location.

Absent Sitter (Proxy Sittings)   A person for whom a reading is performed but who is not present with the reader.

Agent   (1) In parapsychology, a person who attempts to make psychic communication. (2) The subject of a psychokinesis experiment. (3) A person who is the target of poltergeist activity. (4) A person (real or phantasm) who appears to communicate important information to someone in a trance state.

Alpha Rhythm   The measurable electrical activity in the brain during deep relaxation. In such a state the brain maintains about 10 cycles per second.

Altered State of Consciousness   A general term for any mental state different from either normal wakefulness or normal sleep. These include trance states of various kinds (meditative, hypnotic, etc.), drug-induced hallucinatory states, ecstasy (sexual, religious, etc.), and similar states.

Ancestor Worship   Any of the world's many religious practices in which the dead are venerated. The belief is that the dead have passed to higher states of awareness and when prayed to will sometimes share knowledge of enlightenment.

Animal Magnetism   One of the many phrases used to describe charisma. The phrase was coined by Franz Anton Mesmer (1734–1815), the forefather of modern hypnosis.

Animal Psi (Anpsi)   Psychic abilities demonstrated by animals. Horses and dogs are widely believed to possess strong psychic powers.

Anniversary Ghost (also **recurring ghost, echo ghost)**   An apparition that appears on the anniversary of an event such as a death, birthday, or battle.

Announcing Dream   A vision sent in the form of a dream to announce a birth. Such dreams are common when important persons are incarnating, such as lamas.

Anomalous Experience   Any experience that cannot be explained scientifically.

Anomalous Phenomena   Any observable incident that has no obvious scientific explanation.

Apparition   A vision, sighting, or hallucination by a nonsleeping person of something that is not tangibly there. There are many kinds of apparitions, some of which foretell disaster (see CRISIS APPARITION), some of which provide insight, while others remain inexplicable.

⊰ 13 CLASSIC ⊱ GHOST FLICKS

1. *A Christmas Carol* (various) This classic Christmas story is certainly a spooky and tragic ghost story about the consequences of one's actions. The two best are the 1951 Alistair Sim's version (which is the most popular and includes a bravura performance by Sim) and the 1984 George C. Scott production (which offers the best performances across the board).   *(continued)*

2. *Blithe Spirit* (1945) Rex Harrison and Constance Cummings in a David Lean film based on the Noel Coward play. A man and his new wife are haunted by the spirit of the first wife. Funny, touching, and too often forgotten.

3. *Carnival of Souls* (1962) Candace Hilligoss plays a woman who survives a car crash and then begins seeing some very strange things. Are they ghosts? Is *she* a ghost? This weird, wonderful low-budget lost classic is worth tracking down on DVD.

4. *Curse of the Cat People* (1944) Little Amy Reed has a new friend—her name is Irena, a ghost (played by Simone Simon). Irena was the doomed werecat of the classic *Cat People* (1942) film, but this charming little film doesn't touch on that. *Curse of the Cat People* is about the girl's friendship and the sadness of the ghost who now sees her husband happily remarried.

5. *Ghost Breakers* (1940) Though dated in many ways (especially when it comes to the portrayal of African Americans!) *Ghost Breakers* is a classic horror-comedy, with Bob Hope as a skeptic trying to disprove a haunting in a creepy Cuban castle.

6. *House on Haunted Hill* (1959) Though not truly a supernatural film, this Vincent Price classic uses all of the trappings of the "haunted house" motif to create chills and laughs.

7. *Portrait of Jenny* (1948) Joseph Cotten plays a painter who meets a woman (played by the gorgeous Jennifer Jones) who may, or may not, be the ghost of the woman

he once loved. Like many classic ghost films, this one leaves a lot to the viewer's imagination.

8. *The Ghost and Mrs. Muir* (1947) Rex Harrison is the ghost of a crotchety old sea captain and Gene Tierney is the lovely young woman who now occupies his house. They meet, they fall in love, but he's dead . . . so she waits until she passes on so they can be together for eternity. Funny, moving, and a genuine tear-jerker.

9. *The Haunting* (1963) A researcher brings a group of psychics to a haunted house to conduct parapsychological experiments. Then things go quickly and horribly wrong. This film, based on Shirley Jackson's novel *The Haunting of Hill House,* appears frequently on top ten lists for the best horror film of all time.

10. *The Legend of Hell House* (1973) Based on a story by Richard Matheson, *Hell House* tweaks the model established in *The Haunting,* and goes even further into dark territory. Regarded by many to be Roddy McDowall's best and most understated performance.

11. *The Old Dark House* (1932) The prototype for the creepy, haunted-mansion story. Even after all these years, this James Whale classic still provides some chills, and a few laughs.

12. *The Turn of the Screw* (various) The 1898 Henry James novella has been filmed a number of times, both under the original title (in 1974, with Eva Griffith; in 1984, with Magdalena Vasaryova; in 1990, with Amy Irving; in 1992, with Patsy Kensit; and in 1999, with Jodhi May), both un-

(continued)

der this name and as *The Innocents* (1961, starring Deborah Kerr). The story deals with a young governess in a rural English manor house who becomes convinced that something supernatural is corrupting the children in her charge. Is she right, or is she mad?

13. *The Uninvited* (1944) Ray Milland and Ruth Hussey play siblings who move into a creepy house that might well be haunted.

Artifact   Physical items found at the scene of a psychic event, which prove not to be true evidence of a said event.

Astral Body   The spiritual aspect of a person that resides within the physical body, but is not permanently encased therein. In some psychic and/or spiritual practices, the astral body can leave the physical and travel through strength of will.

Astral Projection   Also known as OBE (Out of Body Experience), astral projection involves the astral body separating from the physical body, whether by accident (as in the case of some near-death experiences or through deliberate means (as with very advanced forms of meditation).

Atmospheric Ghost (also **replaying ghost, residual haunting)**   An apparition that appears in a single location (as opposed to a roaming, historical, or traveling ghost). It repeats certain actions over and over again, suggesting that it is a kind of signal or energy pattern somehow stored in the materials of the vicinity (rocks, metals, etc.). Parapsychologists generally believe that this kind of spirit has no consciousness and is merely a kind of psychic projection.

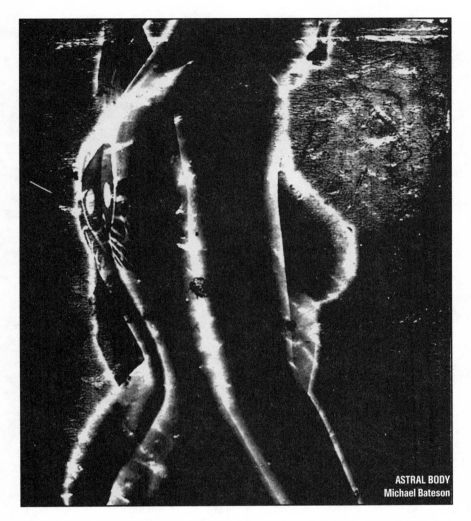

ASTRAL BODY
Michael Bateson

Aura   The spiritual energy field of the human body, and the essential substance of the astral body. It has been speculated that the aura is created by the electrochemical process of living, since all living things have one (trees, flowers, etc.). Another theory is that the aura is created by molecular movement, and that even something as apparently inert as a rock has an aura because even it has some movement on the molecular level.

Automatic Art   Drawing or painting accomplished while in a psychic trance. In such cases the subject is often channeling the thoughts of a spiritual being.

Automatic Writing   Writing accomplished, generally, while in a psychic trance.

Automatism   Movements of the arm during psychic trances in which the subject draws, writes, or otherwise attempts to communicate.

Autoscopy   The event of seeing one's physical body while in astral form during an OBE (out-of-body experience).

Billet Reading   A trick used by stage magicians and mentalists in which they ostensibly use psychic abilities to read a message written on a slip of paper in a sealed envelope.

Bilocation   The act of being in two places at the same time.

Blind   A control used in scientific experiments. Subjects are not informed of certain vital aspects of the tests, so that they do not consciously or psychosomatically influence the outcome of the test.

Book Test   A psi experiment in which the sitter looks at a specific page of a book and attempts to psychically send the page number or text to the subject.

Cabinet   A sealed box or test cubicle in which a physical medium sits during a psychic test. The cabinet is designed to isolate the medium, so that any manifesting phenomena can be verified as having originated from him or her.

Calling Ghost   There are two types of calling ghost. The first is a supernatural predator (a ghost, demon, or other spirit) who uses various ploys to lure humans to them—usually by getting them to follow calls or apparitions to secluded spots. It can then attack them to steal life essence, breath, or other energies. The second kind of calling ghost is less deliberately vicious, though still unpleasant. It is a messenger ghost sent by some otherworldly power to tell a person that they are doomed to die. Some of these spirits also act as guides to the underworld. (See PSYCHOPOMP).

Card-Guessing A commonly used psi test in which a subject attempts to guess the content on a card. Generally, the back of the card is shown to the subject. In some experiments, however, a sitter looks at the card in a separate room or a screen blocks the subject. Sometimes standard playing cards are used, and at other times Zener cards are used.

Chance Random and unpredictable influences on events. They are often mistaken for luck, divine influence, or as examples of psychic ability. ESP researchers have to allow for mere chance when collecting and analyzing data from psi testing.

Channeling The belief and practice of receiving messages, thoughts, and inspirations from nonphysical entities (demons, gods, aliens, spirits). ESP researchers are notoriously skeptical of channeling claims, though many have advanced the theory that channels are actually telepaths picking up thoughts from living persons. Overall, the jury is still out on the subject for most parapsychologists.

Cipher Test A code or coded message agreed upon between two persons,

CALLING GHOST

particularly when one is dying. After death the cipher test will signal communication between the spirit world and the physical one.

Circle   A group of people, generally seated around a table, who conduct a séance.

Clairaudience   The psychic ability to receive information by means of sounds or voices.

Clairvoyance   The ability to receive images and information through psychic means rather than normal sensory perception. The person possessing these powers is known as a clairvoyant.

Closed Deck   A deck of cards used specifically in ESP testing; there is a fixed number of cards for each image or value. The frequency with which the card is correctly guessed or identified via ESP is factored along with statistical probabilities to determine the presence, accuracy, and strength of the subject's psi powers.

Coincidence (also **synchronicity)**   When two or more seemingly related events occur in a short period of time, but with no apparent causal connection, it is considered a "coincidence." Like chance, coincidence is often mistaken for a psychic or spiritual event.

Cold Reading   A psychic reading given by a subject with no previous knowledge of the sitter.

Collective Apparition   An apparition seen simultaneously by two or more people. These events are very rare and are among the most compelling in parapsychology. Some of these events have been upheld by religious communities as spiritual or holy visions.

Communication   A message received by a medium that is believed to have come from a nonphysical entity.

Communicator   A nonphysical entity that communicates with a living medium.

Control   A process of ESP testing in which all experiments are conducted under strict laboratory conditions, thus reducing data pollution from nonrelated incidental factors.

Control Group   A group of nontest subjects whose reactions and performance is compared with those of the actual subjects. The intention is to identify naturally occurring or chance phenomena.

Crisis Apparition   A spiritual image or being that appears to a person shortly before death; or a similar image that appears to warn of impending sickness, disaster, or death.

CRISIS APPARITION
Jason Beam

Cross-Correspondence   Information received from two unrelated or independent mediums, which separately is nonsensical but when combined form a cohesive message.

Cryptomnesia   Information a person acquires without conscious awareness of its source. This phenomenon is often found at the heart of psychic investigations.

Death Image   A kind of crisis apparition that appears in the form of a death's head, skull, or angel of death.

Death Warning   An apparition where someone "sees" a person whom they later learn has recently died. This belief has been reported in most countries and cultures.

Decline Effect   In ESP testing, the measurable decrease in a subject's accuracy as a test is repeated.

Deja Vu   The feeling a person has that a currently unfolding event has been experienced before.

Dematerialization   The fading or disappearance of a physical object accomplished through psychic or spiritual means.

Deport   The movement of an object from inside a secured test space (or cabinet) using purely psychic means.

Dice Test   A test of psychokinetic ability in which the subject attempts to control the fall of rolled dice.

Direct Voice   A voice heard during a séance that does not appear to originate from any visible person. Ostensibly this is the voice of a nonphysical entity.

Discarnate Entity   Another of the many terms used to describe an entity that has no apparent physical form. More commonly known as a nonphysical

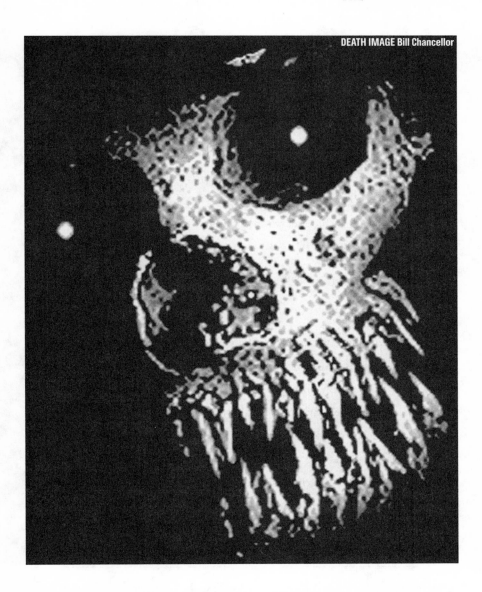

DEATH IMAGE Bill Chancellor

entity, these may include ghosts, spirits of undefined nature, aliens, gods, demons, and more.

Divination: Methods by which psychics and/or spiritual mediums read signs of various kinds to obtain knowledge.[21]

21. See chapter 4 for a complete list of divination methods.

Down Through Technique (DT)   A psi test in which the subject attempts to guess or identify a number of stacked objects from top to bottom. Cards are most often used during this technique. The reverse experiment is called "up through technique."

Drop-in Communicator   A nonphysical entity who attempts to speak through a medium at a sitting or séance, but who is not the intended target of the communication.

Ectoplasm   A dense bioenergy that emanates from living beings during psychic events. While similar to the aura, ectoplasm is more tangible and visible.

Empath   A psychic possessing the ability to feel the emotions of another.

ESP   Extrasensory perception; a catch-all name for psychic abilities.

Exorcism   A religious ritual used by various faiths to drive out unwanted nonphysical entities. In most cases there is a belief that a demon has taken possession of the victim, though in recent decades belief has shifted (for the most part) to an understanding that aberrant behavior on the part of the victim may, in fact, be symptomatic of psychological disorders. In parapsychology, there are mixed feelings on the subject, with some researchers suggesting that possession might be the result of psychic abilities blossoming without any self-awareness or filters. Though not frequently practiced, there are some standard religious exorcisms being practiced in modern times.

◁ EXORCISM ▷

This is a true personal experience regarding modern-day exorcism (name withheld by request):

I started sleepwalking when I was about seven. At least that's when I noticed it. I'd wake up in the tree outside my window quite regularly, and many other places as well. My parents tried locking me in my room at first, but that only resulted in broken windows. Admittedly on more than one occasion it was quite deliberate—I had some "behavior issues" as a child. I often went out anyway, and I don't think my waking self was any more tolerant of confinement than the sleepwalker was. This went on with little interruption until I was eleven when my father started dragging me to see a priest he knew. Funny how a man who believes in possession would refer to psychotherapy as black magic or hokum, isn't it?

After a few visits the priest referred my father to an exorcist because he thought I was possessed by an evil spirit, possibly a werewolf. The next two weeks were spent being subjected to some rituals that were truly painful—emotionally as well as physically. I really don't know how to describe it without getting angry. After finally giving up for lack of any result, the priest recommended that I be institutionalized. My father was against it, but gave in after an hour of trying to get me to speak to him. I was there for two months.

I managed to keep from my nightly wandering for about three weeks after my release.

Experimental Parapsychology   ESP research using new (hence experimental) methods rather than the established scientific data-collecting methods.

Faith Healing   The capacity, generated either by psychic ability or via some spiritual connection, to cure injuries and disease.

False Awakening   A psychic event in which a person believes he or she has awakened but is still sleeping.

FAITH HEALER
Rita Isabel Sancho

Family Ghost   A spirit that appears to be attached to the members of a particular family. In folklore many of these ghosts are CRISIS APPARITIONS. Family ghosts are not necessarily the surviving spirits of deceased family members, and there are several accounts of ghostly animals attached to specific families.

⊰ LIVING WITH LIZZIE ⊱

This is a personal encounter story as told by Elyssa Noonan, cofounder of the Paranormal Hunters of Indiana:

For a while I was a stay-at-home mom, caring for my kids, Torin, 3, and Brianna 2. As soon as the kids went to bed, I would go off to la-la land myself. One night I had a dream that was strikingly real. I heard the phone ring, I felt myself pick it up, and I said, hello. I heard a middle-aged woman's voice asking, 'Hello, is Elizabeth there?'

I answered back, somewhat annoyed at being called and jolted awake at this hour, 'No, there is no Elizabeth here.'

Abruptly the woman's voice turned harsh and snapped: 'Yes there is—look in the basement!'

I woke up thinking that this had been a pretty strange dream, and it left me with a weird feeling. The next day, I was looking for Brianna only to hear her carrying on a full conversation in my room. Expecting Torin to be in there with her, I walked back to find her in there all alone on the end of the bed, seemingly talking to someone beside her (though there was no one there). When I asked her who she was talking to, my two-year-old replied, 'Ewizabet . . . she's nice.'

Naturally, I freaked out. But after a while I realized that there was some kind of spirit in the house. We began noticing a lot of things moved and other pranks—the kind a playful poltergeist might do. The spirit of that little ghostly girl was with us for years, and when she'd pull one of her pranks we'd talk to her as if she were real (or alive). She seemed to listen, too, because the pranks would stop after we "talked" to her.

Sadly, we moved from that house after ten years of living with Elizabeth to find a smaller, less expensive place. The house still stands, I wonder if the new owners have met Lizzie yet!

Focal Person   A person to whom poltergeist activity is apparently directed.

GESP (General Extrasensory Perception)   A term used to describe apparent psychic events in which the specific type of psi ability (telepathy, empathy, precognition, etc.) is uncertain.

Ghost   A spirit or energy pattern of a dead person. There are many theories within the spiritual and parapsychological communities to explain the nature of ghosts, many of which conflict radically. Crews of ghost hunters abound, many of them using advanced sensory and recording equipment to collect field evidence.

Glossolalia   Popularly known as "speaking in tongues," glossolalia is the apparently patternless speech uttered during trance states. Within the religious community there is a belief that this is the language of the angels.

Goat   Nickname for an ESP test subject who does not actually believe in psychic abilities.

Guide   A nonphysical entity that aids a person through a spiritual journey or other experience.

Hallucination   An experience in which a person perceives events or phenomena, but which are not actually related to their physical senses.

Haunted Object   Any item that apparently stores psychic energy and perhaps some consciousness.

Haunting   A paranormal event in which unexplained sounds, sights, movements, or other phenomena occur. As far as the parapsychology community is concerned, the jury is still out as to whether these phenomena are in any way related to surviving spirits, ghosts, or other nonphysical beings.

Healer   In the world of the paranormal, a healer is a person who uses psychic or spiritual powers to affect a cure. See also FAITH HEALER, PSYCHIC HEALING, SPIRIT CURES.

Hellstromism   A process of ESP testing in which all experiments are conducted under strict laboratory conditions, thus reducing data pollution by nonrelated incidental factors.

Historical Ghost   A kind of atmospheric ghost who is seen in multiple locations.

⊰ 13 RECENT GREAT ⊱ GHOST MOVIES

1. *Below* (2002) A vastly underrated thriller set on a haunted ship during World War II. Is it a ghost story or isn't it? It's definitely worth watching to find out.

2. *Chinese Ghost Story* (1987) A terrific remake of Li Han-shiang's *Enchanting Shadow* (itself an adaptation of writer Pu Song-ling's *The Magic Sword*). It tells the story of a fox spirit who falls in love with a mortal.

3. *Ghost* (1990) One of the most beloved love stories of the 90s dealt with a ghost, Patrick Swayze, and his attempts to solve his own murder. He also tried to contact his wife (Demi Moore), with a little help from medium Whoopi Goldberg.

4. *Ghost Story* (1981) Peter Straub's powerful novel undergoes a plot makeover (read the book, watch the film, and decide which you prefer). The strong performers include Fred Astaire, John Houseman, Douglas Fairbanks, Jr., Melvyn Douglas, and Alice Krige as a sexually compelling specter.

5. *Ghostbusters* (1984) Though by no means serious, this

(continued)

Dan Ackroyd, Bill Murray, Sigourney Weaver comedy did a lot to raise awareness of parapsychology as an actual science.

6. *Poltergeist* (1982) A chilling classic that pitted a team of parapsychologist parents (Craig T. Nelson and JoBeth Williams) against some very nasty ghosts. This is the film that put the phrase, "Don't go into the light!" into common usage.

7. *Stir of Echoes* (1999) Kevin Bacon turns in a fantastic performance as an average Joe who channels a vengeful spirit in this modern ghost story by Richard Matheson.

8. *The Grudge* (2004) Screenwriter Stephen Susco nails the mood and emotion of the Japanese original *(Ju On)* in this nasty ghost story set in contemporary Japan. Sarah Michelle Geller (Buffy, the Vampire Slayer) is the young woman whose life is tortured by a revenge-hungry spirit. The sequel, *The Grudge 2* (2006) picked up the story with the sister of Geller's character trying to unravel the deadly mystery.

9. *The Others* (2001) Nicole Kidman turned in one of her most compelling performances as a young mother trying to protect her children from some otherworldly goings on.

10. *The Shining* (1980) Stephen King has scared a lot of people with his books, but rarely have his works been translated to the screen with all of the jolts intact. Stanley Kubrick managed it, however, with a little manic help from Jack Nicholson.

11. *The Sixth Sense* (1999) M. Night Shyamalan burst onto

the film scene with this riveting tale of a little boy (Haley Joel Osment) who sees dead people; and Bruce Willis, a child psychologist, has his own supernatural issues to sort out.

12. *Truly, Madly, Deeply* (1991) Juliet Stevenson does an outstanding job as a teacher trying to pick up the pieces of her life after the love of her life dies. Alan Rickman's performance as the ghost of her lover is funny and heartbreaking at the same time.

13. *What Lies Beneath* (2000) Michelle Pfeiffer and Harrison Ford in a tale of twisted love, guilt, murder, and supernatural revenge.

Hot Reading   A psychic reading in which the subject has previous knowledge of the sitter. These readings are almost always frauds and generally pollute the attempt to understand and verify actual psychic skills.

Hyperaesthesia   A condition in which one or more of a person's senses are unnaturally acute. Some medical conditions can account for incidents of this, though some are currently inexplicable and are being studied by parapsychologists.

Hypnagogic Imagery   Visual events that occur just as someone is dropping off to sleep, which may or may not have connections to psychic or spiritual phenomena.

Hypnopompic Imagery   Visual events occurring at the point when a person is just waking up.

Hypnosis   A form of mental control where a person is induced into a trancelike state, so that he or she will be receptive to suggestion. There are

EVIL HAUNTING
Ken Meyer, Jr.

scores of methods of practicing hypnosis, from cheap parlor tricks to therapeutic methods used during healing.

Illusion   (1) A visual phenomena—either naturally occurring (but unusual) or a misperception (that leads a person to make incorrect assumptions). Mirages are perfect examples. (2) In stage magic, the illusion is intentionally created for entertainment purposes.

Incline Effect   A marked increase in the accuracy of a subject's psychic performance during repeated testing.

Intelligent Ghost   Apparitions that appear to possess memory, conscious (though often limited) control over its actions, intelligence, and an awareness of the living. Poltergeists are one kind of intelligent ghost.

Intuition   A nonpsychic talent for making accurate decisions based on a variety of overt of subtle sensory and informational input. Unusually perceptive persons are often mistaken for having a degree of psychic ability. Actual psychic ability is variously known as clairvoyance or precognition.

Kirlian Photography   A photographic method developed by S.D. & V. Kirlian in the Soviet Union to photograph the aura surrounding objects.

Laying on of Hands   A name given to faith healing in which the healer's hands touch the aura or physical body of the patient.

Levitation   The telekinetic ability to raise objects into the air.

Lucid Dreaming   A dream state in which the sleeper is conscious of what he is dreaming. Sometimes he or she can even direct the focus of those dreams.

Lucid Painting   An advanced form of lucid dreaming in which the sleeper can preplan a dream before going to sleep and then experience that specific dream.

Marian Spirit   A ghost who takes the form of the Virgin Mary, or in some cases one of the saints.

Matching Test   A card-guessing test using key cards.

Materialization   The psychic ability to create tangible objects out of thin air.

MCE (Mean Chance Expectation)   The name given for the most probable score in any given ESP test, which is based solely on the randomness of chance.

Medium   A psychic who acts as an intermediary between humans and non-physical entities.

Mental Medium   A psychic capable of hearing, speaking to, or otherwise contacting the spirit world.

Mentalism   A branch of stage magic that relies (or purports to rely) on some degree of actual psychic ability.

Mesmerism   A technique of mentalism developed by F. A. Mesmer in which the subject is placed into a trance in order to transfer ANIMAL MAGNETISM.

Metal Bending   The ability, popularized by Uri Geller, in which a physical medium attempts to bend metal objects, such as spoons.

Mind Reading   Commonplace nickname for telepathy.

Misdirection   A deceptive technique used by stage magicians to distract the attention of the audience in order to disguise another movement, such as pulling a bird out of a sleeve.

Menmonist   A person (psychic or otherwise) who possesses the ability to remember unusual amounts of information, including complex numbers and patterns.

Messenger   A spirit who conveys important information to the living, such as a warning (see CRISIS APPARITION).

Mystic   A person who has, or attempts to have, experiences and interactions with the spiritual plane. Generally mystics are less involved in the discovery of the science behind the experience, preferring instead to accept the events as spiritual or religious events.

NDE (Near-Death Experience)   Many thousands of people have reported that they had visions or astral projections during the short time their bodies were lingering on the edge of death. Quite a few NDEs have been reported by accident victims who claim to have floated about the accident scene, or surgical patients who witnessed their surgeries while separated from their physical form. NDEs are often life-changing events.

Necromancy   A form of black magic in which a sorcerer communicates with the dead. It may well be that the legends of necromancy are based on poor reportage of early spiritualists and mental mediums.

Newspaper Test   A psychic test in which the subject attempts to predict the headlines of a newspaper sometime in the future.

OBE (Out-of-Body Experience)   A psychic event in which a person's astral body becomes detached from the physical form, either by accident (as with many near-death experiences) or through self-induced trance states.

Occam's Razor   The tenet that we should always seek the simplest explanation for any given occurrence. A fundamental rule in parapsychological research.

Occult   Literally "hidden"; a word used broadly to describe anything that is unknown but sought.

Open Deck   A card-guessing test in which cards are pulled randomly from a deck.

Ouija Board   A board on which the alphabet, numbers 0–10, and the words, "Yes," "No," and "Goodbye" are printed. One or more subjects lightly place their fingers on a planchette (a small, easily moveable board on raised legs) and nonphysical entities are supposed to guide it around the board, so that words or number patterns are spelled out. The board gets its name from the French and German words for "Yes."

Paranormal   A catch-all term for anything involving ghosts, psychic ability, channeling, or other such phenomena.

Paranormal Dream   A dream in which secrets and information are revealed, which could only have been obtained through some kind of psychic ability.

Parapsychology   A term coined by J. B. Rhine to describe the quantitative scientific study of the paranormal.

Past-life Memories   Images and information in one's mind, which appear to be the actual memories of a former incarnation.

Past-life Regression   A hypnosis technique in which a person is regressed to a former incarnation.

Percipient   Another name for the subject in a psychic experiment.

Phantasm   An apparition.

Phantom   A spirit who resembles a living being so closely that it is difficult to detect it as an apparition.

Phenomenology   The scientific study of a person's psychic experiences.

Photographic Ghosts   A spirit who can be seen in a photograph. Some of the spirits appear after the picture is developed; some are visible prior to the shot, but do not appear in the picture; and some are clearly spirits and can be photographed as normally as a physical object.

Phrenology   The psychic skill of reading a person's character through the shape of his or her skull.

Physical Medium   A psychic capable of physical manifestations, such as moving objects, materialization, telekinesis, pyrokinesis, levitation, and so on. Most physical mediums can only accomplish these feats while in a trance state.

Placement Test   A test for psychokinetic ability in which the subject is asked to influence the way objects, such as dice, land. Also known as the dice test.

Poltergeist   A German word, which translates as "noisy spirit." The term is used to describe a nonphysical entity with disruptive (and sometimes destructive) psychokinetic abilities. Some poltergeists make noise, others hurl objects around the room; a few have even attacked people, causing injury.

⊰ THE DIFFERENCE ⊱ BETWEEN A HAUNTING AND A POLTERGEIST

A ghostly entity may rattle a chain or knock on a table, but that doesn't qualify it as a poltergeist. There are differences between a "true haunting" and an incident of poltergeist activity.

- *Hauntings:* When the spirit of a deceased person lingers in a specific place that is known as a haunting. Spirits do not always manifest themselves in physical form, and even when they do, they are generally only partial apparitions. A head and torso is most common. Hauntings often occur in the place where a person has died and, therefore, the ghost is generally accepted to be the lingering spirit of that specific person. In some cases a ghost has become stuck in a place in which its former (living) self was strongly tied, even though that is not actually the place of its death. Hauntings are continuous events and have rarely (if ever) been reliably tied to violence of any kind.

- *Poltergeists:* Though they are invisible and unearthly, poltergeists may not actually be the spirits of the

(continued)

dead. Many parapsychologists believe that poltergeist activity is based more on explainable phenomenon than on otherworldly. These scientists believe that poltergeists are likely a form of energetic charge—perhaps even static electricity—that for reasons not yet known stay in a certain place. A house, for example, becomes the battery that stores this charge. Humans are electro-chemical beings, and each person's frequency is a bit different. It is thought that certain "charges" in people within a house of this kind cause a reaction that triggers a discharge of energy. Sometimes this is small and merely moves an object; sometimes the discharge is massive and causes great damage. Poltergeists are frequently linked directly to a specific person or object. Also, like many static charges, poltergeist activity builds up over a period of time, reaches a point of maximum destructive discharge, and then settles down to begin building again. Some psychologists are studying the link between emotional trauma and this unleashing of energy because studies have shown that poltergeist activity is often greatest during times of stress and emotional/psychological upheaval.

On the other hand: Making absolute statements about the Larger World is risky because there are often exceptions to any rule. In some cases, for example, poltergeists have indeed manifested in physical forms, and in those cases there are often odors (ozone, burned oranges, and so on) associated with the activity.

Precognition   The psychic ability to foretell the future.

Prediction   Any statement that purports to foretell the future, but which may be an example of good guessing.

Premonition   A psychic event of precognition.

Presence   A nonphysical entity that is sensed but not actually seen.

Prophecy   Precognition accomplished through spiritual rather than psychic means.

PSI   A nickname for any psychic ability. More commonly used in the scientific community; whereas ESP is used more often in pop culture.

Psychic   A person with extrasensory abilities.

Psychical Research   A nineteenth century nickname for what is now called parapsychology.

Psychic Healing   Any of the forms of healing, which use psychic abilities, including laying on of hands, psychic surgery, and so on.

Psychic Photography   The psychic skill of creating images on photographic film.

Psychic Surgery   A form of healing using psychic abilities rather than conventional medical or surgical techniques.

Psychokinesis   The psi ability to manipulate physical objects.

Psychometry   The psi skill of learning information by touching physical objects. Also known as "object reading," psychometry has even been used by police departments in the solving of crimes.

Psychopomp   A spiritual being who, according to various world religions and myths, escorts newly deceased souls to the afterworld.

Quickflash   A psychic ability in which a mental medium meets a stranger and instantly obtains extensive personal knowledge of that person.

Rapping   Unexplained sounds that occur in the presence of a physical medium. It is an open question as to whether the medium creates these sounds or attracts nonphysical entities that then make them as a means to communicate.

Raudive Voices   Voices inexplicably recorded on magnetic tape that speak intelligibly. This phenomenon was first discovered by Konstantin Raudive.

Reading   A session during which a psychic attempts to gather information about or for a sitter.

RSPK (recurrent spontaneous psychokinesis)   The term in parapsychology for poltergeist activity.

Regression   A hypnotic technique in which a person is induced to mentally return to an earlier point in their life.

Remote Viewing   A psychic technique for viewing objects at a distance. This is a technique highly sought after by governments for the purpose of espionage.

Residual Haunting (also imprint haunting)   A ghostly image or voice not perceived at the time of a recording, but which later shows up on film, tape, or other media.

Retrocognition   Psychic knowledge of past events at which a subject was not present.

Second Sight   Archaic name for clairvoyance.

Sender   Another name for subject or psychic who can psychically transmit to a psychic receiver.

Sensitive   Another name for a subject or psychic.

Sheep   Nickname given to a subject who already believes in his psychic ability. The opposite of GOAT.

Sheep-Goat Effect   The statistical anomaly identified by parapsychologist Gertrude Schmeidler, which clearly indicates sheep score significantly higher than goats in psychic testing.

Simultaneous Dreaming   A psychic event in which two or more persons share the same dream.

Sitter   A person who has a session with a subject, or psychic.

Sitting   A séance.

Sixth Sense   Pop-culture term for psychic ability.

Speaking in Tongues   See GLOSSOLALIA

Spirit   A common name for a nonphysical entity.

Spirit Cure   Any healing accomplished because of psychic or spiritual means.

Spirit Photography   Photos in which dead persons inexplicably appear.

Spiritualism   Religious belief used to explain psychic phenomena.

⊰ GHOSTS GONE ⊱
WILD—CAUGHT ON FILM

This is a personal encounter story related by screenwriter and film producer Joe Augustyn:[22]

Halloween holds many special memories for me, from trick-or-treating as a kid (when it was still safe to go out sans parent or

(continued)

---

22. *Night of the Demons* (1987), *Night Angel* (1990), *Night of the Demons 2* (1994), and *Exit* (1996).

guardian) to ultra-high-spirited party hopping in L.A. But one Halloween tops them all. The night my friends, John and John, threw a shindig in their haunted house.

They own a rustic cabin nestled in the hills of Eagle Rock, one of the funkier suburbs of Los Angeles. In a town where real estate is sold by the inch, they found a great deal on a huge double lot; and their little house sat snugly in a patch of dense woods that's so quiet and secluded it's easy to forget you're in a city.

Their house was investigated by Kerry Gaynor (of Entity fame) and psychic Peter James. I was present when the Sightings TV crew videotaped some remarkable footage. They handed one of the Johns a sealed-and-numbered pack of Polaroids from a case shipped directly from the company. He loaded it on-camera.

A question was asked, "Are you connected to this house or to a person in it?" John clicked and the Polaroid popped out, and when it developed there were wispy words suspended in the air: "Genius loci." The translation from Latin: "A spirit attached to a place or person."

The next Halloween they threw a big party, and guests brought their own cameras. Things started slow, a relaxed affair, but suddenly the atmosphere turned. The volume of chatter soared. The air seemed electric. I watched as one guest snapped a picture of another. When it developed there were dozens of tiny ectoplasmic squiggles over his image, which formed a splatter pattern spreading upward from his neck. It looked like his head had been shotgun blasted. The guest promptly left the party. Thoroughly unnerved.

> *Dozens of photos were snapped that night, by various guests, using cameras and film stock of their own. Most contained ghostly images. That was a great Halloween party.*

Spontaneous Cases   Paranormal events occurring in everyday life.

SHC (Spontaneous Human Combustion)   The inexplicable bursting into flames of a human body, generally with little or no spreading of the fire beyond the victim's remains.

Stigmata   The sudden appearance of bleeding wounds that correspond to the wounds of Christ.

Subject   A psychic participating in a parapsychological experiment.

Survival   The belief that the nonphysical or spiritual aspects of a person can (or do) survive after death. Some psychics and spiritualists believe that surviving spirits retain all of their previous memories and, at the same time, acquire a broader cosmic consciousness; other parapsychologists believe that surviving spirits are a form of energy that does not necessarily retain consciousness. Both sides bring good arguments to the table.

Synchronicity   A Jungian term for events occurring simultaneously. Although they happen randomly there is a significant connection.

Target   The object or goal of a psychic test.

Telekineses (also known as telekinetics)   The ability to move objects using psychic powers.

Telepathy   The psychic ability to communicate mind to mind rather than through speech, writing, or gestures. Telepathy varies from a sharing of emotions (empathy) to the actual projection and/or reading of thoughts.

Teleportation   The psychic ability to transport items using only the power of the mind.

Teletemporarianation   The psychic ability to move through time.

Trance Medium   A person who manifests psychic powers only when in a trance, whether it is induced by hypnosis or meditation.

Traveling Clairvoyance   An archaic term for OBEs, or out-of-body experiences.

Traveling Ghost   An apparition who appears to travelers, often in the form of a hitchhiker. Many urban legends are built around these spirits.

⊰ HAVE YOU HEARD THE ⊱ ONE ABOUT THE PHANTOM HITCHHIKER?

Urban legends abound worldwide. Although there are plenty involving mad killers with hooks for hands, by far the majority of these tales involve ghosts. There are three basic subgroups to these roving specters: phantom travelers, and phantom hitchhikers.

•Phantom travelers are not necessarily threatening, and often appear as a person waiting for some form of transportation (car, boat, plane, and so on). Most phantom travelers do not interact with humans and appear to be a kind of randomly repeated energy pattern (see HISTORICAL GHOST). Some travelers appear on the anniversary of their deaths, and generally those deaths involved travel disasters, such as car wrecks or plane crashes.

•Phantom hitchhikers are far more interactive ghosts who take rides, usually on the anniversary of their deaths. The ghosts are usually tragic and they tell the driver their sad story (fatal drag races, disastrous prom nights, and so on) before mysteriously vanishing.

•Phantom drivers: A twist on the hitchhiker stories is the ghostly vehicle that stops to pick up a human. Despite the potential for disaster, these tales are generally nonviolent and involve some kind of spiritual life lesson imparted by the ghost to his passenger. This legend was used as the basis for the classic 1967 hit song, *Phantom 309* by Red Sovine.

Up Through Technique   A psi test in which the subject attempts to guess or identify a number of objects in correct order, beginning with the bottommost and working upward.

Veridical Dream   A psychic dream that corresponds to an actual real-world event, but which could not have been known to the dreamer at the time.

Vision   An apparition of a religious nature.

White Noise   This hissing sound generated by a combination of all audible frequencies. Several different psi phenomena have been discerned while subjects listened to white noise.

Xenoglossy   The inexplicable ability to write or speak in a language the subject has never learned.

Yoga   A religious philosophy that teaches, among other things, meditation and spirituality.

Zener Cards   A set of twenty-five cards created by perceptual psychologist Karl Zener for use in card-guessing psychic tests. There are five each of the following: circle, square, five-pointed star, three wavy lines, and the greek cross.

— *Chapter Seven* —
HERBS AND STONES

⊰ HEALING WITH HERBS ⊱

The tapestry of herbal medicine, like so many of its sisterly beliefs, began to unravel in Europe in the 1600s. The power of the university and the church (which were most often one in the same) began to systematically eliminate any practice, medical or otherwise, that they didn't sanction. Undoubtedly, the first to go were the midwives. The practice of midwifery was a double slap in the face of the church in that it gave mortals sway over the power and circumstance of birth, and worse yet, the mortals in question were women. Women who practiced these crucial techniques were branded as witches and cast out of their villages—or worse, persecuted, tortured, arrested without trial, and often executed. Much of the world's knowledge of natural medicine has been lost to the persecution of wise women.

Luckily some of these dedicated herbalists were as hardy as some of the plants in their charge—and these practices and ideals survive. In Asia, Africa, South America, and elsewhere folk medicine flourished, there are efforts to decrypt old herbal-based medical texts from the Mayans and similar extinct cultures.

On its surface, the practice of herbal medicine differs little from the practice of agriculture. It's simply a matter of choosing what to grow, when it must be harvested, and how it must be processed for the greatest effect.

Most herbs are prepared as follows: First, the material is cut into small parts and tied into bundles with twine or string. These bundles can be hung in a cool, dry spot for a while to give the leaves time to dry. Depending upon the herbs and the amounts, this could take anywhere between a few days to a few weeks.

Herbs for medicinal use can be processed for use in any of the following ways:

• *Pulverization:* Once the leaves have dried, a mortar and pestle can easily grind them into powder for use in tinctures, teas, or even poured into empty gelatin capsules for do-it-yourself pills and supplements for those on the go!

• *Extraction:* Herbs can be *decocted,* or extracted with boiling water; *infused,* by mixing the herbs with alcohol and keeping them in a tightly sealed container; or *macerated,* by adding water of a temperature less than boiling (thus separating the needed contents).

• *Filtration:* This process is similar to maceration, but involves either the use of some medium (even if it's simply filter paper) to keep the elements separate.

• *Clarification:* The process of repeatedly boiling a substance and collecting the "skin" or sediment that rises to the top.

• *Expression:* When a device similar to a wine press is used to literally squeeze the needed elements from herbs and plant material.

And now for the bad news. Any good book on herbalism or natural remedies, no matter how learned the source, is quick to dissuade readers from heading out to their gardens with a pair of scissors and some plastic bags—and this book is no exception. Plants that are useful in healing can be extremely dangerous. Preparation and proper handling are crucial.

Misuse is another problem. Like traditional medicines, herbs can often cause symptoms such as elevated heart rate or blood pressure. Those who suffer from these conditions should consult a doctor before beginning a regimen of herbal remedies. While your doctor may not agree that the old ways are best, he or she can arm you with information so that you won't be walking blindly into earth's garden.

Most herbs are dietary supplements rather than medicines. Of the many herbal remedies on the market, more than 50 percent are based on these eight herbs: echinacea, ephedra, garlic, ginko, ginseng, kava, St. John's wort, and valerian. Most, or all of these herbs, despite their beneficial properties, can interfere with pre- and post-surgical health. Bottom line: Find out about them first before swallowing anything!

The following is a quick guide to the healing power of herbs:

Agar Derived from seaweed and algae, this material can be used like gelatin for purposes ranging from the culinary to the medical. Agar can be used to create the medium surface for petri dishes to grow molds and cultures for scientific experimentation. It is popular as a diet aid in Asia due to both its laxative and water-absorbing properties, and unlike most other such aids, it does indeed have nutritional value.

◄ INCENSE ►

Incense can be made from a wide variety of plants, but the best incense for healing, spiritual practice, or protection is made from one or more of the following: agarwood, gum benzoin, clove, camphor, cedar, copal, cypress, frankincense, juniper, labdanum or ladanum, myrrh, nutmeg, patchouli, sage, sandalwood, star anise, or storax.

INCENSE AND HEALING CRYSTALS
Sara Jo West

Agrimony   A plant with yellow flowers that grows throughout temperate areas of the northern hemisphere. In Wicca, it's a popular practice to slip some dried leaves of agrimony into the pillow of someone who is sick to ensure that they can rest. Agrimony can also be used internally to improve liver function and soothe the stomach and bowels.

Alfalfa   Widely known as the stuff of feed for cattle and domestic animals throughout the world, alfalfa sprouts also make for an agreeable addition to salads. The working witch, however, might opt to create an all-around health tonic from the plant, but its value is clearly more nutritional than magickal.

Angelica   The leaves, flowers, and roots of this widely available herb can treat disorders of the kidneys. Angelica cleanses and detoxifies, as it promotes sweating. It has a long history of use by Native American tribes for rituals and medicine, as well as being consumed as food.

Anise   Treasured for its use in the creation of sweets and liquors like Greek ouzo, the seeds of this plant can also stimulate the function of the liver, treat asthma and bronchial disorders, cataracts, coughs and colic in infants, prevent nausea, and cure insomnia.

Barberry   There are nearly 500 varieties of these shrubs growing through-out North and South America, Asia, Africa, and Europe. It can be used to help limit bleeding in wounds or as a laxative. The bark of the plant can also be used to reduce fever, and the berries can be distilled into a soothing paste for sore throats.

Bayberry   These shrubs are common throughout the Americas, Africa, Asia, and Europe. Their unique fruits have been crafted into candles and can also be used as an effective insect repellent. It is both an astringent and a stimulant, so it can be used to soothe disorders of the stomach such as diarrhea and dysentery.

Black Cohosh   Also known by the much cooler monikers of "black bug-bane" or "snakeroot," this plant has been used throughout history by women to aid in the symptoms of premenstrual syndrome, the onset of menopause, and other female issues. It can also be instilled into a tonic to treat sore throats and coughs.

Blackberry   In English folklore, blackberries shouldn't be picked after mid-September because they have been coveted by the devil, who has left his mark upon them. It's still wise to keep this in mind as the later blackberries are har-vested the more prone to blight and mold. The leaves of the blackberry and blackcurrant can be used to treat diarrhea and as a general health tonic. The bark of the plant can be dried and made into a valuable tea that can treat stomach disorders, and even whooping cough.

Blessed Thistle   With a nod to true dichotomy, this plant is also known as "cursed thistle," and grows throughout the Mediterranean and Western Europe. It can be used by women to promote lactation and instilled into a tonic to soothe the stomach and increase the appetite. Blessed thistle can be used externally to dress wounds and treat skin ulcers. The plant was once touted as a cure for smallpox, most likely because it promotes sweating and can clear up some of the sores that are symptoms of the disease.

Boneset (also **thoroughwort)**   Generally considered poisonous, Boneset is used for its laxative and stimulating properties. It can also ease the symptoms of rheumatism and the common cold.

Buchu   In Europe, the leaves of this South African plant were treasured as recently as the nineteenth century for their ability to treat infections of the urinary tract (and kidney stones) by increasing the flow of urine. Since that time, sythethic versions of drugs have been created, but the effects of buchu were certainly a guideline for their creation.

Burdock   The roots of these thistled plants can be eaten and are still a popular dish in Japan. The leaves and seeds are also prized in herbal medicine for their blood purifying attributes; they can also stimulate hair growth and treat diseases of the scalp. The plant reproduces with tough burrs that get tangled in the fur of animals or clothes of people. In the 1940s, Swiss inventor Georges de Mestral pulled yet another round of them from his dog when he was struck with inspiration—the result was the invention of velcro.

Calendula   This beautiful marigold grows throughout the Mediterranean, Mexico, and Central America. It has great natural antibiotic properties, and can be made into an ointment, which soothes burns and clears up acne. The leaves and petals of this flower are also used as an ingredient in salads, but they tend to taste bitter.

Caraway   The "caraway seed" that can be found in spice shops and special-ity stores is actually a misnomer—it's actually the fruit of the plant native to Europe and Asia. A tea distilled from caraway fruit is a useful tonic to cure colic in infants—as well as to flavor medicines to make them more palatable for children and adults alike. Fans of rye bread are very familiar with caraway, and it also can be used as an all around cooking spice, or to flavor liquors, cheeses, and dishes of all types.

Cardamom   The fruit from this plant is seed like, very similar to the fruit of the caraway. The plant originated in India, but it was brought to the new world in the 1200s, where it flourished and found new uses in herbal medicine. In India, the fruit was used to treat diseases of the gums, teeth and throat, for coughs and congestion, and even as an antivenom for snake bites and scorpion stings. The Chinese used it to treat disorders of the stomach, as well as in their cooking.

Catnip   While most widely known for its effects in the domestic feline, this herb has been used medicinally since the Middle Ages to promote sweating and treat diseases of the digestive system. It can also calm the nerves and be used as an all around sedative. The use of this herb, however, is probably best limited to stuffed mice and scratching posts.

Chamomile   The German variety of this plant has a beautiful yellow bulb surrounded with white petals. They can be dried and made into teas or pow-ders. Chamomile has been used for centuries to soothe the stomach and as a sleep aid. In our modern world, chamomile tea is as popular a beverage as it has ever been. The plant is also used in the cosmetics industry for its benefit of intensifying the luster of blond hair—yet another shining example of why they have more fun than the rest of us.

Cloves   Few herbs have touched the lives of so very many as that of the humble clove. Anyone who has had a potentially painful dental procedure under the influence of the numbing bliss of novocaine can attest to this. In ancient days cloves were traded like precious currency, and were highly coveted by the wealthy for cooking and incense. Medical uses of cloves are as an anasthetic mostly, but it can act as an astringent, ease nausea, and even work as an expectorant to treat coughs. Denizens of clubs catering to the gothic scene are familiar with the pungent odor of clove cigarettes, which are also popular diversions throughout Europe and Asia. Cloves can also be mixed with marijuana to highten the effects of the drug, and the stronger smell of burning cloves will mask the smell of this drug (illegal throughout most of the world).

Coltsfoot (also **ass's foot, bull's foot, butterbur, coughwort, farfara, foal's foot, foalswort)**   This yellow flowering plant has been used for centuries to treat asthma. It also can be used as an expectorant and cough suppressant. Oddly enough, the preferred method of treatment for all these conditions is to smoke the dried leaves—probably an ill-advised move for someone with chronic lung conditions. Crushing the flowers also releases a powerful emollient that can cure some skin conditions.

Damiana   This intriguing Central and South American shrub is highly regarded as an aphrodisiac and relaxing all-around recreational drug with purported effects similar to that of marijunana. The leaves can be made into tea or simply smoked. The plant has also been distilled into liquor. The intoxicating effects may be exaggerated, however, as they seem to have no chemical basis—and the belief could very well be based on people's experiences with damiana tonics, which are most likely more alcoholic than herbal.

Dandelion   Regarded as a menacing weed to that wily creature, "Suburban Man." The dandelion grows in abundance throughout the world and can be eaten, cooked or raw, as part of soups or salads, or even made into wine. The root makes for a potent natural diuretic, and it can increase the production of bile in the liver and even balance blood sugar to combat diabetes. As "weeds" go, it is one of the most useful and versatile. Due to its prevalance and relative safety (even in high doses), dandelion is a fine starting point for the fledgling herbalist.

Don Quai   The Chinese have used this herb for centuries, distilling it into a tonic to regulate the menstrual cycle and to treat hypertension. In can also ease the symptoms of menapause and prementstrual syndrome. Some studies suggest it can actually effect hormonal balance and prevent female conditions like ovarian cysts. Stateside it can be readily found in pill form as an active ingredient in herbal supplements—and is most likely available at your local natural foods store.

Echinacea   These widely growing plants have been used for centuries in herbal medicines and tonics of many varieties by Native American tribes, as well as throughout Europe. The name comes from the Greek *echinos,* meaning hedgehog, because of the flower's prickly center. It's most likely the herb was used as a general cure-all to treat maladies from scarlet fever and malaria to the common cold. Some research has suggested that it can fight infection to a modest extent. Medical studies as recent as 2003, however, have found that echinacea taken for colds will either help you, or possibly not.

Elderberry   Nothing goes to waste in the medicinal use of this humble North American tree and its significantly taller European, Asian, and African cousins. The bark, berries, leaves, and roots all have important roles in folk medicine going back to the days of the pharoahs. The berries are rich in vitamins A, B, and C and have enough food value to keep a wayward traveler going. Care must be taken, however, not ingest the seeds, which will make you sick. Elderberry has been used to treat nerves, chronic pain of the back, and to reduce inflammation. It has even been distilled into wines and liqueurs. The leaves can be used to clear the skin, and it's a valuable ingredient in restorative ointments for cuts and burns.

Elecampane   This yellow, flowering plant grows in Europe and some parts of Asia. Breaking the root of these blooms will yield a camphor smelling, astringent liquid, and tonics made from it are said to aid the flow of our many organs that secrete (thyroid, adrenal, pituatary, and so on). The flowers are also known as "horse-heal" and a drug made from the plant is still used in the practice of veterinary medicine, but not very widely.

Ephedra   This widely growing shrub called *ma-huang* by the Chinese has had some bad press lately. The active ingredients in the plant are ephedrine and pseudoephedrine, which are used in decongestants and can elevate heart rate and blood pressure. They are also the building blocks for the illegal and highly dangerous drug methamphetamine. Additionally, ephedra was marketed as an active ingredient in herbal diet aids. The Food and Drug Administration (FDA), however, banned the sale of the plant on December 30, 2003—linking it to 155 cardiac or stroke deaths. Diet aids and stimulants containing ephedra or ephedra-like compounds are still widely available, though. People with elevated heart rate or high blood pressure should definitely steer clear of them. These days, the name is most often uttered in athletic doping scandals as ephedra is often used in the sports community as a "performance enhancing drug."

Fennel   In addition to flavoring Indian, Middle Eastern, and Mediterranean cooking, the leaves and seeds of this popular spice were used in the Middle Ages to ward off evil spirits. This belief probably stems from the fact that when burned, fennel is an effective insect repellant. It was also used medicinally as an antispasmodic, to relieve disorders of the digestive tract and even as an aphrodisiac.

Feverfew   These small, flowering bushes are also known as featherfew and "batchelor's buttons" and were brought to America from Europe initially for their beauty. They are a potent medicinal however, and have been used to treat headaches and migraines, the chronic inflammation that comes with conditions such as arthritis, to lower blood pressure, soothe the stomach and stimulate the appetite and even to alleviate dizziness and ringing in the ears.

Ginseng   The name of this well-known substance comes from the Chinese term meaning "man root"—which clearly describes its unmistakably human shape. While mainly thought of as an Asian herbal remedy, Native Americans also utilized a North American version of this unique plant—which is still widely available in Chinese grocery stores and restaurants. Ginseng is sold and used heavily thoughout Asia and touted to cure impotence, prevent cancer, and generally stimulate the body and mind. It is believed that the American version of the root improves the yin (female) aspects, and the Asian variety, the yang (male). As is the case with many other herbs and natural substances, the "rights" to ginseng can't be held exclusively. So, with no big money to be made, there's also no impetus to fund expensive medical studies in substantiating its effects. Like so many other entries in *Cryptopedia,* this one needs to be taken on faith.

Goldenseal   This white flowering cousin to the buttercup grows throughout North America. In paste form, the root acts as a local antibiotic—and can clear up skin disorders such as eczema, athlete's foot, ringworm, and psoriasis. It has also been used internally as an aid to digestion, to ease inflammation of the eyes and mouth, and even as an effective douche to treat yeast infections. Great care needs to be taken with goldenseal, as high doses can be toxic—but in the hands of the learned herbalist, its effects cannot be denied.

Hawthorn   The berries of the hawthorne—a beautiful perennial with white flowers—can increase the flow of blood, and have been used in folk medicine since the Middle Ages. It also acts as a powerful antioxidant and diuretic—and can be useful for weight loss and all-around cleansing in the body.

Hops   Before beer brewers knew what they were missing, these aromatic buds were used as a sedative. They could also treat anxiety, nervousness, and were sometimes simply placed into a pillow to treat insomnia. Hops also will cleanse the blood and promote the production of bile.

Licorice   This familiar flavoring agent is actually a legume, and is more closely related to beans than herbs. The roots of the plant are boiled to distill a syryp for use in candies and cooking. But this tasty treat also has great medicinal value. Licorice taken internally acts as a powerful expectorant and can be used to soothe coughs. Even in the present day, many prepared cough syryps and medicines still have a familiar licorice flavor to them, whether or not it is one of the active ingredients. Licorice, in powdered form, can be used orally as a toothache remedy, or to cure ulcers and sores in the mouth. In the stomach, it can have both a laxative and soothing effect (and seems to be a good all around bellyache remedy). Like so many other herbs and plants in our list, licorice is also touted to be a potent aphrodisiac—but one would probably be better served by finding a lover with a sweet tooth rather than relying on its magickal reputation.

Mandrake   A plant that has a long and storied history as an object of ritual magick and power. Myths and legends encompass every aspect of the mandrake, even the manner is which it must be harvested in order to avoid harm. Legend says it will emit a hideous shriek when removed from the earth, which can kill man or beast. When harvesting the root, one must dig carefully around it until it is almost exposed. Then, a rope is tied around the neck of a dog, and the other end fashioned around the root. Protecting the ears from the coming scream, a person then walks (or more likely runs) away, and the dog is compelled to follow. This allows the rope to sever the root with a person at a safe distance. Unfortunately, the hideous bellow will kill the canine. The mandrake is mentioned in stories from biblical times to the heyday of witchcraft in the Middle Ages, even as part of the curriculum at the Hogwart's School for Wizards in the *Harry Potter* series of books.

Mugwort (also **wormwood)**   Growing throughout Europe and Asia, the herb is used both to flavor foods and in folk medicine. Similar to the cocao plant of South America, mugwort leaves were chewed by travelers as a stimulant. Mugwort can also be smoked, and it can have introspective and dreamy effects similar to those associated with marijuana. In witchcraft, mugwort is not surprisingly used for relaxation and can raise the consciousness needed for astral projection, lucid dreaming, and midnight screenings of *Pink Floyd: The Wall.*

Myrrh   A powder created from the dried sap of an East African tree, this substance is most widely thought of as a birthday present of some reknown (along with gold and Frankincense, of course). The name comes from the Hebrew *maror,* or bitter, and is frequently misidentified as the bitter herb served during the Jewish tradition of Passover, but not so. Its medicinal uses were limited to salves and ointments, but myrrh was most highly prized as incense—and was burned by the Romans to keep the smell of the dead at bay.

⊰ ANCIENT MEDICINE ⊱

The Egyptians did more than build and bury, they also healed. Imhotep, who lived in 2980 B.C.E. is the man regarded as the founder of Egyptian medicine, and his writings show exact methods for examination, diagnosis, treatment, and prognosis. Many of Imhotep's medical writings have been translated from a document dating to 1600 (itself a translation of much earlier documents). Known as the Edwin Smith Papyrus (named for the famed Egyptologist), these writings show that there was a strong and accurate understanding of organ functions,

(continued)

of the circulatory system, the respiratory process, and many other aspects of human anatomy. During the First Dynasty (Imhotep's era) hospitals were being invented and medicine was being taught. By 2750 B.C.E., Egyptians were performing surgery. Women, as well as men, were being trained as physicians.

Astoundingly, recent archeological evidence has revealed that the ancient Indians were practicing medicine even earlier, at least as early as 3300 B.C.E., and probably earlier. Artifacts discovered in 2001 C.E. revealed that active dentistry was being performed as early as 9,000 years ago.

The Chinese were also practicing refined medicine as early as the reign of the Yellow Emperor (2696 to 2598 B.C.E.).

Pennyroyal   This herb, similar to mint, has been long used as part of folk medicine for female-related issues. However, this often dangerous substance works from both ends of the spectrum. Pennyroyal made into tea can increase and promote the menstrual flow, but the more potent oil can cause spontaneous abortions. As recently as 1994, countless women died from the practice by overdose.

Sage   This stout evergreen shrub grows throughout Europe and Mediterranean regions. The herb is used widely in cookng for marinades, soups, and sauces, and to flavor cheeses and sausage. In tea form, sage can soothe the stomach, and has aromatic and astringent properties. It can also be used to create a tonic that has a generally relaxing effect.

Slippery Elm   This variety of elm tree grows throughout the northeastern and southern areas of North America. The bark of the tree in powder form can me made into a tea, which soothes coughs and sore throat. The bark is also rich in nutrients, and can be prepared to treat inflammation of the stomach lining or irritable bowels.

Stinking Helbore   The names refers to the stink that comes when the leaves are crushed, even just by hand. While purportedly used in folk medicine, it's unclear just what such a noxious plant could treat. The leaves are used routinely in magical conjuring. The plant is frequently mentioned in Christian and Greek mythology.

St. John's Wort   These yellow flowering plants grow wild throughout Europe and North America. The plant is named for St. John's Day on June 24, when it is traditionally harvested. In homeopathic medicine, St. John's Wort is used as an antidepressant or mood stabilizer, a benefit recently supported by clinical trials.

Valerian   This flowering plant has a very strong, yet sweet, smell. In folk medicine, it was used to sedate, and even to treat epilepsy, though the efficacy of this is uncertain. If valerian is taken in large doses, it becomes addictive, and will cause symptoms of withdrawal if usage is stopped. In the domestic cat, valerian has an effect that is similar to catnip.

Witch Hazel   These shrubs grow in North America, Japan, and China. The bark and leaves of witch hazel are distilled for their astringent properties—and are used for liniments and lotions. The word "witch" comes from the Middle English *wice,* meaning pliable—also the source of the words "wicker" and "weak."

⊰ SPIRITUAL QUALITIES OF ⊱ CRYSTALS AND STONES

The belief that stones—parts of the very earth—held energy, life, and magick is older than civilization. Many modern folks, however, scoff at New Agers for their beliefs in the healing and spiritual properties of these minerals as if this is something new and off the wall. Someone is out of touch (and it probably *isn't* the New Ager).

Looking from a big picture perspective at world cultures, one finds that different cultures often used the same types of minerals to alleviate the same conditions or to protect against the same kinds of evil. Suggestive, isn't it?

These days, crystals that heal, ground, uplift, strengthen, unify and bring luck, love, and lust are an intrinsic part of the New Age movement, which in case you haven't been reading closely, is just as intrinsic a part of the Old Age movement from which it spawned. This further suggests a cyclic nature to spirtuality itself—making it round like the shape of our earth, which for all intents and purposes is just another really big rock in the quarry of the universe.

Following is a guide to the qualities of stones and minerals:

Agate   The family of agate minerals are beautifully colored stones named for the Sicilian river Achates, were they were first discovered. In pratical magick, these stones have many purposes. They can aid the workings of spells dealing with love, envy, strength, bravery, protection, or bitterness of the heart. The powers of the agate can ensure a bountiful garden, and the stone itself can be worn as an amulet, which compels the wearer to speak the truth on all matters. Various types of this mineral also have medical applications and have been used to combat the symptoms of Alzheimer's, improve circulation, soothe coughs, ease the pain of childbirth, reduce fevers, quell earaches, and even help eating disorders, such as bulimia and anorexia.

Amethyst This beautiful violet or purple form of quartz has been cherished for centuries for its beauty and power. It is the stone of royalty and has been coveted by kings as well as those with a lust to rule. It is the February birthstone, though it is associated with both Aquarius and Sagittarius in the zodiac. Among its magickal properties are the sharpening of psychic abilities, protection, peace, healing, courage, love, and happiness. In some cultures, the stone is regarded as an aphrodisiac and has even been used to deter acne. Perhaps one of the few stones with no negative aspects, the amethyst can attract love, soothe the mind and body, and inspire happiness. It is associated with the fifth element, also called Akasha, which translates to "ether" in ancient Hindi.

Amazonite A semi-precious gemstone, amazonite has long been associated with good luck. The stone makes a fine talisman and all around good luck charm for the gambler or those who play games of chance. It also possesses soothing and healing properties, and can bring balance, both physical and spiritual, to those who would wear it. It's also used to bolster metabolism.

Amber A fossil resin, this mineral is created from the secretions of once-living plants and animals. Its beauty has made it a popular decorative gemstone for centuries. The mineral is also referred to as *kahroba*, a Persian term meaning "that which attracts straw." This strange description most likely comes from the evidence of static electricity that builds up in the stones when friction is applied. Not surprisingly, Amber is regarded as a stone of great power, and it has been used to inspire strength, healing, protection, power, love, and luck. It can strengthen the spell of any conjurer, and is representative of the balance of inner and outer beauty. It has also been used to treat asthma, diseases of the bladder and bones, convulsions, and earaches.

Aquamarine This stone, "water of the sea," is a variety of the mineral beryl. The birthstone for March, aquamarine can sharpen psychic abilities and is associated with peace, courage, and purifcation. If worn as a charm, the stone can ensure health, quell fear, and calm emotional difficulties. It allows for better communication between the conscious and unconscious mind, so it is coveted for ritual magick. It is often placed beside a basin or tub where a practioner ritually cleanses him- or herself, where its purifying and soothing properties can be maximized. It is also used to treat swollen glands, hair loss, liver disease, and neuralgia, the intense pain associated with shingles.

Apache Tear   A form of obsidian, or glass created by volcanic activity and lava flows. Apache tear is a dark and mysterious mineral that can be used for divination, offer protection, bring good luck, and offer comfort in times of great grief or stress.

Apophyllite   The mineral can foster the connection between the physical and the spiritual, a tantamount element needed in rituals of magick. Apophyllite is also used to promote astral transferrence and travel and can prepare one to commune with the cosmos. It is associated with the chakra of the third eye and the astrological figures of Libra and Gemini.

Aragonite   Created by the shells of mollusks, aragonite is present in vast, oceanic caves. The mineral sets free the third chakra, which inspires confidence, opens communication, and clears the mind, so that it is more receptive to ideas that come from a higher plain of thinking. Aragonite is also used to soothe everyday aches and pains, as well as diseases of the skin, liver, and kidneys.

Aventurine   A form of quartz that is most often a shimmering green, but can also be brown, orange, blue, yellow, or gray. Even the name of this stone, from the Italian "a ventura" or "by chance," suggests that these gems are literally storehouses of good luck and intention. It is a highly coveted talisman for those who seek wealth and fortune, and can ensure success in gambling ventures and games of chance. It is also capable of bringing all the auras into proper alignment, as well as stimulating the chakra of the heart. This soothing mineral can quell a bad temper, lower blood pressure, inspire creativity, aid in making decisions, clear up eczema, improve eyesight, reduce fever, and has been distilled as an all-around health tonic.

Black Obsidian   Because obsidian flaked easily when struck with a harder stone, it could be made into lethal spear heads and other important tools. Therefore it was essential to prehistoric man. With regard to magickal uses, the stone can repel the negative and protect the bearer from hexes, jinxes, and other curses. The mere touch of this sleek and beautiful stone can align the body and mind, inspire self-control, and it can be used for divination. Even today obsidian is used in the creation of ultrasharp scalpels that can mean the difference between life and death in crucial surgical procedures.

Blue Lace Agate   Prized for its azure tones, this agate can soothe the mind and body and promote healing. As a talisman, this gem can bring the wearer peace and happiness, and downplay anger. The stone can instill mental acuity and clear thinking.

Blue Topaz   This stone is used as a talisman for protection and healing, and can even attract love. It is a powerful defense against the negative, whether such negativity comes by spell, emotion, or disease. It has also been used for psychic development, afflictions to taste, infections of the throat, varicose veins, whooping cough, influenza, and colds. Blue topaz also aids in concentration and can inspire creativity.

Bloodstone   A more common term for the quartz chalcedony, for centuries this stone has been highly coveted for magick and rituals. The Babylonians used it to aid in their fight against enemies human and ethereal. The ancient Egyptians used the gem to rend bonds, shatter the seals on doors, and cause great walls to tumble. The stone made a popular talisman for the soldier, and was not only purported to ensure victory, but also quell the bleeding of wounds received in battle. In a nonmilitary vein, the stone was used as a good-luck charm by athletic competitors, as well as for good fortune in legal matters, business and agriculture.

Botswana Agate   This type of agate mineral is associated with physical strength, protection, longevity, endurance, stamina, and libido. The stone is said to stimulate the crown chakra, energize the aura, and balance the yin and yang aspects of the human condition.

Carnelian   A variation of bloodstone, the Egyptians used this gem to quell anger and protect against the evil eye. It is said that if you place this stone at your bedside, you will be free from nightmares. While the stone can inspire eloquence, create joy, and place one in touch with his or her inner child, it is also used medicinally to boost energy, treat infertility and impotence, reduce fever, fight against heart disease, boost immunity, and cure infection and diseases of the kidney.

Citrine   The November birthstone, this amber-colored quartz is another protection gem. Citrine can ensure a good night's sleep free of worry or nightmare, promote optimism, and open the lines of communication. In this latter capacity it is often the favored good-luck charm of speechmakers and those who need to sway the thinking of others. Its medical applications include the treatment of anemia, anxiety and depression, circulatory disorders, digestion and constipation, and headache. Citrine also bolsters confidence, improves mental clarity to make learning easier, and can foster a connection with the divine.

Dalmation Jasper   This quartz gem looks a great deal like its canine namesake, white with black splotches of varying sizes—its name in Greek even means "spotted stone." Dalmation jasper can be used for general protection, and it can foster awareness. During astral projection and travel, this stone can be used for protection; it can also unite the wearer with necessary ethereal energies. To this end, the stone is a useful aid in meditation.

Dolomite   This limestonelike element is also called "Mountain Jade." It can foster strength, quell negative vibrations, and bring the chakras into proper alignment. It is also used medicinally to improve strength and aid in matters of the kidneys and the bladder.

Emerald   These beautiful and verdant gemstones have been prized for centuries, as objects of adoration and as important ingredients in medicine and ritual magick. The stones can inspire intellect and love, and they bring wealth and good fortune. Emeralds protect against mishap during childbirth, assuage storms at sea, aid in prophecy, and guard against demonic possession. They are also used as antidotes to poison, to treat angina, colds and flu, and diseases of the eye. Headaches, heartburn, weak immune system, infections, and even insomnia are helped with emerald.

Fluorite   While also sacrosanct to the dental community, this crystal formed from calcium fluoride can stimulate critical thinking, cure pneumonia, treat viral infections, and stimulate physical energy. It also serves to calm the psyche, and can quell strong emotions that could interfere with ritual magick or the enjoyment of life in general.

Garnets   The January birthstone. Garnet's name comes from the Latin *granatus,* a term suggestive of the pomegranate fruit. The edible seeds look similar to some varieties of the stones. In magick, garnets are associated with energy, healing, and protection. Travelers and magicians alike wear garnets to keep their energy levels high. If you give a gift of a garnet to a friend when you part, it is certain that you will meet again. It is also known as the passion stone.

Goldstone   A brown stone infused with a multitude of golden flecks, the goldstone can offer protection, promote beauty, bring good luck, and it can also be used in healing and to increase energy.

ᐊ STONE MONSTERS ᐅ AT YOUR SERVICE

Gargoyles—those rough beasts carved in stone—have snarled at the world from the corners of buildings since medieval times. However, despite their often fearsome and ferocious appearance, they're protective spirits. The word "gargoyle" comes from the French word *gargouille,* meaning "throat," and true gargoyles are made from stone and have a channel bored through them to catch rainwater. Stone monsters without such waterspouts are more properly known as grostesques.

Stone gargoyles are the most powerful. In the legends of medieval times, it was believed that these monsters would fight to protect the church (or other building on which they were carved). Their appearance was frightening enough to make most demons scamper off; and since they were made from stone, they were impervious to harm from flesh and blood monsters.

Hematite Also called "black diamond," hematite is the mineral form of iron (III) oxide. The stone builds emotional energy, heals tiredness and fatigue, reduces fever, heals bone fractures, headache, diseases of the heart, stems bleeding, alleviates itching, and cures insomnia.

Howlite Named for Henry How, the Nova Scotia geologist who discovered it, howlite is an all-around soothing element that can treat anxiety, quell anger, and promote kindness. It can also serve as an aid to improve memory, inspire creativity, aid in digestion, foster patience, and help in psychic development.

GARGOYLES OF NOTRE DAME
Sam West-Mensch

Ilolite   From the Greek word for "violet," this stone can be used to soothe the mind and body. It can increase mental acuity and alertness, and ilolite can place the bearer in contact with his or her third eye. The gem's electrical properties can replenish the aura and bring love.

Iridescent Obsidian   This smooth and precious black stone is infused with flecks of light. It is valued as a talisman of protection, and iridescent obsidian can defend against negative energies. In this defensive capacity, it can break evil spells and hexes. This glossy gem can also be used for divination.

Jasper   A beautiful, "spotted" quartz mineral, which can be red, yellow, or brown. Jasper has been used for centuries in healing and protection. It can also foster beauty and wealth. While the gem can be used for many maladies including allergies, bronchitis, cancer, constipation, diseases of the bladder, bowels, gall bladder, and heart, diabetes, digestive disorders, epilepsy, and fever, it is perhaps most closely associated with relieving the pangs of child-birth. Jasper can also ease melancholy and soothe a troubled mind. The stone is integral to the practitioner for its grounding and centering abilities, and it can also ward off negative spells and the evil eye.

Jasper (Lizard) Also called Zebra Jasper, this stone is a lush green with white flecks. It is the preferred talisman of travelers for its protective qualities. Like its nonreptilian counterpart, this gem can calm and center the bearer and ease negative emotions. Lizard jasper is useful for healing as well.

Kunzite This pink gem is a powerful love stone that stimulates the heart, crown, solar plexus, and throat chakras. Kunzite can purify and bring peace to the bearer. It can also aid in meditation and astral projection. The stone is also closely associated with Scorpio, Taurus and Leo in the zodiac.

Labradorite This fairly common volcanic stone is quite beautiful, with flashes of pink, blue, yellow, violet, green, and brown. Labradorite can be used to heal, foster energy, understand one's destiny, inspire creativity, aid in diges-tion, and detach one from his or her ego, so that they might establish oneness with God. It can also cleanse and detoxify and bring the energies of the body and mind into proper balance.

Lapis One of the oldest precious gems in recorded history, this beautiful azure stone was coveted by the pharaohs and is frequently found in the ornate burial tombs of ancient Egypt's wealthy and powerful. The ancient Sumerians believed the stone held the souls of the gods within it, and anyone who wielded the stone would be imbued with their powers. The gem can soothe, heal, lift depression, and promote spirituality. The full name of this gem is lapis lazuli, but it is more commonly known by the shortened moniker.

Malachite Another favored talisman of the frequent traveler, this luscious green gem was used extensively in tinctures and dyes through the 1800s. It stores power and energy, and it can aid in rituals and magickal workings.

Malachite can bring peace, prosperity, and love as well. It is purported to cure poisoning, soothe the symptoms of premenstrual syndrome and toothache.

Marble   Though generally not a power stone in itself, marble is nonetheless prized for its ability to endure. Dense, tough, and yet beautiful, marble has been used as funerary markers for centuries.

⊰ GRAVESTONES, ⊱ TOMBSTONES, FOOTSTONES AND HEADSTONES

Nowadays the words "gravestone," "tombstone," and "headstone" are interchangeably used to describe the stone marker at the head of a burial plot; but in former years each had a separate meaning:

- *Tombstone:* Originally this was the flat lid of a stone coffin that was cut so that its weight and density formed an airtight seal.
- *Gravestone:* This was a stone slab laid over the exterior of the grave. It was often carved with the name and likeness of the deceased. Fieldstone was often used to deter animal scavengers.
- *Headstone:* A stone marker (standing or flat) placed at the head of the grave. The size of the stone and the amount of artistic detail used on it became a status symbol. Sandstone was used for quite a while because the soft stone made carving easy, but, after a while, the

(continued)

deterioration of these markers led to the use of marble as the traditional (and enduring) stone of choice.

•*Footstone:* A stone marker placed at the foot of the grave to indicate the boundaries of the burial plot. Footstones were seldom inscribed, and nowadays their use is discouraged (it makes it difficult for the groundskeeper to mow the grass).

Moonstone   These delightful gems look very much like their namesake. They can be either shimmering or translucent, or have a rich, milky quality. It is closely associated with love, and can both attract love, aid in fertility, and strengthen existing relationships. A moonstone placed at one's bedside can ensure a good night's sleep, and it can also aid the dieter in quelling hunger pangs and foster willpower. It is also purported to grant wishes, aid in childbirth, and cleanse and purify. In divination, moonstones can provide emotional balance, bring luck, happiness, and joy, and ease the effects of menopause.

Moss Agate   This crystal is usually white with an interior pattern of gray, black, brown, or red. Closely associated with agriculture, moss agate makes a fine talisman for the farmer or gardener. It can resolve the left and right hemispheres of the brain, and is thusly associated with Gemini in the zodiac. It represents abundance and fortune, can aid in anorexia, move one to forgiveness, heal emotional wounds, open and activate the chakras, and bring wealth and prosperity.

Mother of Pearl (also **nacre, sadaf**)   A unique talisman in that it is created by a living thing, namely oysters and abalone. Outside of the magickal realm, mother of pearl has been used to make buttons, sinks, and basins, and even decorations on saxophones, trumpets, and guitars. Cheaper to produce

GRAVESTONES Fran Kirsch

knockoffs of this mineral are comically known as "mother of toilet seat." Being borne of the ocean, the gem is associated with the sea and is valuable and powerful to the sailor and other seafarers. Mother of pearl is also regarded as a symbol of wealth and power. It can heal fractures, hemorrhoids, intestinal disorders, and aid trouble with knees and other joints.

Moukaite   Also known as "the stones of change," moukaite is a storehouse for the energy of the earth. It aids in healing by stimulating the chakras, and it can be used for protection, grounding the spirit, and bringing good luck. The gem is associated with the zodiac signs of Cancer and Leo. The influence of this stone can inspire one to expand horizons, as well as alleviate fears and concerns pertaining to future events.

Onyx   This sleek, black mineral is prized as a powerful stone of protection. It can also ban negative energy. Onyx stimulates the root chakra and helps the bearer to realize his or her dreams and goals. The stone is closely associated with Saturn and Capricorn in the zodiac. In India, the stone is used to cool the hot tempers that love can bring. Onyx can also be used to treat addiction and alcoholism; banish grief; strengthen bones; treat breathing disorders, such as asthma and bronchitis; and soothe earaches.

Opal   From the Latin *opalus* or "precious stone," the opal is a powerful stone associated with astral projection and the development of psychic abilities. It is said that the opal contains the color and the power of all stones. It can be charged with many kinds of energies and is essential to ritual magick. Opals are also purported to enhance beauty, improve eyesight, reduce fever, and fight infection and kidney disease.

Pyrite   Also called "fool's gold", this stone is very powerful in repelling the negativity of hexes, jinxes, and the evil eye. In ancient Mexico, the stone was used for divination, and it was indispensable to Native American medicine men. Pyrite is also purported to cure influenza, tonsillitis, fever, brain disorders, and bronchitis. It can foster connection with the divine, and manifest goals and desires, so that they can be more easily attained.

Periodot   The August birthstone, these beautiful and verdant gems can be used for healing or simply for good luck. Periodot can repel the evil eye and attract love. It can also be an aid in releasing anger, foster detachment from the ego, and provide balance in interpersonal relationships. In a medical capacity, it can ease the pain of childbirth, detoxify the blood, aid in digestion, and soothe heartburn, improve poor eyesight, and reduce fever.

Quartz Crystal   Anyone who doubts the veracity of the claims made about gems and crystals in this section need only look to their wristwatches and radios to know that minerals are as alive as anything else in the natural world. Quartz can both emit and receive electromagnetic waves, and it is used abundantly in the world of electronics. These unique attributes were also exploited in past centuries when quartz crystals were used in alchemy, divination, and magick. The stone can stimulate the chakras and is easily charged with energy; it can also provide grounding and balance.

Quartz (Rose)   This beautiful and popular pink version of quartz can affect the heart chakra and attract love. It can also restore peace to stormy interpersonal relationships. In this capacity rose quartz can also serve as a potent aphrodisiac. It will soothe common aches, pains, bruises, and burns, release anger, provide balance, and cure anorexia and asthma.

Quartz (Smoky)   Like its quartz cousins, this stone can be charged with all manner of energies. It can be used for luck, healing, divination, and various rituals of magick. Smoky quartz is also purported to aid disorders of the abdomen, kidneys, pancreas, ovaries, and testicles, as well as soothe the effects of premenstrual syndrome. It can help build willpower in the face of addiction, lift depression, overcome fear, clear up infection, and even treat cancer.

Rhodocrosite   These rose red or pink minerals can store energy and foster feelings of peace and love. Rhodocrosite is highly regarded for its calming and grounding effects and is the favorite lodestone of those who work love magick. These minerals can rejuvenate the cells, banish despair, and soothe disorders of the inner ear.

Serpentine   This term actually refers to a group of minerals that can clear and purge the chakras and bring balance. The stone can also foster relationships and provide clear methods of communication. Serpentine even aids the symptoms of diabetes.

Sodalite   This rich, royal blue mineral is valued for its calming effects and aids meditation. Sodalite also builds endurance, banishes fear, doubt, and guilt, aids in hearing difficulties, impotence, and insomnia. It soothes sore throats and diseases of the mouth and helps poor circulation and high blood pressure.

Snowflake Obsidian   This form of obsidian is black with large silver and white flecks that resemble snowflakes. The stone is valued for its grounding elements, and it can be used for divination, fostering changes in bad habits and behavioral patterns, better digestion, and detaching from one's ego. Snowflake obsidian helps provide emotional balance, improves eyesight, and confidence.

Sunstone   These vibrant red stones are valued as much for their beauty as for their magickal properties. They can stimulate the chakras, build physical energy, foster a positive outlook, build self-discipline, strengthen courage, aid in making difficult decisions, and cleanse and purify.

Tiger's Eye   These gorgeous yellow and brown gems look, not surprisingly, like a tiger's eye when polished. As such, it is coveted as a powerful good-luck charm, which can attract wealth. It can also build the bearer's confidence and strengthen his or her convictions. Tiger's eye can promote mental clarity, cure disorders of the mouth, ignite dormant passions, and build willpower. The stone is also valuable in divination, and it can aid in past-life regression.

Topaz   This protective stone is associated with the Egyptian god Ra. It's purported to cure rheumatism and arthritis, aid in digestion, lift depression, help willpower during a diet, provide emotional detachment when needed, improve poor eyesight, alleviate swollen glands, and cure insomnia. Topaz can also be used to attract love.

Tourmaline   In Egyptian legend, these gems traveled to earth by rainbow, which is responsible for their striking and colorful patterns and layers. This gem can attract love, wealth, luck, courage, and success in business matters. It can also aid in astral projection, and is purported to cure anemia, maintain even blood pressure, sooth an earache, and to treat epilepsy and laryngitis.

Turquoise   Long sacred to Native American tribes, these beautiful blue-green minerals are synonymous with tribal jewelry. They're also important to the workings of healing and magick. The name comes from the French for

"Turkish Stone." Although they aren't found in Turkey, they were extensively traded there. Turquoise aids in anorexia, fosters communication and a connection with the divine, builds courage and energy, inspires faith and honesty, eases headaches, and stimulates the intellect.

Unakite This innocuous looking quartz mineral is a powerful grounding element that can disperse blockages and negative energies. It can increase mental acuity and banish forgetfulness. With many health benefits exclusive to women, unakite makes a marvelous talisman for the mother-to-be, as well as for the hopeful.

Yellow Jade Another mineral that has served man throughout history in all capacities. It makes for a sharp and lethal spearhead, intricate statuary, or just a sensible pair of earrings. Slipped into the pocket of the traveler, this charm offers protection from falls and other mishaps on the road. It can boost the immune system, treat infertility, cure disorders of the kidneys, and attract love.

— *Chapter Eight* —
MYTHOLOGY

FOR EVERY CIVILIZATION THERE ARE TWO versions of history: what's provable (wars, the line of kings and queens, heroes and villains, the arts, science) and the other is the larger story of its creation and the structure of the universe (gods, demons, angels, and monsters). This latter, the mythology of each culture, is as important as the verifiable history.

But why does mythology persist? Why, after centuries or even millennia, do we continue to remember, investigate, explore and appreciate the myths and legends of the past? What is there for us in stories of ancient gods and kingdoms in the clouds? Do we secretly yearn to believe that there was once an age of titans? Does it make our lives more livable if we hold to the belief that a vast pantheon of gods and spirits oversaw the mundane minutiae of everyday life?

All of that is almost certainly true, but the value of myth goes even deeper than that, especially when we step back and look at the big picture to realize that what we now call myth was once the religion of our ancestors. It is what they *believed*, as fervently as anyone of faith believes today; and belief was far more widespread. There were few openly avowed atheists or agnostics in, say, Norse culture. Doubting the existence of Odin might not have resulted in a lightning strike, but it might earn a head-tap with a war hammer.

Mythology is the way in which our ancestors made sense of the wonder of life, of its complexity, of its balance. Without a deep knowledge of science, evo-

lution, bacteria, physics—the world was too large, too frightening to accept unless there was some guiding force behind it. This thinking, by the way, has not
exactly evolved out of our consciousness. When the tsunami of 2005 hit Indonesia, many people openly wondered about the wrath of God; or prayed to
God (or gods) to save them; or thanked the heavens that they were spared.
Even the most sober of statesmen and TV anchormen asked people to pray for
those affected by that catastrophe. In a thousand years, or five thousand, will
our descendants look back on that and consider it to be some kind of pagan
worship? Will they think we're less advanced people and wonder how their
own ancestors could have been so misinformed about the nature of the universe?

Or will the future humans look back and understand, more clearly than
we do, that the universe is too vast, too complex, to be able to make any statements as short-sighted or arrogant as "The gods are only myth and everything
in the universe belongs to science—no guiding hands were ever present."

In the ongoing and very heated debate between scientists who believe that
the universe just *happened* and those who believe in deliberate creation, there is
actually a vast middle ground. The extremists on either side are not the majority. Between them is the vast bulk of humanity who believe, to one degree or
another, that the universe is larger than science will ever be capable of measur-
ing. There are more people living today who believe in celestial or supernatural forces than those who don't—by a ratio of many hundreds to one. The
thing is—and it is a marvelously encouraging and fascinating point—no one
can prove that they are completely right, or completely wrong.

Mythology is there to help us understand where we come from. While often not useful as a true history, the myths of our ancestors were often moral-
ity tales, and from these we learned so much about the cause and effect of
human actions. Myths offer ways of ordering experience. Myths provide an understandable vision of the basic structure of reality, as seen in the founding
myths or creation myths. They help us understand our own nature and iden-

tity, especially in relation to our culture and family lines. They teach lessons about how to hold a community together. Myths express a sense of cosmic balance, which is crucial to help us through times of crisis; if we know that there is a fundamental universal balance then the pendulum of fate will swing back the other way. Myths show that there are patterns to human action and this allows us to understand and even predict our future interactions with others.

In this chapter you'll meet some of the key figures in world mythology: gods and goddesses, heroes and monsters.

⊰ GREEK GODS ⊱

Aphrodite   The Goddess of Love from Greek myth is an icon of female beauty. She was born as an adult (there are no references of any kind to a childhood) and is thus a symbol for adult womanhood. Aphrodite is one of the few goddesses of the Greek pantheon to have married, although she frequently cheated on her husband (the immortal blacksmith Hephaestus). She is depicted as vain, short-tempered, easily offended, and dangerously meddlesome (if you read Homer it was Aphrodite who offered Helen of Troy to Paris, thus kicking off the whole Trojan War). In Aphrodite's temples ritual prostitution was not only allowed but also encouraged. However Aphrodite did have a softer side as seen when the loveless sculptor Pygmalion carved a statue inspired by a dream of the goddess; moved by this devotion Aphrodite breathed life into the statue and thus the woman, Galatea was created; the couple lived happily ever after.

Apollo   One of the most important and progressive deities in both the Greek and the Roman pantheons. Apollo was the god of music, the sun, prophecy, archery, poetry, and light. He was the son of Zeus and Leto, and the Oracle of Delphi was devoted to his influence. He was also the leader of the Muses, which gave the gift of artistic expression to humankind.

Ares   Ares was the god of war and the son of Zeus and Hera. He was a patron deity to the warlike residents of Sparta, where there was a huge statue of him bound up in chains. This represented his spirit never leaving the city. In legend, Ares had a massive chariot drawn by four horses that were the offspring of the steeds of Apollo (who drew the sun across the sky each day).

Artemis   Twin sister of Apollo, Artemis was goddess of the hunt, the open wilderness, fertility, and childbirth. In this last respect, she was known as a protector of women, and, like her Roman counterpart Diana, her name and concepts are still associated with feminist issues. In art, she is generally portrayed as carrying a bow and accompanied alternately by a fox, stag, leopard, or lion.

Athena   The goddess of wisdom, art, war, weaving, and industry. Athena possessed a goatskin breastplate called the aegis given to her by her father Zeus. The word has since become synonymous with protection. She is often depicted wearing a helmet and carrying a shield, which bears the severed head of the gorgon Medusa. She is most revered in her role as protector of the city that is her namesake, Athens. In legend, a woman named Arachne boasted that she was better at weaving, and Athena appeared to her disguised as an old woman and asked her to recant. After Athena revealed herself, the defiant Arachne challenged her to a contest. Though the contest was never decided, Arachne later hanged herself out of guilt. At the last moment, Athena spared her life and transformed her into the first spider—which since that time has had to weave webs to catch prey.

Demeter   The goddess of agriculture and farming. Demeter preserved youth and oversaw the cycle of life, death, and the changing of the seasons. For those who feel that breakfast is the most important meal of the day, Demeter was responsible for bringing the gift of cereal—as is reflected by the Latin name of her Roman counterpart, Ceres. She taught humankind to farm and work the earth. Her daughter Persephone was doomed to spend part of each year as a consort to Hades, the god of the underworld. While Demeter pines away for her daughter for half the year, she neglects her duties, and the world is thrust into the harshness of winter.

Dionysus The god of wine and agriculture, his cult of worship is similar to that of the Roman Bacchus. Ceremonies to honor him, therefore, were essentially state-sanctioned drunken orgies. In Greek mythology, it was Dionysus who gave the golden touch to King Midas, after keeping him entertained for ten days and nights—a gift that ended up being slightly dubious.

Enyo A lesser-known goddess of war to the Greeks, she is described as either mother or sister to Ares. In art, she is often depicted covered in blood and carrying various weapons of battle.

Hades The name of both the god of the underworld and the region over which he had dominion. Despite the name's use as a mild way to express the idea of hell in speech—Hades was the resting-place for all souls—from heroes and great men to despots and criminals. Fortunately, Hades was segregated—the Elysian Fields were the home of pure souls, and the wicked were sent to Tartarus.

Helios The god who is responsible for ferrying the sun across the skies in a great chariot each day. In art, he is often depicted with a halo or crest around his head, bearing the earth in his arms. Perhaps the most widely known legend associated with him was when his son Phaeton stole his chariot for a little joyride—the results were scorching. Teenagers.

Hephaestus The god of blacksmiths, sculptors and artisans, brother to Ares and son of Hera. Hephaestus was not the son of Zeus, however, as he and his brother Ares were the products of a Grecian take on immaculate conception: Hera got pregnant with no male assistance and bore the two gods. Unlike his warlike brother, Hephaestus was good-natured and patient, useful traits for the god married to the fiery and unfaithful Aphrodite (who was dallying with Ares)! Among the magical metal-crafts created by Hephaestus were the winged helmet and sandals worn by Hermes, the impenetrable aegis breastplate given to Athenam, the armor worn by Achilles, and Helios' celestial chariot.

Hera The wife and sister of Zeus, and queen of the gods of the Greek pantheon. She is also the patron goddess of marriage and was especially adored by the ancient city-states of Argos and Mycenae. Her presence abounds in legend, perhaps most notably for suggesting the twelve labors of Hercules. To modern pagans, Hera still represents a powerful and maternal spirit of woman that instills domesticity, love, and monogamy.

Hermes A god who wore many hats other than the famous and familiar one with the wings. He was the patron of shepherds, speechmakers, writers and poets, athletics, weights and measures, and commerce. Due to his cunning nature, he was also the patron god of thieves.

Hestia The goddess of home, hearth, and family, she always received the first offering each time a sacrifice was made in a household or temple. Greeks often kept their fires perpetually burning in tribute to her. This concept of an eternally burning flame has carried over into Judeo-Christianity and other systems of belief, and is commonly seen on the graves of fallen heroes, heads of state, and at the sites of significant events. The first American eternal flame was lit on John F. Kennedy's grave, and one burns at Ground Zero in New York.

Persephone The queen of the underworld and the beloved daughter of the goddess Demeter. According to legend, she was abducted by Hades and brought to the underworld. With her absence, Demeter became more and more distraught and plunged the world into chilling winter. While his prisoner, Hades tricks Persephone into eating four seeds of a pomegranate. Though Zeus intervenes and finally releases Persephone, she must spend four months each year in the underworld, at which time the seasons of fall and winter occur, while Demeter grieves for her daughter.

Pan   The Greek god who protects shepherds and their flocks. Over time, however, the concept of Pan has evolved into something far less wholesome. As a satyr, with horns and the lower half of a goat, his visage has become synonymous with the devil. His name means "all," as does the prefix (i.e., pantheism [accepting of all faiths]; panorama [a representation of an entire landscape]). He was also known for inspiring fear in people when enclosed in small spaces—called "panic." To modern pagans, he represents the libido and the potency of male sexuality.

Poseidon   The familiar trident-bearing god of the seas, storms, horses and earthquakes. Sailors offered up great sacrifices to him to ensure the safety of their sea voyages. In art he is often depicted with the tail of a great fish, riding a chariot pulled alternately by hippopotamus, horses, or dolphins. He dwells beneath the ocean in a great palace of coral.

Selene   The goddess of the moon. Selene is often depicted in art as being beautiful, riding a chariot pulled by oxen or riding a horse or bull (with a crescent moon above her head). Today, the study of the geography of the moon is called *selenology.*

Zeus   The king of the Greek gods and the ruler of Olympus, Zeus embodied dignity (at times), power (all the time), humor (occasionally), and lust (frequently). There are tales of Zeus playing pranks on both humans and other gods. There are hundreds of tales of Zeus' wisdom and just as many that told of his wrath—which he enforced with thunderbolts. There are stories of him seducing women of all kinds, frequently while wearing disguises, such as when he came to Leda in the form of a great swan. His children—legitimate and not—include Athena, Apollo and Artemis, Hermes, Persephone, Dionysus, Perseus, Heracles, Helen, Minos, the Muses (by Mnemosyne).

⊰ ROMAN GODS ⊱

Apollo   A counterpart god to the Greek Apollo

Bacchus   A counterpart to the Greek Dionysus.

Bellona   A counterpart goddess to the Greek Enyo.

Ceres   A counterpart to the Greek Demeter.

Cupid   This familiar symbol of St. Valentine's Day is the Roman god of love. Like Venus, his cult of worship was dedicated to erotic love. He is portrayed as a naked young boy with wings carrying a bow and a quiver of arrows—which inspire love and adoration when fired at the unwary. While a Greco/Roman concept, the idea was co-opted by Judeo-Christianity in its description of the cherubim order of angels.

Diana   A companion goddess to the Greek Artemis.

Faunus   A companion god to the Greek Pan.

Flora   The goddess of flowers, whose name has become synonymous with the study of plant life.

Janus   The god of gates, doorways, and of endings and beginnings. Janus was often depicted as having two faces, one clean-shaven and the other with a beard. As such, he was worshipped as the overseer of transitions. Janus was invoked at the beginning of the harvest season, as well as at births and marriages. The month of January is named for him.

Juno   A counterpart goddess to the Greek Hera.

Jupiter   A counterpart god to the Greek Zeus.

Lares   A collection of Roman gods that protected the household, family, the crossroads, the sea, the state, land, and travelers. They are comparable to "house sprites," such as faeries or brownies, which are part of European folk-lore.

Mars   This well-known god of war actually had more humble beginnings as a fertility god who protected crops and livestock. Later he became associated with the martial. The month of March is named for him, as is the fourth planet from the sun in our solar system.

Mercury   A counterpart god to the Greek Hermes.

Minerva   The goddess of crafts and wisdom, she was the daughter of Jupiter and Metis. She was also the patron goddess of poets, military men, medicine, and business—and gave humankind the gift of music. She is comparable to Athena.

Neptune   A counterpart god to the Greek Poseidon.

Ops   A goddess of fertility and agriculture, her name is Latin for "plenty." Her husband was Saturn. In art, she is often depicted seated and holding a scepter or a stalk of corn.

Pales   A god of shepherds and their flocks, Pales is depicted as either male or female, and, in some cases, as a pair of deities rather than one. A festival in his honor was held each year on April 21, where cattle and livestock were driven through the flames of a bonfire to purify them.

Pluto   A counterpart god to the Greek Hades.

Pomona   The Roman goddess of fruit trees. She has since become associated with the idea of plenty. In advertisements and packaging in the 1800s, her image was often seen carrying a horn of plenty.

Proserpine   A counterpart goddess to the Greek Persephone.

Saturn   A god of agriculture and a protector of seeds and crops. His wife was the fertility goddess Ops. An annual feast in his honor, Saturnalia, was held on December 23. Evidence would suggest that this pagan celebration was what eventually became the observance of Christmas. Saturday and the planet Saturn are named for him.

Venus   A counterpart goddess to the Greek Aphrodite.

Vertumnus   The god associated with the changing seasons. Vertumnus could transform himself at will, and used his power to gain the upper hand on those that would oppose him.

Vesta   A counterpart goddess to the Greek Hestia.

Vulcan   A counterpart god to the Greek Hephestus.

⊰ NORSE GODS ⊱

Aesir   The better-known clan of gods in the Norse pantheon. Their counterparts are called the Vanir.

Andhrimnir   The cook or chef of the Aesir clan of gods. Each day he slays the boar, Saehrimnir, and cooks it in a magical cauldron called Eldhrimnir. Each night the boar is reborn to be slaughtered again the next day. Andhrimnir is also responsible for creating the mead consumed by the gods.

Angrboda   One of a race of female giants in Norse mythology. Angrboda is mother to the god Fenrir and the wife of the trickster god Loki.

Balder   The god of innocence, purity, and beauty, he is Odin's second son. According to legend, Loki tricked Balder's blind brother Hoor into killing him with a dart made of mistletoe—the one substance that could hurt him (despite the assurance of all of nature that no harm would come to him).

Borr   Sometimes written as Burr, Bor, or Buri, he is the father of Odin. However, this seems to be the first and only mention of him in Norse lore.

Bragi   He is the god of poetry and son of Odin. The Norse word for poetry is "bragir," although he is also referred to as "the long bearded god."

Dagr   The god of the day. He is son of Delling, god of twilight, and Nott, goddess of the night. Each day, Dagr rides across the heavens on his horse Skinfaxi, whose mane gleams with a light that illuminates the earth.

Delling   The god of the dawn and father to Dagr.

Eir   The goddess of healing and medicine, she also has the power to raise the dead. According to legend, Eir would only share the secrets of healing with women. Hence, at the time, only women were allowed to practice the healing arts.

Elli   The goddess and personification of old age. She is perhaps best known for defeating the god Thor in a wrestling match.

Forseti   The god of truth, justice, and peace. Forseti is the son of Balder and Nanna. He also served as arbiter of disputes in heaven and on earth.

Freyja   Though generally regarded as the goddess of fertility, Freyja also has close associations with love, sex, war, beauty, and sexual attraction. She is equally as important to the soldier as the lover, and could often be found riding a boar named Hildisvin into battle. Freyja is also responsible for choosing some of the battle slain that will go to Valhalla.

Freyr   One of the vanir, and brother of Freyja. He is the god of fertility and protector of crops and fields. In art, Freyr is often depicted standing beside a giant boar and carrying a magic sword, which can fight on its own. He also possesses a ship that creates its own wind and can be carried in a small satchel until needed.

Frigg The wife of Odin and goddess of marriage, motherhood, and domesticity. Frigg is regarded as the queen of the Norse gods. Her children are Balder and Hoor, and the goddess Eir serves as her consort and personal doctor.

Gefjun (also Gefjon, Gefyon, Gefn) She is regarded as the goddess of the plow, virginity, and good fortune. In Norse mythology, women who die as virgins are sent to her abode to become her servants in the afterlife.

Hel She is the queen of Hel, the underworld of Norse mythology. Hel is the daughter of Loki and Angrboda. Her name, of course, is the root of "hell." Also, as in Judeo-Christian beliefs, Odin banished the children of Loki to the underworld, where the souls of those who did not die in battle were sent to eternally languish.

Heimdall The gatekeeper and guard of Asgard, the realm of the gods. Heimdall blows his great horn, Gjallahorn, should any danger approach. As a guardian, it is said that his senses are so acute that he can hear the growing of the grass and never requires any sleep.

Hoor The blind god of winter who was tricked by Loki into slaying his brother Balder with a dart made of mistletoe. After the killing occurred, Odin and a giant named Rindr gave birth to Vali, who grew into adulthood in one day and slew Hoor.

Iounn The goddess of spring. She was also the keeper of the apples the Aesir used to maintain their eternal youth.

Jord The goddess of the earth, daughter of Odin and the mother of Thor.

Kvasir The wisest god of the Aesir. Kvasir was created from the saliva of all the other Norse gods. He was killed by two dwarves, Fjalar and Galar, who mixed his blood with honey to create a mead that could provide inspiration to poets and writers. It was used by the Valkyries to raise the dead upon their arrival in Valhalla.

Lofn   The goddess of forbidden love, and the protector of illicit affairs of the heart.

Loki   This god of mischief, and foster brother to Odin, had quite a reputation for trouble. In his meddlesome capacity, he could transform into many types of animals to escape detection. He is perhaps most known for tricking the blind god Hoor into slaying his brother Balder with a dart of mistletoe, the one substance that could harm him. Loki had three children: Jormungandr, a giant sea serpent; Fenrir, a giant wolf who would devour Odin himself at Ragnarok (Norse apocalypse); and Hel, the ruler of the underworld.

Mani   The god who bears the moon each night across the skies. He was ever pursued by the wolf, Hati, but each time the wolf came close, Mani caused a lunar eclipse. Children would often bang pots together to scare the wolf away from the moon.

Meili   One of the Aesir and brother of the god Thor.

Mimir   A god of great knowledge and wisdom who was often regarded as one of the wisest of the Aesir, Odin once drank from his magical well in order to gain his wisdom. As punishment, Odin had to pluck out one of his eyes. Mimir's severed head later was used as an oracle at Asgard—either severed by Odin himself or sent to him during the battle of the Aesir and the Vanir.

Nanna   Goddess and wife of Balder, who in legend cast herself upon her husband's funeral pyre in grief over his murder.

Nerthus (also **Herta)**   She is a goddess of fertility.

Njord   A Norse god of the Vanir whose domain was the verdant and fertile lands that line the coast. He was also the patron of sailors.

Nott   The Norse goddess who is the personification of the night.

Odin   The chief god of Norse mythology and the leader of the Aesir. He is also viewed as a god of war and warriors. His spirit is embodied by neopagans and those who identify with Viking or Scandinavian heritage.

Sif   A Norse goddess of fertility and wife to Thor. Her hair was purported to be made of gold. The trickster god Loki cut it off as joke, and Thor demanded that Loki replace her locks with ones crafted by dwarves from gold. Norse legends and sagas often refer to gold as the "hair of Sif."

Sleipnir   Not a god, but worthy of mention. He is the eight-legged horse that Odin rode. The name translates as "smooth" and is the source of the English word "slippery."

Sol   The Norse goddess, and personification, of the sun.

Syn   A Norse goddess of the legal persuasion, her spirit was invoked by defendants while on trial.

Thor   Another of the most recognizable of the Norse gods. This red-haired and bearded god of thunder drives a chariot drawn by two goats: Tanngrisnir and Tanngnjostr. His famed hammer is called Mjollnir and when thrown at an enemy, it returns like a boomerang. In order to wield this mighty weapon, Thor possesses gauntlets and a belt that increase his strength.

Tyr   One of the older Norse gods associated with the glories of battle in single combat.

Ull   Son of the goddess Sif, he is associated with skiing and skill with a bow.

Vali   Son of Odin, Vali was created solely for the purpose of slaying the god Hoor whom Loki had tricked into killing his brother Balder. Vali grew to adulthood in just one day.

Valkyries   Servants of Odin, these beautiful creatures rode either on winged horses or wolves, searching the battle slain for the bravest warriors to take back to Valhalla. These souls then became part of the Einherjar, an elite army of the dead. Eternity was spent alternately getting drunk out of their skulls on mead or joyously cutting one another to pieces on the battlefield, only to be reborn the next dawn.

Vanir   The lesser-known clan of gods in the Norse pantheon; their counterparts are called the Aesir.

⊰ CELTIC GODS ⊱

Aine   The Celtic goddess of love, plenty, livestock, and the day.

Airmid   The Celtic goddess of healing and medicine, she is often associated with the practice of herbalism.

Angus Og   A Celtic god of love, youth, and beauty.

Arawn   The Welsh god of the underworld, which was called Annwn. He is known to ride through the skies of autumn, winter, and spring with a collection of red-eared white dogs.

Artio   The Celtic goddess of the bear and the creatures of the open wilderness.

Balor   The king of a race of giants called Fomorians. Balor possessed an evil eye that could kill anyone who gazed upon it.

Branwen   The Celtic goddess of love and beauty.

Bridgid   A Celtic "triple goddess" who combined the three aspects of a woman's life: maiden, mother, and crone. This idea is also embraced in Wicca and Neopagan beliefs as the "earth mother."

Cyhiraeth   While originally the Celtic goddess of streams, she later became regarded as a demonic figure.

CREATURES OF AIR AND WATER
Alan F. Beck

Dagda   The Celtic father god and leader of the Tuatha Dé Danann order of gods who inhabited ancient Ireland. He is depicted as being armed with an enchanted club that could kill nine men at once and also raise the dead. The Dagda also possessed a magical cauldron that had no bottom and could potentially feed an entire army.

Danu   The maternal Celtic goddess and queen of the Tuatha Dé Danann.

Dewi   An ancient Welsh god in the form of a giant red serpent. The name is Welsh for "David" and could be an early rendition of St. David. This symbol still exists today as the emblem for the nation of Wales.

Diancecht   The Celtic god of healing and medicine.

Druantia   Associated with the Druids, this goddess is protector of the trees. She is also closely linked with tree spirits called Dryads, and might have been their queen.

Giobhniu   The Celtic god of smiths and weaponry.

Gwyn Ap Nudd   The Welsh god who escorted the souls of the dead to the underworld accompanied by a group of ghostly canines.

Manannan Mac Lir   The Irish god of the seas and the weather.

Morrigan   Once a Celtic goddess, Morrigan was later regarded as the terrifying "phantom queen." She is associated with female demonic figures such as Lilith, the Furies, or as a deity of war, similar to the Valkyries of Norse mythology.

Nemian   A Celtic goddess of war that may very well be the warlike aspect of the Morrigan.

⊰ JAPANESE GODS ⊱

Aizen-Myoo   The Japanese god of lust and love, he is generally portrayed as a red-skinned man with a dour expression on his face.

Amaterasu   The Japanese goddess of the sun, she was born from the left eye of the god Izanagi.

Amatsu Mikaboshi   The "August Star of Heaven," he is the god of evil and of the stars in the sky. Amatsu Mikaboshi represents more the antithesis of the positive, rather than a demonic figure per se—providing a balancing element, rather than embodying evil.

Azumi-No-Isora   The Japanese god of the seashore.

Benzaiten   The Japanese conception of the Hindu goddess Sarasvati. Benzaiten is the overseer of that which flows—whether it be water, eloquent speech, wisdom, poetry, or the arts. She is one of the seven gods of fortune.

Bishamonten   Another of the seven gods of fortune, he is the patron of soldiers and warriors.

Butsu   A term that is interchangeable with Buddha (one who has been enlightened). Buddhists acknowledge twenty-eight Buddhas throughout history.

Chimata-No-Kami   The Japanese god of the highways, crossroads, and footpaths traveled by man. He was originally regarded as a phallic god, and phallic symbols were often left at crossroads as an offering to him.

Chup-Kamui   Originally regarded as the goddess of the moon. It was said that she could not bear to look down and witness the adultery that took place on the earth each night. She begged her brother the sun to switch places with her, which he kindly did.

Daikoku   Another of the seven gods of fortune. Daikoku is the god of wealth and the harvest. He is also protector of the household. In art, holding a golden mallet, he is often depicted as a smiling figure, seated on bales of rice and surrounded by mice. Rather than infestation, the appearance of the mice symbolizes an abundance of food.

Ebisu   Another of the seven gods of fortune, Ebisu is the patron of fishermen, good fortune, and of the working man. In art, he is depicted as carrying a fishing rod and a fresh catch. Ebisu is also associated with jellyfish, and some seafood restaurants in Japan still use images of Ebisu in their décor.

Emma-O   The Japanese god who judges all of the souls of the dead and decides their eventual fate. The punished may be sent to naraka, more similar to purgatory than hell, or given the chance to return to earth in another form.

Fudo   The Japanese god of wisdom and fire. His aid is often invoked during times of great danger and strife.

Fujin   The Japanese god of the wind and one of the eldest gods in the pantheon. In art, Fujin is depicted as a monstrous, demonic figure clad in a leopard skin who carries an immense sack filled with the winds of the world.

Fukurokuju   Another of the seven gods of fortune, he is the god of happiness, wealth, and longevity. In art, he is depicted as bald, but with a long beard. Fukurokuju carries a staff to which a large book is tied. A crane and a turtle—which persist as Japanese symbols of a long life—generally accompany him.

Hachiman   The Japanese god of war and the country's patron and protector.

Hotei   The familiar "laughing Buddha" that can be found on statuary and art in Chinese and Japanese restaurants and architecture. He represents joy and contentment. He is also one of the seven gods of fortune.

Inari   The Japanese god of fertility and rice. He is the patron of foxes. Temples devoted to Inari's worship are surrounded by red torii (the familiar Japanese arch).

Izanagi   A Japanese elder god responsible for the creation of many other deities and islands. He created the sun goddess, Amaterasu, from his left eye; the moon god, Tsukiyomi, from his right; and Susanoo, the god of storms, from his nose.

Izanami   The Japanese goddess of creation who was once the wife of Izanagi—or more exactly, the female aspect of the god.

Juroujin   One of the seven gods of fortune and the Japanese god of longevity.

Kojin   The Japanese goddess of trees and the hearth. It is believed that she dwells in enoki trees. It is customary not to discard old dolls in Japan, but to offer them up to the goddess by placing them at the base of an enoki tree.

FAITH HEALER RITA ISABEL SANCHO

ARMAITA Angel of Light MICHAEL BATESON

GANESHA LEO PLAW

CRISIS APPARITION JASON BEAM

OWL SHAMAN LEO PLAW

EARTH MOTHER GODDESS HERVÉ SCOTT FLAMENT

CERBERUS ADAM GARLAND

ANAHITA Angel of Fertility JASON BEAM

Ryujin   The Japanese "dragon god" of the sea. Ryujin lives under the sea in a massive palace constructed of coral where he controls the tides. He can also transform into a human at will.

Raiden   The Japanese god of thunder and lightning. His name is probably more familiar to videogame fanatics as the fighter who can wield lightning bolts in *Mortal Combat.* Oddly enough, he is also purported to feast upon the navels and bellies of children.

Shinda   The god of fertility worshipped by the Ainu of northern Japan.

Suijin   The Japanese god of the waters, this term can also be used to describe any number of water spirits and magical beings related to rivers or streams.

Tenjin   The Japanese god of scholarship, language, and writing. To this day Tenjin is invoked by Japanese students to help them pass their often grueling exams.

Uke Mochi   The Japanese goddess of food.

Yama-No-Kami   The Japanese god of the mountains.

⊰ HINDU GODS ⊱

Agni   The Hindu god of fire. Agni also served as a messenger. He is associated with fire, lightning, and the sun. In art, he is depicted with two faces, three legs, and seven arms riding alternately upon a ram or in a chariot ferried by a team of goats.

Aditya   A group of seven Hindu deities associated with the sun.

Brahma   A deity of the Trimurti, a sort of Hindu Trinity. Brahma is considered a god of creation, crafting the ten *Prajapatis,* the creation gods who served as the basis of the human race.

Devi   The Hindu goddess that encompassed the female aspects of god. She is the mother of all living things.

Durga   A Hindu goddess depicted in art as a beautiful woman with many arms riding atop a lion and making various mystical gestures with her hands. She was created to be a warrior to battle the demon Mahishasura.

Ganesha (Also **Ganesa, Ganesh, Ganapati)**   Perhaps one of the most well-known gods in the Hindu pantheon. Ganesha is the lord of good fortune, wisdom, and intellect—and is the remover of obstacles. He is generally depicted with an ample belly, yellow, or crimson skin, the head of an elephant and with four arms. Ganesha represents the male and female aspects of humanity in perfect balance.

Indra   The Hindu god of war and weather, and the lord of Svarga, a Hindu heaven where souls dwell before they reincarnate.

Kali   As goddesses go, Kali doesn't make for a pretty picture. In art, she is depicted as a terrifying woman with black skin, wild, tangled hair, wearing a necklace made of human skulls and entrails. However, she is only the wild and unkempt aspect of the goddess Devi, consort of Shiva.

Krishna   In Sanskrit, his name means "black" or "dark one." This description most likely springs from his dark complexion of blue or black, which appears in artwork and various depictions of him. He is regarded as a supreme god.

Lakshmi   The lovely Hindu goddess of beauty, good fortune, and fertility, she is often depicted with four arms seated on a lotus.

Mariamman   The Hindu goddess of fertility and healing. Mariamman is mainly worshipped in the south of India. Her favor is said to cure poxes and diseases of the skin.

GANESHA Leo Plaw

Parvati   This Hindu goddess is the patron of married women, and they often enlist her aid to prolong the lives of their husbands.

Prajapati   The Hindu god of animals.

Prithvi   The Hindu mother goddess of the earth.

Rudra   The Hindu god of storms, winds, nature, death, and the hunt. In art, he is depicted as bearing arrows that can inflict disease on man or beast.

Saraswati   The last of the three main Hindu goddesses, she is the consort of Brahma. Saraswati is the goddess of music, arts, speech, and rivers.

Shiva   The third aspect of the Hindu trinity or trimurti. He is seen as "the destroyer" while the other aspects of the trinity are viewed as aspects of creation and preservation. Shiva is the supreme god in the Shaivism Hindu sect.

Vishnu   In the Hindu trinity, or trimurti, Vishnu represents the second aspect of god and acts as a counterpart to Brahma and Shiva. Those who follow him practice a belief called Vaishmavism. While Vishnu has been depicted in art, he is generally regarded as having no physical form.

⊰ SLAVIC GODS ⊱

Belobog   The Slavic "white god" of light and the day. He is the counterpart to Crnobog, who rules the darkness and night.

Berstuk   An evil Slavic god who dwells in the forest.

Crnobog (also **Czernobog or Zernebog)**   The Slavic "dark god" of the darkness and night. He is the counterpart to Belobog, who rules the light and the day.

Dazbog   The Slavic god of the sun.

Dziewona   A Slavic goddess who is the equivalent of the Roman Diana, portrayed as a virginal goddess adept at hunting.

Flins   The Slavic god of death.

Hors   The Slavic god associated with the sun in winter.

Jarilo   The Slavic god of vegetation, fertility, and the springtime. Jarilo is also associated with war, however, and the reaping that comes with the harvest.

Juthrbog   The Slavic god of the moon.

Lada/Lado   A Slavic goddess of mirth, harmony, youth, love, and beauty. Lada is also the name of a popular Russian car manufacturer.

Marowit   The Slavic god of nightmares.

Marzanna   The Slavic goddess of the harvest often associated with witchcraft. In Poland and Slovakia, a folk tradition still exists where straw dolls, in her image, are burnt to banish the winter and welcome the springtime.

Matka Gabia   The Polish goddess and protector of domesticity, home, and hearth.

Matka Ziemia   The Slavic version of the "Mother Earth" concept. Matka Ziemba encompassed the creation aspect and, after the advent of Christianity, was associated with Mary as a maternal figure.

Perun   A major god and the highest member of the Slavic pantheon. He is associated with thunder and lightning, mountains, trees, and weapons made of stone and metal.

Podaga   The Slavic god of weather, fishing, hunting, and agriculture.

Porewit   The five-headed Slavic god of law, order, and judgement. Porewit is patron to the town of Korzenica in Poland.

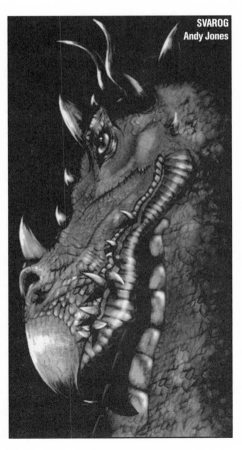

SVAROG
Andy Jones

Siebog   The Slavic god of love and marriage.

Stribog   The Slavic god of the sky and winds.

Svarog   The Slavic god who personifies fire. He is often portrayed as a winged, fire-breathing dragon.

Svetovid   The Slavic deity of war and divination. Svetovid is portrayed as having four heads, one of each looking to the north, south, east, and west. This may also reflect the four seasons of the year.

Veles A Slavic god of the waters, the earth, and the underworld. He is associated with magic, livestock, dragons, music, riches, and deceit. Veles's opponent is the thunder god Perun.

Zirnitra A Slavic god of sorcery who took the form of an immense black dragon.

⊰ AZTEC GODS ⊱

Acolmiztli The Aztec god of the underworld.

Amimitl The Aztec god of lakes, and a patron to fishermen.

Atl (also **Atlaua)** The Aztec god of water and patron of both archers and fishermen.

Atlacamani The Aztec goddess of storms and hurricanes.

Atlacoya The Aztec goddess associated with drought.

Atlatonin The Aztec mother goddess.

Ayauhteotl The Aztec goddess associated with fog at twilight, and of vanity and fame.

Camaxtli The Aztec god of the hunt, war, fate, and fire. He is one of the four gods who created the earth. Sacrifices to him were often of the human variety.

Chalchiuhtecolotl The Aztec god associated with owls and the night.

Chalchiuhtlicue The Aztec patron goddess of lakes and streams. She was also the patron of childbirth and was invoked during "baptisms." Her name means "she of the jade skirt," and as such, she is often depicted wearing a green skirt with newborn babies springing from it.

Chalchiuhtotolin The Aztec god of disease and of mystery.

Chalmecatl   The Aztec god of the dead.

Chantico   The Aztec goddess of domesticity, home, and hearth.

Chicomecoatl   The Aztec goddess of food and produce; each September a young girl was decapitated and offered to her as a sacrifice.

Chicomexochtli   The Aztec patron god of artists of all persuasions.

Chiconahui   An Aztec goddess associated with fertility and protector of homes.

Chiconahuiehecatl   An Aztec god associated with the creation of the world.

Cihuacoatl   An Aztec goddess associated with fertility and motherhood. Cihuacoatl is the patroness of midwives.

Centeotl   The Aztec god of corn.

Citlalicue   The Aztec goddess who created the stars and placed them in the heavens.

Coatlicue   The Aztec "lady of the serpent" who gave birth to much of creation and to the gods of the sun and war.

Cochimetl   The Aztec god of merchants and business.

Coyolxauhqui   The Aztec goddess of the moon.

Ehecatl   The Aztec god whose breath was the wind. It was said that he gave mankind the ability to love, so that he could win the affections of a human woman.

Huehuecoyotl   An Aztec trickster god associated with the coyote. He is often portrayed as one, but with human hands and feet.

Huitzilopchtli   The Aztec god of the sun and patron of the city of Tenochtitlan, the former capital of the Aztec empire.

Huixtocihuatl   The Aztec goddess of fertility, salt, and salt water.

Illamatecuhtli   The Aztec goddess who created the stars.

Itzli   The Aztec god of stone, he is most often associated with the sharpened stone knives used for human sacrifices.

Itzpaplotl   The goddess who ruled over Tomoanchan, the Aztec conception of heaven or paradise. She is most often depicted in skeletal form.

Ixtlilton   The Aztec god of healing and medicine.

Macuil-Tochtli   The Aztec god of alcoholic beverages.

Malinalxochi   The Aztec goddess associated with snakes, scorpions, and other creepy-crawly creatures of the Mexican desert.

Metzlti   The Aztec god of the night, the moon, and farming.

Mextli   The Aztec god of storms and war, and root of the word "Mexico."

Mictecacihuatl   The Aztec goddess of death and the underworld, called Mictlan. Rituals devoted to Mictecacihuatl's honor are the precursor to Mexico's Day of the Dead held each year. Her husband was Mictlantecuhtli.

Mictlantecuhtli   The Aztec god of death and the underworld whose wife was Mictecacihuatl. He is often depicted wearing a necklace made of human eyes.

Mixcoatl   The Aztec god of war and hunting. Mixcoatl was associated with the Milky Way.

Nanauatzin   The Aztec god of the sun who sacrificed himself to the flames, so that the sun would light the world during the day.

Opochtli   The Aztec god of hunting and fishing.

Patecatl   The Aztec god of healing. He was also responsible for discovering peyote—a flowering cactus that causes psychoactive effects when ingested.

Quetzalcoatl   The Aztec "feathered serpent" that still survives today as a symbol of Mexico, most notably on the country's flag.

Temazcalteci   The Aztec goddess of steams baths and medicine.

Teoyaomqui   The Aztec god of dead warriors and patron to those who have died in battle.

Tepeyollotl   The Aztec god of jaguars, echoes, and earthquakes. Tepeyollotl is often depicted in jaguar form, lunging his way toward the sun.

Tepoztecatl   The Aztec god of drunkenness and fertility.

Teteoinnan   The Aztec mother god, she represents the power of nature.

Tezcatlipoca   The Aztec god of the north, the night, sorcery, temptation, beauty, and war. He possessed a magic mirror in which he watched the actions of humankind. Tezcatlipoca carried four arrows to punish sinners.

Tlahuizcalpantecuhtli   The Aztec god of the morning star.

Toci   The Aztec goddess of the earth and protector of injured animals and people.

Tonacatecuhtli   The Aztec god who divided the world into areas of land and sea. He is also associated with fertility.

Tonantzin   An Aztec moon goddess.

Xipe Totec   His name means "the flayed one." In order to give food to humankind, Xipe Totec sacrificed himself by his own flaying. Unfortunately for those who were sacrificed to him, they were also ritually flayed—and to add insult to injury, their skins were worn by the attending priests.

Xochipilli   The Aztec god of corn, beauty, love, and flowers.

Xochiquetzal   An Aztec goddess of love and the moon, and a patron of prostitutes, artisans, and expectant mothers.

Xochiquetzal   An Aztec god associated with fire and the stars.

Xolotl   The Aztec god of lightning who escorted the souls of the newly deceased to the Mictlan, the underworld.

Xochipilli   The Aztec god of the harvest, singing, love, competition, beauty, and dance. Xochipilli means "flower prince."

Yacatecuhtli   The Aztec god of commerce and merchants.

⊰ᅦ MONSTERS AND OTHER ⊱ CREATURES OF GREEK AND ROMAN MYTHOLOGY

Achlys   A female evil spirit who embodied misery and the idea of eternal darkness. She is also regarded as the patron goddess of poisons.

Automatoi   Rather than traditional monsters, these creatures were animated metal statues of men, monsters, or animals created by Hephaestus. Once activated, these creatures served as powerful, ever watchful guardians or were offered as royal wedding gifts. Perhaps the most famous of these creatures is the Kaukasian Eagle, a bird statue of bronze that tormented the bound Prometheus each day by devouring his liver. Each night the organ would regenerate, and the torture would begin anew at dawn.

Amphisbaina   A fabled serpent with two heads, one in the normal location and another at the end of its tail. It was said that this creature often chased down its prey by placing one head in the opposite mouth and rolling quickly across the terrain like a hoop—a scary prospect indeed.

Baliskos   A fearsome serpent that could kill its victims with a single glance.

Campe   A female dragonlike creature with a head similar to a gorgon and the tail of a scorpion. Her main purpose was to guard the twin giants Hecatonchires and Tartarus after the god Cronus imprisoned them. She was killed by Zeus, and the giants were rescued.

Centaur   A half-human, half-horse creature from Greek myth who possesses a turbulent, wild, and often hostile nature. Centaurs were the offspring of Ixion, king of Thessaly and Nephele, goddess of the clouds.

Cerberus   The famous three-headed dog, with a lion's claws and the tail of a serpent that guards the gates of Hades, the Greek Underworld.

Cercopes   In Greek myth, the Cercopes were a pair of forest creatures that caused havoc and mischief wherever they traveled. They have often been described in simian terms, because according to legend, Zeus changed the duo into monkeys for their transgressions—which gives us the term for the genus of Old World monkeys, *Cercopithecus*.

Ceryneian Hind   One of the five giant deer sacred to the goddess Artemis. They were said to have antlers of gold and hooves made of bronze. These creatures were so swift they could outrun an arrow in flight. One of the twelve labors of Heracles was to capture one of the beasts, and he pursued it on foot for more than a year.

Chimera   A horrible, Frankensteinesque monster that was a patchwork of many different creatures. It has been depicted as having the body of a goat, the tail of a serpent, and a lion's head. This terrible creature could also breathe fire,

CREATURES OF GREEK MYTH Lee Moyer

and catching a glimpse of one was a sure sign of disaster. In modern usage, the term "chimera" describes anything that possesses attributes from multiple sources.

Cyclops   This term refers to any of the race of one-eyed giants from Greek mythology. Perhaps the most famous legend about them is Homer's *Odyssey*, where the hero and his men find themselves trapped in the cave of a cyclops and use trickery to escape.

Drakones Aithiopes A breed of giant, man-eating serpents native to Ethiopia.

Empousa A female demon notorious for harassing and attacking wayward travelers. It either scares them to death or kills and devours them outright. Though these hideous demons had flaming hair and the legs of a donkey, they could transform into beautiful women to entice their prey.

Eurynomos A demon of the Greek underworld, Eurynomos was an eater of carrion and the patron of flies, maggots, vultures, and other creatures that feast upon the dead.

Gorgon Like many other monsters of mythology, our perceptions of the gorgon are so entrenched in film and literature that the term Medusa is often used instead. The gorgons have been described as serpentine woman-creatures with hair of writhing serpents. Others say they are winged creatures with boar-like tusks who can cast fire from their fingertips. With a single glance they can all turn men to stone. In the legend of Perseus— there were three gorgons: Stheno, Euryale, and Medusa. Being the

MEDUSA
Lilian Broca

only mortal sister of the three, Medusa was slain and her head placed on the shield of the goddess Athena.

Griffin Another classic creature of Greek mythology, the griffin is generally depicted as a winged creature with the body of a lion, sometimes with the tail of a serpent.

Harpy Originally, these creatures were beautiful, winged women. Their depiction in the legend of Jason and the Argonauts however led them to be regarded as ugly, flying monsters who spread filth and disease. In modern usage, the term "harpy" is used to describe a shrewish, heartless woman.

Hydra Perhaps one of the most famous monsters in Greek mythology, this nine-headed serpent was a fearsome creature indeed. Said to be brethren to the Chimera and Cerberus, the creature was slain by Heracles as one of his twelve labors. Like many other Greek monsters, after its death, it was consigned to the heavens as the Hydra constellation, one of the largest star systems.

Karkinos A giant crab that came to the aid of the Hydra in its battle with Heracles. Though the unfortunate crustacean was crushed under the heel of the great warrior, its place in history was sealed when the goddess Hera consigned it to the skies as the constellation of Cancer.

Keres These female spirits of death are described as dark and monstrous, with sharpened teeth and claws. Prowling fields of battle in search of the dead and the dying, they then feast upon them. During the Greek festival of Anthesteria, the Keres' evil influence may be banished.

Katoblepone A monstrous, bull-like animal that can kill its victims with a single glance, or with its noxious breath.

Leukrokotai A large, hoofed animal that can mimic the sound of humans to lure their prey to them (most likely inspired by the African hyena).

Minotaur   While this term is used to describe any creature that is a man-bull hybrid, like Medusa it is the proper name of one monster in particular. The god Poseidon sent a gift of a white bull to the king of Minos to be sacrificed in his honor. The king was so taken with this animal that he sacrificed another in its place. Enraged, Poseidon caused the king's wife Pasiphae to fall in love with the bull. With the help of Daedalus, a device was constructed which helped consummate the relationship. The Minotaur was the result of this unholy union.

Pegasi   Although "pegasus" is often used as a blanket term to denote any sort of flying horse—the pegasi were a tribe of flying horses. In legends, it was Pegasus who grabbed all the glory.

Satyrs   These were the half-man, half-goat companions of Pan and Dionysus, and they are the original party animals. Lovers of wine, women, and song, the satyrs exemplify celebration in all its glorious excesses.

Sirens   The sirens were beautiful sea-nymphs with the heads of women and the bodies of birds who lived on the island of Sirenum, which was surrounded by dangerous reefs and jagged rocks. It was said that when a ship approached, the sirens would sing, and their beautiful voices would draw the helpless sailors and their ships to certain doom.

Tauroi Aithiopes   Also called the "bronze bulls," these creatures possessed tough hides that were said to be impervious to all human weaponry. The monsters were twice the size of their domestic counterparts, and the flesh of man was a familiar and coveted source of food for them.

⊰ MONSTERS AND OTHER ⊱ CREATURES OF NORSE MYTHOLOGY

Arvak and Alsvid   Twin horses who pulled the chariot bearing the sun across the skies each day.

Blodughofi   A horse whose name means "bloody hoof," purported to be able to gallop across flame.

Audhumia   The "primeval cow" of Norse mythology responsible for creating the world.

Fenris   A giant wolf that was the offspring of a female giant and the trickster god Loki. Though the gods have imprisoned him in chains, he is destined to grow too large for his bonds, break free, and devour Odin at the end of time.

Geri and Freki   A pair of wolves that served as devoted companions to Odin.

Gullinkambi   In Valhalla, this golden rooster crowed each morning to rouse the sleeping einherjar—the souls of those who died bravely in battle—so that they could begin a new day of feasting, drinking, and fighting with one another. His crowing will also herald the coming of Ragnarok, the end of time.

Garm   A mammoth hound similar to Cerberus, who guards the gates of Hel, the Norse underworld.

Hati   The wolf that chases the moon across the sky each night.

Heidrun   A goat in Valhalla that produces mead for the einherjar, so that they might be eternally drunk.

Hildisvini   The massive boar often ridden by the goddess Freya.

Hugin and Munin   A pair of ravens that served as consorts to Odin. Each day they would fly throughout the world and report news and events to the high god. In art, the pair are often depicted on Odin's shoulders, whispering secrets into his ear.

Jormungandr (also **Midgard** or **World Serpent)**   This massive sea monster was the offspring of Loki and the female giant Angrbooa. It was said that the creature could wrap itself around the earth and grasp its own tail—hence the term World Serpent. His archenemy was the god Thor, and the two were fated to battle at the end of all days.

JORMUNGANDR Leo Plaw

Lindworm   A serpentlike dragon common in Norse and other Germanic mythology. Lindworm stalked the countryside devouring cattle or, sometimes, defiling cemeteries to feast upon the dead.

Nidhogg   A dragon that gnaws at the roots of Yggdrasill, the world tree.

Ratatosk   A mystic squirrel whose name means "drilling tooth." Ratatosk would ferry messages and gossip throughout Yggdrasil, the world tree.

Saehrimnir   A magic boar that was slain and consumed each night by the gods, only to be born anew the next day.

Sköll   A great wolf that chases the sun across the sky each day. Brother to Hati, who chases the moon.

Tanngrisnir and **Tanngnjostr**   A pair of magic goats that pulled the chariot of the god Thor.

Valkyries   Servants to Odin, these beautiful creatures rode either on winged horses or wolves, searching the battle slain for the bravest warriors to take back to Valhalla. These souls became part of the einherjar, an elite army of the dead. They then got to spend eternity alternately drunk out of their skulls on mead or joyously cutting one another to pieces on the battlefield, only to be re-born the next dawn.

Ymir   A frost giant slain by Thor. The world—as well as the world tree, Yggdrasil, was purported to have spawned from his remains.

⊰ MONSTERS AND OTHER ⊱ CREATURES OF CELTIC, WELSH, AND IRISH MYTHOLOGY

Ankou　In Celtic mythology, the Ankou is a shadowy figure in a wide-brimmed hat who collects the souls of the dead in a cart and transports them to the afterlife.

Bananach　Female spirits purported to haunt fields of battle.

Baobhan Sith　Also known as the "white women of the Scottish Highlands," these female creatures are similar to vampires or succubi. They appear in the form of beautiful women to seduce men, killing them, and drinking their blood. Despite their beauty, they are said to have feet like those of a deer, which they cover with their verdant gowns.

Bean Nighe　Also known as "the little washer at the ford," this hideous crone is purported to have a single tooth, pendulous breasts, and one nostril. She is a banshee-like creature who washes the blood from the clothing of those who are about to die. In some legends, the Bean Nighe are the spirits of women who died during childbirth.

Boggart　A mischievous sprite or house spirit similar to brownies or hobgoblins. A horseshoe hung on the wall can dispel them. However, these creatures are not always malevolent and can be helpful in the home if appeased with offerings. The modern usage of the term *bogart,* meaning a refusal to share, is actually a corruption of *boggart.*

Cat Sidhe　A ghost of the Scottish Highlands that appeared in the form of a large black cat with a white spot on its breast.

Ceffyl-Dwr　A magical horse that flies, but does not have wings. Also called a "water horse," this creature is found near bodies of water.

Cu Sith   A mammoth spectral hound that haunts the Scottish Highlands.

Dobhar-Chu   A creature that is a hybrid of a dog and an otter—its name means "water hound." This monster has a taste for human flesh and will leap from stream, river, or sea to drag hapless prey beneath to consume.

Leanan Sidhe   These beautiful female spirits are similar to muses, and can offer inspiration to artisans (though sometimes the artist is driven insane in the bargain).

Nuckelavee   In Scottish folklore, the nuckelavee was an elf who lived in the sea and caused crop blight and drought. It has been depicted as centaurlike, but with fins on its legs, a large, gaping mouth, and a single eye. Perhaps the most horrifying aspect of this creature is its lack of skin; those who gaze upon it are repulsed by the sight. Like the classic (yet false) vampire myth, the creature is unable to cross running water.

Redcap   A murderous and evil sprite found in British folklore. These creatures haunt the ruins of castles and villages waiting for hapless travelers to become their prey. After the kill, the creatures stain their hats with the blood of their victims, hence their name. If the blood dries, the creatures die—so they must constantly kill to stay alive. While outrunning these swift creatures is impossible, they may be thwarted by quoting a passage from the Bible.

Sidhe   Not a monster per se, sidhe are mounds of earth regarded as the homes of spirits and other magical beings. They are purported to be the remains of a once great underground kingdom where the creatures who lived in them (also called sidhe) existed long ago.

Sluagh   These vengeful spirits of the dead travel in packs and wreak havoc wherever they roam. Sometimes they enter the house of the dying and attempt to steal the person's soul. In such houses, the westernmost doors were generally kept locked to keep this from occurring.

Y Draig Goch   The "red dragon" of Welsh legend that still exists as a symbol on the current flag of Wales.

◄ MONSTERS AND OTHER ► CREATURES OF JAPANESE MYTHOLOGY

Akaname   Also called the "grime licker," this Japanese spirit has been described as childlike, but with bright red skin. This creature has the dubious habit of licking dirty bathrooms clean. In some legends, any such room becomes tainted by the creature's poisonous saliva, yet others say it is benign.

Amanojaku   A lesser demon of Japanese mythology, it delights in causing havoc and mischief. They are comparable to imps and other tricky creatures of legend.

Amikiri   This bizarre creature is described as a cross between a snake, lobster, and a bird. Rather then being truly malevolent, it is more likely to cut holes in fishing or mosquito netting than harm a person outright.

Baku   These creatures of Japanese and Chinese cultures are similar to the Greek chimera. They have been depicted alternately as having the body of a lion or horse, the head of an elephant, the tail of a cow, and the feet of a tiger. Despite this fearsome combination, baku are benign—they devour bad dreams and can bring good luck. In modern times, plush toys representing the creature can be found in the bedrooms of Asian children.

Chochinobake   The spirits of paper lanterns that have existed for one hundred years or more. According to Japanese mythology, inanimate objects that reach a century become *tsukumogami* (living objects able to think and move of their own accord).

Gaki   The spirits of the jealous and greedy, damned to wander the earth forever in a state of hunger for some object. As part of this punishment, the coveted object might be carrion, excrement, or even human blood. In modern usage, *gaki* can be used to describe a spoiled child.

Hanyo   A term describing the offspring of demons and men.

Harionago   A hideous female ghoul who attacks her victims with her long hair. While its hair seems silken and smells of roses, it is actually tipped with sharp barbs. Harionago may appear to hapless travelers and laugh at them—should they dare laugh back, her tresses will come to life and impale her prey.

Hibagon   This mythical creature is similar to the yeti or Bigfoot, but is purported to be about half the size of their cryptid cousins. Hibagon stands about five feet, but leaves impressive footprints.

Hisa-Me   A female demon comparable to a succubus.

Hitodama   Similar to St. Elmo's fire or a will o' the wisp, this ghostly vapor is said to rise from graves and cause mischief.

Jiangshi   A familiar monster for fans of 1980s Hong Kong horror movies, these "hopping vampires" are reanimated corpses with lolling tongues and long fingernails. Jiangshi get around by hopping—apparently due to their state of rigor mortis. They feed upon the "chi," or life essence, of hapless travelers.

Inugami   An avenging spirit that comes in the form of a dog.

Isonade   A giant shark of Japanese legend that is said to have three tails, dorsal fins, and a sharpened horn like a narwhal.

Ittan-Momen   A flying monster of Japanese mythology that is purported to kill men by wrapping around their heads and suffocating them.

Jikininki   Similar to ghouls and zombies of other cultures. Jikininki are the evil dead who prowl cemeteries at night to devour and loot the deceased of valuable personal items. Like zombies, their rotting form resembles the corpses upon which they feed.

Kappa   A mythical Japanese water spirit about the size of a child and a cross between a frog and a monkey. The strangest aspects of these creatures are their heads, which are said to be concave and able to hold a measure of water. Should it spill, the Kappa loses much of its power. When confronting one of these monsters, an easy trick is simply to offer a deep bow, which the polite creature will be compelled to return.

Karakasa   Another example of a Tsukumogami, or inanimate object that comes alive after one hundred years. Karakasa are the spirits of umbrellas. Like other creatures of this type, they are often depicted with one eye and an open mouth.

Karura   Purported to feed upon dragons, Karura has the body of a man and the head (or just the beak) of an eagle.

Kekkai   An unsavory blood-monster that is created when traditional child-birthing procedures are not followed. The resulting beast is an amorphous blob of blood and afterbirth that terrorizes the populace.

Namazu   A mammoth catfish that is said to live inside the earth. Its motions are said to cause earthquakes.

Nuppeppo   An animated bit of dead flesh that can move on its own. Nuppeppo is said to haunt cemeteries at night.

Oni   Supernatural creatures of Japanese folklore, the oni have been depicted wearing tiger skins, with horns, sharp claws, and gaping mouths. More than simply monsters, the oni are the personification of the dark nature of man and can cause disease. The red- or green-bodied oni prowl the earth in search of sinners. They deliver them by chariot to Enma Daiou, the god of hell (where they live). He judges them with the aid of two decapitated heads.

Onryou A Japanese ghost of vengeance that most often appears in female form. This creature is the basis of the 1998 Japanese horror film *Ringu*—poorly remade with its equally inept sequel, in the United States as *The Ring* (2002).

Orochi An eight-headed serpent creature of Japanese mythology similar to the hydra.

Shachihoko A rather unusual hybrid, this creature has the head of a tiger, the body of a carp, and controls the weather.

Shisa This lion-dog hybrid is a long-adored symbol in Japanese mythology. Statues of this creature have served as potent guardians for centuries—generally in pairs, one with an open mouth, the other closed. They are a counterpart to the "guardian lions" of Chinese culture (a common part of the décor of Chinese restaurants, temples, and other structures and architecture).

Tsuchigumo A giant spider-monster of Japanese folklore.

Tsuchinoko A giant snake-monster of Japanese folklore.

Tsukumogami According to Japanese folklore, inanimate objects a century old are imbued with life and awareness. Lanterns, toys, shoes, umbrellas, weapons, and jewelry all have this potential—and often are slightly malevolent, or even bitter, at being cast away by their owners.

Ushi-Oni A water demon that has the body of a mammoth spider or crab and the head of a cow.

Yama-Uba A hideous creature resembling an old woman similar to the "old hag" legends of many cultures. She can shapeshift into a beautiful woman to lure victims. Once she gains their trust, her hair springs to life (or turns into a mass of writhing snakes), and Yama-Uba pulls her quarry into a gaping maw atop her head.

Yokai   A general term applied to spirits, ghosts, and demonic figures in Japanese mythology.

⊰ MONSTERS AND OTHER ⊱ CREATURES OF AZTEC MYTHOLOGY

Ahuizotl   Described as half human and half monkey, ahuizotl has a grasping human hand at the end of its prehensile tail. The creature has a taste for human flesh, especially coveting teeth, eyes, and fingernails.

Cipactli   A primeval Aztec creature that is part fish and part caiman or crocodile. It is said that the earth was created from his flesh.

Cihuateteo   The Aztecs believed that the birthing process represented a great battle, so women who died in childbirth were honored in the same way as the finest warriors who died in combat. The cihuateteo are the spirits of these women that haunted the night, caused disease, and tempted men.

Chaneque   These implike creatures were the protectors of the natural world, attacking and stealing the souls of those who trespassed on their territory.

Nahual   The Aztec conception of a "guardian angel" that can also transform into an animal and act as a person's familiar.

Tlaltecuhtli   A primeval sea creature that was torn apart by the serpent god Quetzalcoatl and Tezcatlipoca, the god of night. Half of the flesh was thrown upward to form the skies, and the remainder became the land. She is depicted as a crocodile festooned with human skulls.

⊰ MONSTERS AND OTHER ⊱ CREATURES OF SLAVIC MYTHOLOGY

Baba-Yaga   A wild woman of Slavic legend comparable to the "old hag" of other cultures. She is most likely the inspiration for witches in fairy tales. She has been portrayed in the classic form, even flying through the air on a broom. Baba-Yaga will devour the souls of the wicked and is said to dwell in a secluded cabin, surrounded by a fence made of human bones and skulls.

Bannik   The spiritual patron of the bathhouse or sauna in Slavic mythology.

Bies   A malevolent spirit or demon.

Boginki   Polish for "little goddess," these river nymphs were known to snatch away children and replace them with creatures called Odmiences, a "changeling" with a vile temper, voracious appetite and an inability to move.

Domovoi   A "house spirit" of Slavic mythology. These creatures are described as small, hairy old men. Families will often leave offerings to the creatures in the hope that they will not cause mischief.

Drekavac   While descriptions of this mythical monster vary, what does not are tales of its hideous screams emanating from the forest. The monster is used to frighten children into proper behavior, much like bogeymen are in the West.

Karzelek   These dwarves dwell in underground structures. They'll lead miners and other earthworkers to new strains of ore, or aid them when they become lost in caverns. Those who insult or belittle the karzelek might have dirt thrown at them. Should the disrespect continue, they might be unceremoniously pushed into an open hole or off a steep embankment.

Kikimora   The female counterparts to the domovoi, these house spirits often live behind stoves or in deep cellars. Kikimora may look after livestock and perform chores in a clean household—but shoddy housekeeping is bound to incur her ire. A displeased kikimora might harass children and keep them awake at night. Those who see her with her spinning wheel will soon die.

Leszi   Covered with dark hair, this creature serves as the protector of the woodlands and its animal denizens. Leszi can shapeshift into animal form and is often associated with bears, wolves, and other powerful forest animals.

Likho   A creature that is the hideous embodiment of bad luck and misfortune. It has been depicted as an emaciated old woman with a single eye in the middle of her head.

Polevik   A malevolent spirit of the field. Polevik is alternately described as a man or a woman known for annoyances of all varieties, from hair pulling to the strangulation of lazy drunkards who fall asleep in its fields.

Rusalki   These beautiful water nymphs are delicate with long green hair that must remain wet for them to survive. Unlike their mermaid cousins, they have legs and often gather along riverbanks and other bodies of water. If a man should come upon them, he is likely to be enticed, as the lovely creatures caress and dance around him. Before long, however, the victim is tickled to death and taken beneath the waters.

Sudice   Comparable to the Fates of Greek mythology, these spirits bestow fortune and destiny on humankind.

Topielec   The spirits of those who have died by drowning. Now water sprites, Topielec are notorious for dragging unwary travelers, or even domestic animals, into bodies of water to drown them.

Vampir   The Germanic term for vampire.

Wodjanoj   They have been depicted as old, bearded men covered in seaweed (and are sometimes scaled like fish). Fishermen may give offerings of tobacco or butter to the wodjanoj to ensure a bountiful catch.

— *Chapter Nine* —

NEW AGE

THE FIRST THING TO KNOW about the "New Age" movement is that it isn't new. Nor is it necessarily from the current age. New age is a rather inaccurate label broadly stamped over a remarkably diverse and occasionally interlocking set of beliefs, many of which are hundreds and even thousands of years old. It has also become a catchphrase for any concept or belief that is nonstandard with the mainstream mindset. New age combines elements from a number of world religions, ranging from various Native-American faiths to a variety of Eastern ideas, particularly from Buddhism, Hinduism, Taoism, and Zen. But new age reaches far beyond religion and into all aspects of the spiritual, as well as into a variety of meditative techniques, healing modalities, and programs to help with a number of emotional and psychological issues.

Not everyone involved in a new-age type of belief or practice necessarily accepts or even acknowledges all of the beliefs lumped under that name. New age practices range from those that resonate with the common mindset—such as acupuncture, astrology, massage, and meditation—to more arcane practices including light therapy, rebirthing, past-life regression, channeling, and laughter therapy. Each has its followers and its premier thinkers, each has its own history, and each can be followed as a single path or as part of a much more complex avenue of consciousness.

The following are some of the key terms, people, organizations, and methods related to the vast and overlapping areas of the new age. It is vast and undergoing constant change, so there will necessarily be some omissions, but on the whole this chapter will provide a strong perspective into this fascinating, positive-focused world.

Aborigine   A race of people who lived in Australia for over 10,000 years and who maintain a shamanistic culture. They refer to their vast astral/spiritual world as "The Dream Time."

Activation, Law of   The belief that individual human development is possible only through a process of conscious activity and involvement.

Acumassage   A form of bodywork in which massage techniques are applied directly to acupressure/acupuncture points.

Acupressure   A form of massage developed in Asia where pressure is applied to specific energy points on the body to relieve tension, cure sickness, and promote the correct flow of chi (vital energy) along the proper energy pathways (meridians). Shiatsu is one of the oldest forms of acupressure. Other modalities include reflexology and touch therapy.

Acupuncture   An ancient healing method developed more than 5,000 years ago in China. Ultra-thin needles are inserted into specific energy points on the body in order to promote good health or restore a person from sickness or injury. Acupuncture allows the chi (vital energy) to flow correctly along pathways called meridians. Correct flow equals good health; incorrect flow results in sickness, a process emblematic of the yin and yang concept of universal balance. In the late twentieth century, acupuncture came under intense scrutiny from allopathic (Western) medicine, largely in an attempt to discredit it. However, after exhaustive studies this ancient science has not only been proven effective but is gradually being openly endorsed by mainstream medicine. Acupuncture has even been found to be useful, in some cases, as a form of anesthesia.

Adept   An individual who has become extremely skilled and knowledgeable in mystic arts. Adepts that take on students (or *chelas*) are called masters.

Affirmation   A statement or thought that is focused on the positive and generally intended to manifest some good outcome.

Age of Aquarius   A new age of man which starts (depending on who is doing the calculations) somewhere between January 1, 1981 and May 5, 2012. The Age of Aquarius is (or will be) marked by an increase in spiritual awareness.

Age   An astrological division of time corresponding to the twelve houses of the zodiac. Each age lasts approximately two millennia (opinions do vary a bit on this). Depending on whose calculations are the most accurate, we are either at the end of the Age of Pisces or in the early years of the Age of Aquarius.

Agnostic   A person who does not necessarily believe in the existence of God (as opposed to an atheist, who is sure there is no God). Many agnostics are, however, actively spiritual and are looking for proof of God's existence.

Ahimsa   A Sanskrit word meaning "nonviolence." It refers to the practice of not harming any living creature, whether it is a human or a mosquito.

Akashic Records   According to psychic Edgar Cayce, there is a great hall of universal knowledge existing on the fifth plane of existence that contains all knowledge. It is in the Akashic Record that all information about one's past, present and future lives are to be found. It is also the repository of all mystical and magical knowledge. Though not a physical place, the Akashic records can sometimes be accessed through various kinds of meditations and astral travel.

Alchemy   An ancient attempt to understand physics and chemistry in which the pervading belief was that science and mysticism were inextricably linked. Transmutation, the science of turning one thing into another (such as lead into gold), was one of the major branches of alchemy.

Alexander Technique   A bodywork modality developed by F. Matthias Alexander (1869–1955) in the early twentieth century, and primarily intended to improve health by improving posture (and its components: joints, muscles, and so on).

Alignment   (1) The process of synchronizing one's mental and spiritual vibrations with cosmic energies, such as gods, avatars, planets, and so on; (2) The correct positioning of the chakras of the body in order to promote proper flow of energy; (3) A mental process by which a person becomes attuned to a specific path of knowledge—a step that separates a novice from a disciple.

Allopathy   Modern or Western medicine, as distinguished from traditional homeopathy. The term "allopathy" was coined by Dr. Samuel Hahnemann (1755–1843), a German physician of some note. The name conjoins the words *allos* (opposite) and *pathos* (suffering).

All-Power   A general term used to describe a supreme being.

Altered States of Consciousness   A term used to describe the perceptions of a person in a trance state (whether naturally attained or the result of a drug). It is widely believed that things perceived in a trance state are profoundly important, and may be glimpses into other dimensions, higher planes of existence, or similar visionary realms.

Alternative Medicine   A general term for natural methods of healing.

Amulet   (1) An object made and worn for the express purpose of protection. Amulets can be religious or magickal, and are imbued with powers that repel evil. (2) Some cultures believe that naturally occurring objects such as feathers, stones, and crystals possess powers that allow them to function as amulets. In these beliefs any manmade object of protection is called a talisman.

Ancient Astronauts   A pop-culture nickname for aliens who may have visited earth and interacted with ancient human cultures, such as the Aztecs,

ALTERED STATES OF CONSCIOUSNESS Bill Chancellor

Egyptians, and so on. This term became popular during the late 1960s with the publication of Erich von Däniken's best seller, *Chariots of the Gods?*

Angel   Any of a number of ethereal beings found in many world religions. (See Chapter 3.)

Anhata Nada   The Sanskrit word for the "Universal Sound," a vibration created by the organic activity of the entire physical and spiritual cosmos. This is represented by the chanting of the word "aum" (often spelled "om" or "ohm"), which is formed by the seamless pronunciation of three letters, A, U, and M. "A" represents normal consciousness, "U" represents dream consciousness, and "M" represents the deepest dreamless sleep.

Anima Mundi A Latin term meaning "the soul of the world," which is connected to the belief that the earth itself possesses consciousness.

Anima Carl Jung's term for the personification of the feminine nature of a man's unconscious.

Animal Shaman A practice among some new-age groups loosely based on Native-American shamanistic practices. In it a channel becomes psychically and spiritually aligned with an animal spirit rather than a human (or humanoid nonphysical entity). By channeling the animal spirit the shaman shares frequency with that creature's essential qualities (wisdom and mental focus from owls; nobility and family bonding from wolves; and so on). These insights are then shared with the other people involved in the ritual experience.

Animism A belief that everything in the universe, from a stalk of grass to a comet hurtling through space, is imbued with vital force (life force). As a result it has some degree of soul, and possibly mind.

Ank'h The Egyptian symbol of a looped cross, which represents eternal life.

Anthroposophy A form of spiritual study created by Rudolf Steiner (1861–1925), a German mystic, which means "wisdom of man." The core of this belief is that humans possess the truth within themselves, and enlightenment is achieved through introspective practices.

Apocrypha "Lost" or "deliberately excised" books of the Bible. They include the Books of Esdras, Tobit, Judith, Wisdom, Baruch, Song of the Three Children, Song of Susanna, The Idol Bel and the Dragon, Prayer of Manassas, and the Maccabees. There have been debates going back centuries over whether these writings are legitimate. The argument here is that some are

OWL SHAMAN Leo Plaw

clearly written much later than other books, though the counterargument is that they are later copies of earlier writings. Some versions of the Bible include parts of the Apocrypha while others do not, and few include all of these writings.

Applied Kinesiology   Also called "muscle testing," this is a diagnostic technique in which patients are asked to hold health-related items in their hands (such as herbs, vitamins, and so on) while the healer tests the reciprocal strength in the patient's hands, fingers, arms, etc. The degree of resistance helps the healer determine the potential effectiveness of the remedy and the strength of the dose.

Aquarian Gospel of Jesus the Christ   An apocryphal book written by Levi H. Dowling. It purports to tell the story of Jesus based on knowledge drawn from the Akashic records.

Aromatherapy   The practice of using essential oils (from flowers, herbs, plants, and trees) to rejuvenate both physical and spiritual health.

Ascended Masters   Spiritual teachers who are believed to have reached the highest possible level of awareness and enlightenment. These masters generally act as teachers or guides to humankind. Ascended Masters throughout history include Buddha, Mohammad, Jesus, Babaji, Afra, St. Germain, Ramtha, Mafu, Seth, Lady Nada, El Moyra, Lanto, Djwhal Khul, and others.

Ascetics   The practice of achieving enlightenment through strict mental and physical discipline.

Asomatic   The spiritual state of being without a body.

Association for Research and Enlightenment (A.R.E.)   A spiritual organization founded by psychic Edgar Cayce, which is located in Virginia Beach, Virginia.

◃ PERFECT MOMENTS ▹

Perfect moments are those incidents in a person's life where the physical and spiritual worlds overlap. Seekers often go on a variety of pilgrimages or vision quests in order to find them, and there is never a guarantee that

(continued)

they will occur. I stumbled onto one, when I wasn't look-ing, as often happens in spiritual pursuits.

Case in point, my wife wanted to visit the Edgar Cayce Institute in Virginia Beach, and I really didn't want to go. I was always more of a skeptic than she, and thought that a visit to the Cayce library would be a boring waste of my time. I wanted to go swimming in the ocean with my son. Turns out, the library and facility were tranquil, fascinat-ing, and filled with compelling volumes of spiritual and healing information. We were happily lost there for hours, wandering through the books.

Afterward I asked one of the staff where the best swimming spot was, and she suggested we just go down to the beach right outside. We took her advice and, to my surprise, the ocean was filled with dolphins—something I had always wanted to see. So my son and I spent the next few hours swimming with the dolphins. The sub-tlety of the message was not lost on me and sparked a gradual change in my attitude so that now I am far more receptive to spiritual matters. A skeptic might scoff at the connection between my visit to the institute and the dolphins, but the experience has removed me from that mindset. Now I embrace spiritual pursuits and, as a re-sult, marvelous and magical things happen around me all the time.

So much for assumptions, eh?

Astral Body   The spiritual essence of a person that is contained within the physical form. In certain circumstances, it leaves to travel on its own. Some argue that the astral body is the soul itself. Others believe that it is made up of the consciousness, since it retains the memories, thoughts, and personality of the current incarnation.

Astral Plane   The state of consciousness that exists apart from the physical world. Also known as the spiritual plane.

Astral Projection   Also known as OBE (Out-of-Body Experience), astral projection involves the astral body separating from the physical body, whether by accident (as in the case of some near-death experiences) or through deliberate means (as with very advanced forms of meditation).

Astral Travel   The act of moving from one place to another using the astral body. The physical body remains behind. Astral travel can vary from movement within the material plane, between dimensions, or through various spiritual realms.

Atlantis   An island first mentioned by Plato. Many scholars believe it to have been a fictional invention. Within the spiritual community, however, there is a very strong belief that Atlantis existed and was located in the Mid-Atlantic undersea mountain range. Theories about the nature of the Atlanteans contend that they were a very advanced and enlightened race, but were destroyed by a natural disaster 9,000–12,000 years ago.

Another notion holds that Atlantis was actually a much older civilization that was destroyed over time by four earthquakes: 800,000, 200,000 and 75,000 years ago, and in the year 9564 B.C.E.

At-One-Ment   A term first used in Christian Science to describe the spiritual unity between humans and God, a state achieved completely by Jesus Christ. The larger new-age community uses it to identify any perfect, harmonious spiritual connection of humans (singly or in groups) with source energy.

Aura   The spiritual energy field of the human body, and the essential substance of the astral body. It has been speculated that the aura is created by the electrochemical process of living, since all living things have one (trees, flowers, and so on). Another theory is that the aura is created by molecular movement, and that even something as apparently inert as a rock has an aura because there is always some movement on the molecular level.

Some spiritual sensitives can perceive the aura, which can vary in color according to a person's health, psychological condition, spiritual well-being, mood. In the 1930s Valentina and Semyon Kirlian attempted to photograph auras using a special imaging technique, now known as Kirlian Photography.

Aura Balancing   A healing modality in which a person's spiritual energies are realigned, soothed, harmonized, or cleansed.

Aura Reading   A diagnostic technique in which a spiritual sensitive reads the colors, size, and movement of a patient's aura in order to determine the state of his or her health.

Automatic Writing   Writing accomplished while in a spiritual trance. In such cases the subject is often channeling the thoughts of a spiritual being.

Avatar   In the Hindu religion, an avatar refers to the physical manifestation of a higher being (deva) or the supreme being. In the larger new-age community, avatar is used to describe any spiritual being who has manifested in human form, ranging from Vishnu to Jesus.

Ayurveda   Ayurvedic medicine is an alternative approach to healing that predates the birth of the Buddha (circa 520 B.C.E.), and which is based on practices originating in India. Āyur means "life" and Veda means "knowledge." Combined they suggest the essence of the method, which is based on a deep understanding of the union of the mental, physical, and spiritual aspects of the body and how they work in harmony. Sickness is caused by disharmony and can be corrected by a variety of means, from meditation to surgery.[23] One way of considering the Ayurvedic approach is that it concentrates on pleasuring the body back to balance and health.

Bach Flower Remedies Remedies made from flower essences diluted in water, a process developed by Dr. Edward Bach (1886–1936). Similar in some ways to homeopathy, the flower essences are purported to contain the energetic signatures of the flowers, which are sympathetic to certain aspects of human health. There are thirty-eight original Bach remedies plus Rescue Remedy™, which combines rock rose, impatiens, clematis, star of bethlehem, and cherry plum essences.

Bahá'í Also known as the Bahá'u'lláh, this is a religious sect that originated in Islamic Persia and has evolved into a worldwide religion with five-million-plus followers. Bahá'í advocates sexual equality, a single worldwide religion, and a unification of political and economic powers to create a new world order that will eradicate want, hunger, poverty, and war.

Biomagnetics A healing technique that uses magnets to realign the magnetic field of the body.

Biorhythm Short for biological rhythm, this is the understanding of naturally occurring personal rhythms. These rhythmic cycles control various physiological processes, and a study of them helps one to understand—and later influence—one's own health and well-being.

Blind Spring An intersection of ley lines.

Bodhi Hindu term for absolute spiritual enlightenment.

Bodhisattva A person who has attained sufficient enlightenment to enter Nirvana, but who voluntarily elects to remain on earth in order to teach.

---

23. Ayurvedic surgery, known as Shalya, developed centuries ago out of a need to repair injuries sustained in war.

Boji   A healing stone used for easing pain. The Boji is held near the body, or in some cases placed on the body, so that it interacts with the aura.

Book of Dzyan   The (allegedly) ancient Tibetan text forms the basis for *The Secret Doctrine,* a key work for the Theosophical sect, created by Helena Petrovna Blavatsky (1831–1891) in 1875. For many years religious historians disputed the authenticity of this material, claiming that it is an invention by Madame Blavatsky; however more recent investigation suggests that her writings may actually be linked to authentic ancient texts called the *The Kalachakra Tantra. The Secret Doctrine* was published in 1888 in two volumes, *Cosmogenesis* and *Anthropogenesis.* It was a remarkably eloquent attempt to combine modern-age thinking with older, Eastern wisdom.

Book of the Dead   There have been a number of religious and philosophic works using this title, the most famous and influential being *The Egyptian Book of the Dead,*[24] which is really a collection of ancient funerary texts. In Egypt it was called *The Book of Coming Forth By Day.* The more lurid "Book of the Dead" title was given in 1842 by German Egyptologist Karl Richard Lepsius when he published the translations for European readers.

The majority of the texts were translated from scrolls entombed with the bodies and from carvings on crypts and sarcophagi. These writings included much of the structure of Egyptian religious practice and belief. They were created to ready the departing spirit for the afterworld. Charms, passwords, and spells were included, so the deceased would have a kind of spiritual cheat-sheet for the journey to the underworld. Many of these rituals are specific to a given mummy; others were far more general.

In more modern times there was (and is) a belief that these writings hold the keys to understanding the ways in which the spirit and physical worlds interact.

---

24. Known in Arabic as *Kitab al Mawta.*

Brahmins   Priest caste of India. The Brahmins were the highest.

Buddha   Though there are a number of Buddhas (which is Sanskrit for "Enlightened One"), the most famous and influential is Siddhartha Gautama (586–511 B.C.E.). Born to privilege, but sheltered from the harsh realities of life, Siddhartha eventually discovered the real world beyond the palace walls. Appalled, he went in search of the truth, eventually finding it through years of meditation. Siddhartha's insights and teachings had a profound impact on those around him, and they formed the basis for a second major religion (with Hinduism) in India.

Buddhism   The teachings and practices initiated by Siddhartha Gautama Buddha are intended to lead a person to Nirvana, a supreme level of blissful enlightenment. Buddhism teaches the Four Noble Truths (which acknowledge that physical existence is the source of all suffering), and the Eightfold Path (which is built on the correct approach to behavior, meditation, and understanding). Variations on Buddhism include Zen, Nichiren Shoshu, Theravada, Mahayana, and Tibetan Buddhism.

Buffalo   In the faith of the Lakota, the great buffalo is a celestial being who stands at the western gate of the universe and holds back the floodwaters, which occasionally sweep across the world to destroy humanity.

Burning Man Festival   A New Age/Pagan festival held each year during the week before Labor Day. Held in Black Rock Desert, Nevada, the event's climax is the burning of a gigantic wooden effigy. Tens of thousands of people come from around the world to *participate* (spectators are not allowed in). There is even a ban on cash transactions of any kind. The Burning Man Festival is purely about spirit.

Cabalah   See Kabbalah.

Campbell, Joseph (1904–1988)   One of the most beloved and important American writers and thinkers of the twentieth century, Joseph Campbell produced a significant body of work, including the seminal four-volume *Masks of God*,[25] which gives a deeply insightful understanding of world mythology, from ancient to modern times. By analyzing patterns in mythology he was able to codify the central paradigms upon which myths (and beliefs) are built, from folktales to the largest world religions. Another equally significant work was *The Hero with a Thousand Faces* (1949), which discusses the archetype of the hero on the journey from feckless youth to wise adult awareness. It also identifies the three stages of such rite-of-passage journeys, as found in cultures around the world: departure, separation, and return. Campbell's books have collectively served as a major influence on spirituality, as seen from a one-world view. They have also influenced film, fiction, and music. Campbell echoes in everything from *Star Wars* to Harry Potter. One of his key catchphrases, "Follow your bliss," has been taken more or less as a mission statement by the new age movement.

Castenada, Carlos (1931–1988)   A best-selling author and mystic who wrote some of the most influential New Age books of the twentieth century, beginning with *The Teachings of Don Juan: a Yaqui Way of Knowledge* (Simon & Schuster, 1968),[26] which he wrote while still an anthropology student at UCLA. In his books, Castenada describes his meeting with a Yaqui shaman, Don Juan Matus, who led him through a series of mind-altering experiences using peyote. As he grew into a fuller understanding of the Yaqui culture, Castenada inherited the role of "nagual" from Don Juan.[27] The new-age culture's devotion, recognition and acceptance of Native American shamanism owes a great deal to Castenada's books.

Cayce, Edgar (1877–1945)   A psychic and healer known as the "sleeping prophet" because he would enter sleeplike trance states in order to "read" his

---

25. *The Masks of God: Primitive Mythology, vol. I* (1959); *The Masks of God: Oriental Mythology, vol. II* (1962); *The Masks of God: Occidental Mythology, vol III* (1964); and *The Masks of God: Creative Mythology, vol IV* (1968).
26. Books by Castenada include *Journey to Ixtlan, Tales of Power, Power of Silence, Separate Reality, The Art of Dreaming, Fire from Within*, and others.
27. "Nagual" is a Spanish world derived from the older Aztec *Nahuatl nahuall*, a term that can be further translated as seer, witch, shapeshifter, and animal coessence.

patients. His trance readings resulted in an enormous body of written work on nearly every aspect of health, some of it delving into rather arcane herbalism and others overlapping with standard allopathic medicine. Cayce also read the past lives of his patients and left thousands of accounts of their former incarnations. In his trances Cayce spoke clearly and precisely, and a stenographer would record his words, a decades-long process, which resulted in some 30,000 transcripts. His organization, the Association for Research and Enlightenment is located in Virginia Beach, Virginia.

C.E.   Common Era, a non-Christian equivalent to A.D. that has come into common usage in writing and history over the last few decades. Also translated as "Christian Era."

Celibacy   The practice of abstaining from sexual relations as a way of purifying the body and soul. Though a requirement for many religious orders, celibacy is also occasionally practiced in various aspects of both the spiritual and secular communities. This may be due to health reasons, for energy conservation (as seen with professional athletes who widely believe that sex before a game weakens them), or as a meditative practice designed to reduce any stimuli, which may interfere with the process of refining the mind. Conversely, there are an equal number of spiritual, religious, and secular beliefs embracing sexuality for the same reasons.

Centering   The process of becoming grounded, typically through meditation, trance experience, massage, or the practice of spiritual rituals. To become centered is equivalent to stepping onto the correct pathway for one's life, or to regain balance.

Chakra   Any of the several major energy points of the body that serve both to filter out impurities and enhance specific frequencies. *Chakra* is Sanskrit for "circle" or "wheel."

Chakra Balancing　Any of a number of healing methods used to regulate the proper flow of energy through the chakras.

Channel　A person through whom nonphysical entities speak in order to communicate with the physical world. Channels may be "clear" or "cooperative." Technically "spiritual mediums," channels are different in that they can also channel living persons, animals, and alien beings rather than just spiritual entities.

Channeling　The act of allowing a nonphysical entity to speak through a living person. Channeling is often used to impart wisdom, do healings, or reveal spiritual secrets.

⚔ A CHANNEL SPEAKS ⚓

This is a personal encounter from professional medium and channel Francine Blackwell:

I made a house call to do a tarot reading for a client who was concerned about not feeling her newly deceased father around her. As she spoke those words, I heard a voice whisper, "I never left her." It was her dad.

I told her to ask him for a sign. Suddenly, the phone in the bedroom rang. She began laughing, telling me that she didn't have a phone in the bedroom. There wasn't even a phone jack in the bedroom.

He called about five times, letting the phone ring seven times each. I finally yelled, "She's busy. She'll call you back after the reading." Then the ringing stopped. After I left, she called to say that he called back once more that night.

Also, during the reading I clearly saw two people standing in her living room. I described them. She said it was her cousin and her nephew, both of whom had passed recently."

Chanting   A meditative practice using rhythmically repeated sounds or phrases in order to calm the mind, enter a trance stance, or cultivate the positive flow of energy.

Clear Channel   Also known as a "pure channel," this is a spiritual medium who does not interfere with the transmissions of the nonphysical energy for whom they channel.

Cooperative Channel   A channel who interacts with, interprets, or otherwise works with the nonphysical entity that is speaking through them.

Chi   A Chinese term for the vital or intrinsic energy that permeates and flows through all living things. Chi flows along energy pathways called meridians and is the basis for health and well-being. When chi flow is interrupted or blocked health is affected. Healing arts, such as acupuncture, were developed to maintain and strengthen the flow of chi.

Chiropractic   An alternative healing method based on the belief that health is affected by the alignment of the spine.[28] Misalignments, known as vertebral subluxations, interfere with the nervous system, which in turn affects organs and general health. Manipulation, or adjustments, of the spine, neck, and other joints is used to restore balance and, therefore, health.

Christ Consciousness   A spiritual view, rather than a precisely religious one, that Christ, as an avatar, provides a pathway to cosmic consciousness. This concept is widely discussed in the New Age, even among persons of non-denominational spiritual beliefs.

Christian Science   A religion, formally known as the Church of Christ Scientist, founded in Boston by Mary Baker Eddy. In Christian Science prayer is not used to implore divine intervention, but is instead used to try and become

---

28. As opposed to allopathic, or "Western medicine.."

aware of the spiritual reality of God. This process awakens "mortal thought" to the nature of the spiritual world, which in turn aligns the energies necessary for healing (without use of medicines or surgery). Christian Science, and its practices of spiritual healing, have been a significant influence on the development of many New Age schools of thought.

Christianity   A major world religion based on the teachings of Jesus Christ of Nazareth, a Jewish prophet born in Judea during a time of Roman occupation and oppression. Christianity, in theory, preaches freedom, tolerance, and love for all. The writings of the followers of Jesus were gathered together to form the New Testament.

Church of All Worlds   A neopagan religion formed in 1962 by Oberon Zell-Ravenheart (b.1942). It is based on reawakening the Earth Mother goddess, Gaia, and reuniting her with her children through a worldwide network of tribal communities. The group was inspired, in part, by a religion of the same name featured in Robert A. Heinlein's landmark science-fiction novel, *Stranger in a Strange Land*. Church of All Worlds is a pantheistic religion that worships, among others, the Earth Mother Goddess, Sun Father God, the Green God and Goddess, the Horned God and Lady of the Beasts; and it also acknowledges belief in faeries and other spiritual beings.

Church of Jesus Christ of Latter-Day Saints   Also known as the Mormons, the LDS movement was founded in 1839 by Joseph Smith (1805–1844) and is currently based in Salt Lake City. Smith believed God and Jesus appeared to him and charged him with restoring Christianity to its true roots and purpose. LDS does not ascribe to the belief in the Holy Trinity, and takes a different approach to salvation, which depends on good works as much as by the sacrifice of Jesus.

Church of Scientology   A new faith founded by L. Ron Hubbard (1911–1986), an American science-fiction writer. Scientology uses a process called "auditing," which is designed to break through previous religious and philosophical "conditioning" in order to bring its members to higher states of consciousness. The process of auditing often takes several years and is extremely expensive, sometimes running to hundreds of thousands of dollars.

Church Universal and Triumphant   A religious organization founded in 1958 by Mark (1918–1973) and Elizabeth Clare Prophet (b.1939), whose followers believe them to be ascended masters. The movement was developed as an offshoot of the Summit Lighthouse. This teaches that everyone possesses the potential for ascendency to his or her higher self and can be freed of the need for reincarnation. The Church Universal and Triumphant includes many elements from world religions and approaches spiritualism from a tolerant point of view. Chanting and mantras are frequently used for personal growth and to influence positive planetary changes. Despite its generally positive messaging, the church made a couple of forays into militant survivalism. Believing that a global conflict was coming, some church members began stockpiling weapons and building defensive structures on their compound.

Circumambulation   A spiritual purifying practice in which a person walks around a sacred place (or, in some cases, around a person) prior to performing a ritual.

Clearing   A spiritual (or perhaps psychic) ability to remove conscious and/or unconscious obstacles and distractions. Clearing is also a healing method that uses crystals, incense, sage, or other natural objects to restore harmony of spirit and body.

Cognitive Dissonance   A concept initiated by psychologist Leon Festinger (1919–1989) in 1956 after he observed a strange increase in proselytization from members of a UFO cult (even after their leader's doomsday prophecies proved completely unfounded). The prophecy in question had been an alien warning for humankind channeled by a suburban housewife.

Amazingly the group embraced a viewpoint that the aliens spared earth because the cult members' faith was so strong. Festinger, rightly so, saw this as a unique and powerful form of rationalization.

Colonic Irrigation Therapy   A healing method in which purified water is used to cleanse the colon of toxins in order to promote health. This purification process is believed to affect all of the humors and influences and/or restore proper psychological behavior.

Color Therapy   A healing method in which colors are applied to the body in various ways (ranging from scarves to crystals to beams of light) in the belief that the frequencies of each are aligned with different organs, moods, spiritual states, and healing processes.

Contact   A connection of a spiritual nature, either with another person, place, animal, spirits, or nonphysical entity.

Contact High   A euphoric feeling obtained by contact with another person's psychic or spiritual energy.

A Course in Miracles   A form of spiritual psychotherapy put into book form by Helen Schucman (1909–1981) and William Thetford (1923–1988). Its assertion is that the essence of the book was dictated to them through channeling. Known commonly as "the course," it came to public attention in the early to mid 1970s. Since then more than 1.5 million copies have been sold, and it has been translated into more than a dozen languages. The primary theme is that forgiveness is intended to be universal and is directed outward to all, as well as inward. *A Course in Miracles* consists of the text, the workbook for students, and a manual for teachers.

Craniosacral Therapy (also cranial osteopathy, osteopathy in the cranial field, cranial therapy)   This is an alternative healing method pioneered by Dr. John E. Upledger (1932–), who expanded on the theories and research of William Sutherland (1873–1954), osteopath who used an assessment of respiratory mechanisms (including the membranes and cerebrospinal fluid of the central nervous system) to begin a manipulation of a patient's skull and body and bring them back into balance. Upledger set about proving Sutherland's theories of cranial bone movement and his discoveries led to the development of CranioSacral Therapy during Upledger's tenure as Professor of Biomechanics at Michigan State University. The Upledger Institute was founded in 1985 in Palm Beach Gardens, Florida.

Creative Visualization (also **guided imagery)**   A visualization technique where one person (called a facilitator) guides another through a meditative exercise in which specific images are suggested for healing, growth, strength, and other life-affecting goals.

Crystal   A naturally occurring mineral believed to have the ability to store and focus energy, amplify energetic vibrations, and enhance diagnostic and precognitive ESP.

Crystal Healing   A healing method that uses the energetic powers of certain kinds of crystals. These powers help realign the mind, body, and spirit.

Cult   A religious or spiritual group, which has generally split off from a parent organization in order to pursue unique and often extreme practices.

Dalai Lama   The spiritual leader of Tibetan Buddhism. The Dalai Lama is a being of great spiritual purity who embodies all the incarnations of all Buddhas. The current Dalai Lama was born as Tenzin Gyatso in eastern Tibet in 1935. In 1959 he fled his homeland because of Chinese occupation. The Fourteenth Dalai Lama is a great peace advocate who has brought an articulate and profound message to the world community, resulting in a Nobel Peace Prize in 1989.

Darshan   The Hindu concept of attaining enlightenment through being in the presence of one's correct guru. The term is Sanskrit for "seeing."

Dead Sea Scrolls   A group of over eight hundred Jewish texts written between the third century B.C.E. and the first century C.E. The scrolls were discovered between 1947 and 1956 in a network of caves located near the northwestern shore of the Dead Sea. Of these, 157 scrolls relate to events of Judaism and early Christianity.[29] The exact origin of the writings is uncertain, although some scholars and historians believe they were found at a trading outpost or Roman garrison; others claim that it was a hiding place for an early religious group called the Essenes.

Deprogramming   The process, either persuasive or coercive, of forcing a person to abandon their adherence to a cult or religious sect. The deprogramming process is seldom pleasant, and often involves isolation, intensive counseling, and other strategies to bring the person "to their senses." This is usually arranged by family members who believe that one of their own is engaged in dangerous behavior. The benefits of deprogramming are debatable since it depends on whether the family's assessment of the danger of membership is accurate (and not merely different from their own views and beliefs). There have been great successes, where people have been rescued from inarguably dangerous situations, and tragic failures, where the process was nothing more than an attempt to gain control (often for financial reasons).

Detoxing   Any of several methods of eliminating toxins from the body through fasting, enemas, juice diets, or sweats.

Deva   A female Hindu spiritual being of great power and enlightenment.

Dharma   The ongoing process of refining one's perceptions, consciousness, and spirituality.

---

29. The other scrolls include apocryphal writings in Aramaic and Hebrew.

SECRET CULTS Ken Meyer, Jr.

Dimension   A loosely flung-about word that can variously refer to aspects of a single plane of existence (such as height, width, and depth), a process of dimensional motion (time), or entirely separate realities. New-age belief usually includes multiple realities and a multiverse, which involves infinite variations of this universe existing in other dimensions. Various spiritual, psychic, and religious beliefs involve travel between realities. The science of quantum physics is actively exploring the very real possibility of dimensions beyond the four currently known to exist.

Discarnate   The state of being without a physical body. In new-age thought, the spirit endures beyond physical death and may, at times, interact with the physical world.

Divination   Any of the many methods of foretelling the future or acquiring knowledge through spiritual or psychic means.

Don Juan Matus   A Yaqui Indian shaman and Nagual who served as teacher and guide to Carlos Castenada. He was featured in a number of the writer's books. The birth and death dates of Don Juan are unknown.

Dreamtime (also **the dreaming)**   To the Australian Aborigines, dreamtime is a great spiritual concept that explains the unification of all things. Dreamtime has four aspects: the beginning of all things; the lives and experiences of the ancestors; the way of life and death; and where power comes from. In Aboriginal thought, all things, all aspects, all dimensions, and all times are occurring simultaneously.

Druidism   The principle religion of the ancient Celts. The chief priests, or druids, maintained the language, culture, spiritual beliefs, and medical knowledge of the people. This vast body of knowledge was passed down orally and required twenty years of study to memorize and understand. Modern druidic practices differ significantly from the ancient ones as the ancient wisdom is largely unknown.

Dualism   The philosophic concept of mutually inclusive opposites (i.e., yin and yang), and the idea that one aspect cannot exist without its equal counterpart. For example, day cannot exist without night, or it has no context in time. Dualism includes the view that apparently conflicting realities, such as spiritual and physical existence, are not as disparate as they seem, but are parts of a natural whole.

Earth Changes   A belief among many new ager's that a cataclysm (or perhaps a series of them) is imminent. As a result earth will undergo such extensive changes that it will necessitate living in a radically different way. The psychic Edgar Cayce, among others, was a major proponent of this view, and he is often credited with coining the "Earth Changes" phrase. More recently catastrophic ecological problems, such as the ruptures in the ozone layer and global warming, and recent disasters, such as the Tsunami of 2005, Hurricane Katrina, and the increase in storm severity, continue to reinforce the concept. Whitley Strieber and Art Bell coauthored a book on these weather-related changes called *The Coming Global Superstorm*,[30] which in turn inspired a science fiction film, *The Day After Tomorrow*, where a new ice age occurs.

Earth Logos   A vast spiritual being who is the embodiment of all life on earth.

Earth Mother   (1) The belief that the earth itself has a feminine aspect that is infused in all aspects of nature. (2) The goddess being in some beliefs who forms, with Father Sky, one equal half of a dual great being. (3) A woman whose nature is significantly nurturing so that she emanates a healing and healthy energy.

Eckankar   A religion created in 1965 by Paul Twitchell (d.1972). It teaches the art of "soul travel," which is the ability to elevate one's astral body to a higher plane of existence where time and space are meaningless and, therefore, universal travel is possible. At such levels the human spirit can also easily bond with the universal all. Twitchell claims to have built Eckankar on principles of ancient origin.

Eckhart, Johannes (1260–1327)   A German Christian mystic and freethinker who challenged the structures of organized faith, Meister Eckhart drew on the philosophies apparent in the study of world mythology. His writings stand among the most influential in all of spiritual history, and they are directly linked with the later rise of Protestantism, as well as new-age thought. Ultimately put on trial for heresy, Eckhart died before his judgment. In recent years the Catholic Church has actively discussed restoring his name to church history.

30. Diane Publishing Company, 2000.

EARTH MOTHER GODDESS
Hervé Scott Flament

Ecological Responsibility A common and positive New Age belief that we, as parts of the living entity that is planet earth, have a responsibility to work toward the overall health of the planet. This is a view apparently not shared by the industrial community, or much of the political world.

Elemental A spiritual entity that embodies a particular aspect of nature (earth, air, fire, or water).

Elements The four cornerstones of nature: Earth, Air, Fire, and Water, which are believed to share consciousness with various spiritual beings. Many believe that every person has a tendency toward one of these elements, as explored in astrology. These four states of being also have material counterparts: earth (solid), air (gas), fire (plasma) and water (liquid).

Empowerment The process of imbuing or inspiring a person with energy, whether it is spiritual, physical, psychic, or emotional.

Enlightenment An advanced spiritual state in which a person rises above a strict adherence to physical laws and perceives the universal mind with great clarity.

Esalen Institute A new-age center founded in 1962 by Michael Murphy and Richard Price. It serves to both provide education in a variety of overlapping disciplines, as well as act as a facility for serious research. Over the years it has attracted many great visionary thinkers (such as Alan Watts, Joseph Campbell, and others). It is located near Big Sur, California.

Esoteric A general name for profound knowledge that is usually hidden (deliberately or not) from common view (or which is attainable only through a deeper than ordinary study).

Esoteric Movements A catchall term for more serious New Age fields of study.

Essenes A pre-Christian sect of Judaism, which held mystic, eschatological,[31] messianic, and ascetic beliefs. Among the New Age community, there is an abiding belief that the Essenes were the authors of the Dead Sea Scrolls, a belief not generally shared by the scientific community.

EST (Erhard Seminars Training) Known as est,[32] these seminars are the brainchild of Werner Erhard (born John Paul Rosenberg, 1935), which became very popular during the 1970s. The est program borrows heavily from encounter therapy, Zen, mind dynamics, Subud, gestalt therapy, and Scientol-

---

31. The aspect of theology concerned with the End of Days, or the apocalypse.
32. The Erhard organization prefers the lowercase spelling.

ogy. It uses large group training to impart transformational information for management skills, stress reduction, and personal growth. When est was nearly buried under legal and political controversy, the program metamorphosed into a different approach called "The Forum."

Etheric Body   See Astral Body.

Existentialism   A philosophic movement developed early in the twentieth century (most significantly in post World War II Europe). It was inspired by the writings of nineteenth century philosophers Soren Kierkegaard (1813–1855) and Friedrich Nietzsche (1844–1900). Kierkegaard espoused the philosophy of a "leap of faith," while Nietzsche argued that "God was dead." In both cases the thrust of the movement was to discover the meaning in one's own life rather than it its relation to the universe. Existentialism focuses on action, freedom, and decision as the most crucial aspects of human existence. It opposes positivity and rationalization.

Exit Counseling   A less destructive and traumatic form of deprogramming based on voluntary counseling rather than forced incarceration.

Fasting   A cleansing and purification method involving abstinence from food for a specific length of time. In some spiritual practices, fasting lasts until the consciousness rises above the physical body and receives a vision.

Feng Shui   Chinese term for "wind and water," but which refers to the ancient practice of precise arrangements of things within a room or space in order to balance the energies and create harmony.

Fetish   A word derived variously from two Latin words, *facticius* (artificial) and *facere* (to make). Fetish refers to a small item made to be a charm of protection. It can be as small as a carved stone carried in a pocket or as large as an elaborate corn dolly.

Findhorn Foundation   A charitable trust that evolved from an early new-age community located in Findhorn, Scotland. Founded by Eileen and Peter Caddy and Dorothy MacLean in 1962, the group practiced channeling, meditation, chanting, and other rituals in order to cultivate and refine their spirits. They also began an organic farm and believed that they were in communication with earth spirits (faeries and so on) and, as a result, their fields burgeoned with fruits and vegetables of amazing size and taste. In recognition of Findhorn's good works, Eileen Caddy was awarded the Most Excellent Order of the British Empire by Queen Elizabeth.

Firewalking   A ritual test in which a person walks without injury across beds of hot coals.

Flotation Tank   A device in which a person floats in skin-temperature water, with the absence of all sensory input. Also known as a sensory deprivation tank, the experience allows the astral body to separate from the physical in order to explore higher realms of consciousness. On a purely scientific level, the experience has been useful in relaxation therapy, testing the subtleties of perception, and noting various stimuli in the environment, such as tiny water temperature changes, introduction of noises, and so on.

Friends, Society of   Also known as the Quakers, the Friends are a spiritual group dedicated to pacifism and social consciousness.

Gandhi, Mohandas Karamchand   An Indian social reformer who led a nonviolent movement to free India from British rule. Known as Mahatma,[33] Gandhi (1869–1948) was an advocate of a modern form of Hinduism, which rejected the old caste system and concentrated on Truth as God.

Gawain, Shakti (b.1948)   A new-age author and teacher who pioneered and popularized meditation techniques for creative visualization. Her books include *Creative Visualization: Use the Power of Your Imagination to Create What You*

---

33. Sanskrit for "great soul."

Want in Your Life, Awakening: A Daily Guide to Conscious Living, Living in the Light: A Guide to Personal and Planetary Transformation.

Geller, Uri (b.1946)   One of the most celebrated psychics of the twentieth century, known for amazing demonstrations of spoon-bending, telepathy, and dowsing.

Gestalt Therapy   A form of psychotherapy developed by Fritz Perls (1893–1970), Laura Perls (1905–1990), and Paul Goodman (1911–1972) in the 1940s and 1950s. Gestalt focuses on personal responsibility, phenomenology, and self-healing.

Ghost   A nonphysical entity believed to be the surviving spirit of a dead person.

Ghost Dance   A religious ceremony practiced by a number of Native-American cultures. It was inspired by the visions of Wodziwob,[34] a Paiute medicine man and prophet from Nevada who first performed the ritual in 1890. As word of the dance—and its spiritual power—spread to other indigenous cultures, each adapted it to fit their own religious practices. It is now practiced widely throughout the Native-American community. Wodziwob conceived the dance while in a trance state during the solar eclipse of January 1, 1890. He also foresaw a nonviolent end to the conflict between the native peoples (and the forced expansion of the white man).

Gifts   Gifts, or "Spiritual Gifts," are the new-age terms for paranormal abilities, such as empathy, telepathy, and so on. Many within the community believe that every person possesses such abilities.

God   (1) The supreme perfect being; (2) any of a number of powerful supernatural beings who form a pantheon of deities; (3) the term used by some New Agers to describe the universal "All"—whether that force is self-aware or not.

---

34. Also known by the anglicized name of Jack Wilson.

Goddess   A supreme being that possesses distinctly feminine qualities.

Golden Dawn (also **Hermetic Order of the Golden Dawn**)   A late nineteenth century theurgic[35] order that has served as the model for many of the "cults" of the twentieth century. Founded by three Freemasons, Dr. William Robert Woodman (1828–1891), William Wynn Westcott (1848–1925), Samuel Liddell MacGregor Mathers (1854–1918), the Golden Dawn was a pathway to the development of magical powers. Immensely popular for a short time, it attracted members as diverse as William Butler Yeats and Aleister Crowley.

Gospel   The word is derived from the Old English "God Spell,"[36] a phrase used by traditional Christians to refer to Jesus Christ's message of salvation and redemption. The term is also used to describe the first four books of the New Testament (Matthew, Mark, Luke and John), which chronicle the life, teachings, death, and resurrection of Jesus.

Grail (also **Holy Grail**)   The grail is the cup (or plate) Jesus used at the Last Supper. Believed to possess vast supernatural healing powers, the grail has been avidly sought since the twelfth century.

Great Invocation   In 1945, theosophist Alice A. Bailey claimed to have channeled the spirit of Djwhal Khul, an ascended master, also known as "the Tibetan." The prayer was instantly embraced by seekers of spiritualism around the world and has since become a new-age staple that has been translated in dozens of languages around the world. The essence of it is summed up eloquently in its last line: "Let light and love and power restore the plan on earth."

Great White Brotherhood (also **The Universal White Brotherhood**) A concept in Western theosophic beliefs in which a group of ascended masters

---

35. Theurgy is a ritualistic practice performed with the deliberate intention of invoking the power and actions of God.
36. This original spelling was used for the 1971 musical *Godspell* by Stephen Schwartz and John-Michael Tebelak.

exist together on a higher plane and provide wisdom and guidance to humans, often through séances, trances, channeling, and similar psychic means.

Grounding   (1) The act of guiding a person toward emotional, psychic, physical, or spiritual calmness and balance, often through spiritual healing therapies; (2) the act of achieving personal calmness and balance through spiritual or meditative practices.

Gurdjieff, Georges Ivanovitch (1872–1949)   A Greek-Armenian mystic and spiritual teacher. Gurdjieff taught a powerful form of self-awareness, suggesting that humans are asleep and need to be awakened. His methods of teaching and writings have been strong influences on the development of many new-age movements.

Guru   A Hindu spiritual teacher who possesses a high level of consciousness.

Halpern, Steve   A New Age composer and musician often credited as the "founding father of New Age music." His music is widely used for healing, meditation, trance, and relaxation.

Hare Krishna   The common nickname of the International Society for Krishna Consciousness, a religious order founded in 1966 by A. C. Bhaktivedanta Swami Prabhupada.

Harmonic Convergence   A new-age event held on August 17, 1987, that involved millions of people around the world. Participants visited sacred spots, convergences of ley lines, and similar places, in order to combine energies in such a way as to positively affect world consciousness. The date was chosen based on predictions in the Mayan calendar, as well as astrological signs. It remains to be seen if the global awakening desired by this event will catch up to the turbulent and war-torn planet earth.

Hatha Yoga   A yogic practice involving slow stretching movements intended to relax the body and free trapped spiritual energy.

Healthy, Happy, and Holy   A new-age group founded by Dharma Yogi Bhajan in 1968. Its intention was to promote wellness through holistic practices such as kundalini yoga.

Herbalism   A method of natural healing using the curative powers of herbs, plants, molds, and fungi.

Higher Self   Used throughout the new-age community, the term refers to the ultimate spiritual aspect of a person, which is free of petty human desires and is capable of perceiving and understanding universal truths.

Hinduism   The world's third-largest religion, originating in India but now spread globally with more than one billion practitioners. Many Hindus maintain a pantheistic belief in a universe populated with many hundreds of gods (each of which are manifestations of Brahman, the cosmic "All"), while others focus their belief on Brahman as a singular universal deity.

Holism   Everything in the universe is part of a single organic entity. Each separate aspect (humans, animals, rocks, and so on) possesses ties to everything else, even when that connection is not apparent. The name comes from *holos,* the Greek word for "all."

Holistic Healing   An approach to wellness that focuses on the whole self (body, mind, emotions, and spirit). Holistic healing concentrates on the cause of an illness, as well as its symptomatic manifestation.

Homeopathy   This branch of medicine, developed by Samuel Hahnemann[37] (1755–1843) takes its name from the Greek, *hómoios* (similar) and *páthos* (suffering) and is built on the premise that illness can be treated by minute doses of chemicals or herbs that would, at full strength, produce serious side effects when given to a healthy person. These smaller doses are intended to spark the body into naturally fighting the illness.

37. Hahnemann coined the term in 1807, though he had been pursuing this line of reasoning since 1796.

Human Potential Movement A movement of interlocking new-age groups and individuals inspired in large part by the writings of Abraham Maslow (1908–1970). Creator of the "hierarchy of human needs," he presented a pyramid of five levels, the lowest of which involved physiological needs and the topmost, actualization. The human potential movement, which got started in the 1960s, adopted the view that humans seldom reach for their potential, either in physical, spiritual, mental, or emotional terms, and that a serious study, which combined proper health (exercise, nutrition, relaxation, massage, yoga, and so on) coupled with spiritual practices would spark great changes.

"I Am" Activity A spiritual movement founded in 1930 by Guy Ballard (1878–1936) and Edna Ballard (1886–1971). Ballard claimed to have met St. Germain and fostered the belief that he was the earthly messenger for all ascended masters, including Jesus Christ.

I-ching Known as the "Book of Changes" or the "Classic of Changes", the I-Ching is the oldest of Chinese texts. It describes a cosmology upon which Chinese culture is built. The I-Ching's lessons revolve around the premises that the universe is balanced like a set of scales (yin and yang) and that change is inevitable. In Western cultures the I-Ching is often denegrated to a simple foretune-telling method, which misses the point.

Initiation A ritual or event in which a person is admitted into a secret organization, belief, or practice.

Inner Self The aspect of a person that is part of the divine universal force.

Institute of Noetic Sciences A spiritual movement founded in 1973 by astronaut Edgar Mitchell (b.1930), and whose teaching is built on the premise of healing through mind power.

Intention A concept of affirmation in which the focus of a person's conscious, subconscious, and spiritual powers combine to manifest actions or growth. A variation of this, called the Science of Deliberate Creation, is espoused by Esther Hicks (1951–), who channels a group of beings collectively known as Abraham.

Interconnectedness (also **interdependence)**   A new-age concept built on the belief that everything in the universe is part of a single organic entity, and that nothing occurs, which does not, or cannot, affect the whole.

Iridology   A new-age diagnostic method dating back to the ancient Greeks in which a study of the patterns of the iris provide useful insights into the health of the entire body.

Islam   The second largest religion in the world, based on the life and teachings of the prophet Muhammad (570–632). The name Islam means "submission to the will of God," and practitioners of this faith are called Muslims. The Quran, or Koran, is their most holy book, though they also regard the Torah, the Old Testament Psalms, and the New Testament as holy.

Kabbalah (Also **Kabbala, Kabalah, Kabala, Cabala, Cabbala, Cabalah, Cabbalah, Qabala, Qabbala, Qabalah, Qabbalah)**   A generic name for Jewish practices that attempt to unlock the mystical secrets of the Tanakh (Hebrew Bible).

Karma   A belief in Eastern thought that activity of any kind (mental, physical, psychic, spiritual, and so on) influences one's destiny.

Karma Yoga   The practice of doing unselfish actions that benefit others.

Kinesiology   The scientific study of human movement that encompasses anatomy, biochemistry, biomechanics, physiology, exercise psychology, and neuroscience; and that explores the connection between the quality of movement and overall health.

Knight, J. Z. (b.1946)   A psychic who claims to be the channel for Ramtha, an antediluvian warrior from Lemuria. He led his people in a battle against the oppressive Atlanteans 35,000 years ago before being overcome and imprisoned. Ramtha used his time in confinement to develop a variety of advanced psychic skills, including astral projection and spiritual time travel. The documentary, *What the #$*! Do We Know!?*,[38] which features Knight channeling Ramtha, was directed by William Arntz, Betsy Chasse, and Mark Vicente, three students of J. Z. Knight and substantially promotes her views.

Krishnamurti, Jiddi (1895–1986) A Hindu teacher proclaimed by theosophist Annie Besant as the world's true messiah. Though Krishnamurti initially took that role, he later recanted and lived out the rest of his life as a teacher of personal philosophy.

Kundalini A yogic healing practice based on the belief in a female nurturing consciousness, which can lead to health and enlightenment. The name, Kundalini, translates as "coiling like a serpent," and refers to the energies that coil around the muladhara, the chakra located between the genitals and anus. The awakening of this bioenergy is life-changing.

Labyrinth In new age terms, a labyrinth is a pattern or path along which a person walks as part of an energy-cultivating, healing, or purifying ritual.

Lazaris Lazaris is a nonphysical entity channeled by Jach Pursel since 1974,[39] and whose message is about discovering one's own path to self-realization. The Lazaris workshops have attracted huge numbers of people, including celebrities (Sharon Gless, Shirley MacLaine, among others).

Leary, Dr. Timothy (1920–1996) Leary was a legend both inside and outside of the pre-new-age movement of the early 1960s. Fearless and infinitely curious, he used himself (and a number of his friends, students, and colleagues) as a guinea pig in his quest to map the terrain of altered states of consciousness (accessible through the use of psychedelic drugs). He advocated

---

38. Also known as *What the Bleep Do We Know?*
39. Born John W. Pursel. The name change was based on numerological calculations.

both the therapeutic, spiritual, and recreational use of mind-altering substances, believing that a person should monitor his or her own use (and abuse) rather than be restricted by prohibitive laws. He particularly argued that LSD (lysergic acid diethylamide), could—under the right conditions and with proper guidance—alter the mind and perceptions in ways that would easily allow people to gain useful mental and spiritual insights.

⊰ PSYCHEDELICS— ⊱ ALTERED STATES IN TABLET FORM

In the 1960s, as the new age was revving into high gear, a number of free-thinkers were experimenting with various kinds of mind-altering drugs. Generally known as psychedelics, these were psychoactive or psychotropic drugs such as stimulants, antidepressants, hallucinogens, and antipsychotics. Popular favorites among the psychedelics were (and are) LSD (acid), psilocybin (psychedelic mushrooms), mescaline (peyote), LSA (morning glory seeds), Ayahuasca (yage), MDMA (ecstasy), 2C-B (nexus), DOM (STP) and 5-MeO-DIPT (Foxy Methoxy), and the old favorite, cannabis (marijuana).

Probably the greatest American champion of the wonders and benefits of psychedelics was the eminent writer and psychologist Dr. Timothy Leary, who began experimenting with entheogen (psychoactive material derived from plant matter—such as *Psilocybe mexicana*, better known as "magic mushrooms"). Leary said that he

(continued)

learned more about his own brain and about psychology after five hours of tripping on psilocybin then he did in the previous fifteen years of purely academic study.

Nowadays, all of the psychedelics are illegal and the new-age community has to rely on fasting, vision quests, astral projection, and other nonhallucinogen-based pathways in order to achieve altered states of consciousness.

Ley Lines   These are lines of energy that criss-cross the world as completely as lines of latitude and longitude. Along them flow various frequencies of energy (negative, positive, and neutral). Though widely believed, or intuited, for centuries, their existence was brought to public light in 1921 by amateur archaeologist Alfred Watkins (1855–1935) through his book, *The Old Straight Track*. Many New Agers and Wiccans believe that nexus points—where ley lines converge—are centers of great power. Stonehenge is believed to sit on such a power nexus.

Lightbody   Another of the many names for the astral body.

Lightworker   A person who actively works on a spiritual project, such as cultivating personal healing. Often used to describe those persons using new-age methods to heal others.

Lucid Dreaming   The phenomena of being aware that one is dreaming while the dream is still unfolding. This can happen by accident or, more often, as a result of spiritual exercises designed to combine the conscious and unconscious minds.

Macrobiotics   A nutrition philosophy and practice whose name, meaning "the great life," was coined by German physician Christoph Wilhelm Hufeland

(1762–1836).[40] The macrobiotic diet is designed to restore and maintain health by understanding the "energetic qualities" of foods. It also analyzes how diet is part of an entire lifestyle (what we do, where we live, how we eat, and so on). Macrobiotics focuses on the expansive and contractive energies inherent in different foods. It is an approach that consists of a nondairy, wholefoods, vegetarian (except for a little fish) diet.

Magnetic Therapy   A new-age healing method, inspired and partly based on ancient Asian techniques, where magnets are placed on (or held near) the body to heal and restore health.

Maharishi Mahesh Yogi   Founder of Transcendental Meditation.

Mahasamadhi   A concept in Buddhist and Hindu philosophies that means "making firm," and which postulates that the spirit is conscious at the moment of death and rises to become one with the divine.

Mandala   A circular pattern used in Hindu and Buddhist meditations to draw a person's entire attention to a single point.

Mantra   A word, sound, or phrase used in meditation. It is uttered in rhythmic chanting in order to clarify the mind, elevate the spirit, and open the consciousness to universal connection.

Mass Incarnation   A new-age belief which states that Christ Consciousness is being simultaneously incarnated on a global scale.

Meridians   Pathways in the human body along which intrinsic energy flows.

Metaphysics   Literally "beyond physics," this is the study of spiritual, psychic, and related themes.

40. From his book, *Makrobiotik, oder die Kunst das menschliche Leben zu verlängern (Macrobiotics, or the Art of Extending Human Life)*, published in 1796.

Mind Sciences   A general new-age term for the various beliefs that human beings are inherently divine and that practices which separate (or elevate) the spirit above the physical will reconnect these sparks of the divine with the "universal all."

Mohammed   The prophet who founded Islam.

Monism   The belief that everything in existence is a manifestation of the divine.

Myofascial Release   A healing therapy similar to massage and acupressure using gentle pressure. Subtle skin and joint stretching restore health and balance.

Mysticism   From the Greek *mystikos* ("to originate"), this is the study for truth and the unlocking of secrets by delving into religion, spirituality, parapsychology, philosophy, and (occasionally) physics.

Namasté (or Namaskar)   A formal and reverential greeting, originating in India. The word has a variety of subtle meanings, including "the spirit in me meets the same spirit in you," and "I bow to the divine in you."

Native-American Beliefs   The religious and spiritual practices of the many Native American cultures have had a profound impact on new-age beliefs. Many of these rituals, both specific to individual societies or general to the collective indigenous cultures of North America (and to a lesser degree South America), have been adopted and adapted for use in new-age rituals, including the rain dance, smoke lodges, vision quests, the ghost dance, the use of sage as a purifying agent, and peyote ceremonies, among others.

Naturopathy   An approach to healing in which natural substances (herbs, for example), the environment (clean water, fresh air, sunshine), and whole foods are used to increase wellness and improve the quality of life.

Neopaganism   A modern recreation of pagan practices, generally with an emphasis on newer Wiccan rituals, goddess worship, positive-energy creation, ecological recovery, and nature worship.

Neuro-Linguistic Programming (NLP)   A counseling approach developed in the early 1970s by Richard Bandler (b.1950), John Grinder (b.1940), based on the work of Milton H. Erickson (1902–1980) and Gregory Bateson (1904–1980), among others. In the development of NLP, the relations of how speech and language patterns (linguistics) interact with the mind and the nervous system ("neuro") are studied to help people create new patterns of speech and action, which will improve overall mental and spiritual health.

Neuromuscular Therapy   A massage modality that combines deep tissue and acupressure practices (in order to break the stress-tension-pain cycle).

New-age Movement   A general term for the many and varied groups and individuals whose focus is improvement of self through natural lifestyles, healthy living, spiritual explorations, and self-realization.

New Age Music   Any of the many forms of music intended to raise the consciousness of the listener, facilitate meditation, provide a calm place for the mind, or otherwise aid in healing and stress reduction.

New World Order   A new-age belief that a cosmic change will occur, which will realign the spiritual harmonics of earth and its people. It will also raise consciousness significantly. Many believe that this process is already under way (see HARMONIC CONVERGENCE), while some believe that it will come about through natural catastrophes (see EARTH CHANGES).

Nirvana   The state of enlightenment according to Hinduism.

OBE   Out-of-body experience; another name for astral projection, whether through deliberate or accidental means.

Om Mane Padme Hum: A Sanskrit mantra used in Tibetan Buddhism meaning, "Hail to the jewel in the lotus." In Nichiren the phrase is translated in Japanese as "Nam Myoho Renge Kyo."

Orgone Box (also **orgone accumulator)**   A device invented by Wilhelm Reich (1897–1957), which he claimed collects a previously unknown form of universal energy called "orgone." According to Reich, the most potent form of orgone could only be generated and collected at the point of orgasm. It was his view that diseases such as cancer were the result of orgone deficiencies in the body.

Pantheism   The belief that everything in the universe is part of God and that God transcends all limits, bounds, or dimensions.

Parmahansa Yogananda (1893–1952)   One of the most important and influential yogis of the twentieth century, and certainly the person most eminently responsible for the worldwide spread of yoga and vedic philosophy. Yogananda is also the author of the classic *Autobiography of a Yogi,* published in 1946 (still in print and selling very well). The book made the practice and devotion to yoga accessible to tens of millions.

Paranormal   Literally "beyond normal," a term used to describe actions, beings, events, or abilities that are beyond normal human ability, perception, or understanding.

Past-Life Regression   A hypnosis technique in which a person is regressed to a former incarnation.

Patañjali   A second century B.C.E. yogi who wrote the Yoga Sutra. As a result he is often called the "founder of yoga," though, in truth, yoga predates his lifetime by generations.

Peale, Norman Vincent (1898–1993)   A Christian cleric and author who espoused "the power of positive thinking." His book of the same name is considered one of the most important pre-New Age books of the twentieth century.

Perennial Philosophy   A concept created by writer Aldous Huxley, author of *Brave New World*, which states that the essential and immutable truth of the universe is woven throughout the fabric of all religions and spiritual practices. Even if approaches and methods vary (even radically), the truth is always there and, ultimately, it is the same. This concept perfectly supports the new-age approach to spirituality.

Personal Transformation   The new-age term for an epiphany that opens a person to a broader view of the spiritual connection of all things.

Peyote   A small, spineless cactus *(lophophora williamsii)* possessing strong hallucinogenic properties. It is used in a number of Native American and new-age ceremonies as a way of opening the mind to visions. The Native American Church, which is also known as the Peyote Church or simply Peyotism, uses peyote as a sacrament.

Philosophical Research Society   A spiritual organization founded by Manly Palmer Hall (1901–1990)[41] in 1934, and which has helped to promote a better understanding of the many paths to enlightenment and understanding. Hall's writings are so influential that even Carl Jung (1875–1961) borrowed from them when writing his famous *Psychology and Alchemy*.

Polarity Therapy   A new-age healing method created in the mid-twentieth century by Randolph Stone, DO, NC, ND[42] and built on the concept of balancing the positive and negative energies in the body. The process involves various forms of bodywork, diet, and some exercise. It is used for pain management and other complaints. Dr. Stone has published seven books on the subject of polarity therapy.

Prana   Sanskrit word for intrinsic energy or "Life-breath."

41. Hall is best known as the author of *The Secret Teaching of All Ages: An Encyclopedic Outline of Masonic, Hermetic, Qabbalistic, and Rosicrucian Symbolical Philosophy*, which he self-published in 1928, but which has since been republished many times.
42. NC—Doctor of Chiropractic; ND—Doctor of Naturopathic medicine

Pranayama   A Sanskrit term for controlling the breath—a technique used widely in yoga and similar practices.

Prophet   A person who possesses knowledge of the future or of spiritual matters; generally prophets are tied to religions, which distinguishes them from clairvoyants, who are psychic without any specific spiritual ties.

Psychic Birth   A new-age phrase denoting a sudden or profound advancement in spiritual power, enlightenment, or understanding, which, in turn, changes the course of one's life.

Psychic Consultant (also **psychic counselor**)   A person who uses psychic abilities as part of an instructional, guidance, or healing process. This can range from divination to life counseling.

Psychic Energy   The as yet unknown source of psychic abilities.

Psychic Healer   A person capable of using either psychic abilities or spiritual powers to cure injuries and disease.

Psychic Massage   A healing method in which a person psychically connects with another in order to help balance energies and encourage mental and physical wellness.

Psychic Vampire (also **energy vampire, pranic vampire, empathic vampire, energy predator, psy/psi-vamp, energy parasite, psionic vampire, emotional vampire**)   A person who feeds off of the mental, emotional, or spiritual energies of others. In some cases this is an unconscious act, in others it's deliberate.

Psychodrama   A form of psychotherapy developed by Jacob L. Moreno (1889–1974) in which group therapy is transformed into a mutual-issue resolution session. Psychodrama uses theater techniques such as improvisation, role-playing, use of props, some scripting, and games. In this way all patients/players become part of the analyses and healing processes.

Psychosynthesis   A form of transpersonal psychology,[43] which forms the fourth substantial approach to psychology, along with psychoanalysis, behaviorism, and humanistic psychology. Psychosynthesis evolved out of earlier forms of psychotherapy, guided along by men like William James (1842–1910), Sigmund Freud (1856–1939), Carl Jung (1875–1961), Abraham Maslow (1908–1970), and Roberto Assagioli (1888–1974). In 1969, Maslow, Stanislav Grof (b.1931) and Anthony Sutich (b.1944) launched the *Journal of Transpersonal Psychology,* the leading academic journal in the field. Unlike the other approaches, psychosynthesis takes into account religious conversion, enlightenment, spiritual growth, and altered states of consciousness when providing therapy for patients.

Pyramid Power (also **form resonance)**   A term coined in 1973 by American inventor Patrick Flanagan (b.1944). He used it to describe the spiritual qualities inherent in pyramid-shaped structures, whether the Egyptian pyramids or smaller models or buildings. The study and practice of using these structures to generate, cultivate, and enhance personal spiritual capabilities became known as pyramidology.

Quakers   See Friends.

Quantum Healing   A concept created by Deepak Chopra (1946–) in which the possibilities for self-healing are explored. His book of the same name was a best seller.

Quimby, Phineas P. (1802–1866)   A spiritual healer and mesmerist whose methods influenced the development of Mary Baker Eddy's Christian Science movement, as well as other new-age and new-thought groups.

Qur'an (also **Koran)**   The holy scriptures of Islam. The name is Arabic for "recital."

43. A branch of psychology that studies the spiritual aspects, beliefs and potential of human beings.

Ram Dass   Born Richard Alpert in 1931, Ram Dass (literarily, "servant of God") is a popular spiritual leader of the new-age movement. He studied yoga and meditation under Neem Karoli Baba (generally known as Maharaji), and combined these teachings with his own. Ram Dass has worked with prison inmates to cultivate spirituality as a way of changing their life paths; investigated the spiritual benefits of psychedelic drugs; and wrote extensively, including publishing the landmark million-plus copy best seller, *Be Here Now*.

Raël   The spiritual name for Frenchman Claude Vorilhon, who claims that an alien race appointed him to be their spokesperson.

Reading   (1) A general term for the process of spiritual diagnostics. (2) The process of discovering information through divination.

Rebirthing (also **rebirthing-breathwork, conscious breathing**)   A form of alternative medicine developed by spiritualist Leonard Orr (b.1938) between 1962 and 1974. It is built on several interlocking concepts, including: Birth memories are not lost and can be recovered; Rebirthing can help a person access memories of past lives; Memory is stored in cells, as well as in the brain; The birth process, being traumatic, leaves damage that can be repaired; and so on. Rebirthing breathing exercises help uncover old trauma and realign the body and mind into a more harmonious state.

Reconciliation   A goal in many new-age therapeutic methods is the removing of an aspect of tension between two individuals, so that a more harmonious relationship can proceed from that point.

Reflexology (also **zone therapy**)   An early new-age alternative-medicine practice developed in the 1930s by Eunice Ingham (1889–1974). It is built on earlier experiments by Dr. William Fitzgerald. Fitzgerald discovered that different body parts, particularly organs and glands, have corresponding points on the foot, and that massage, pressure, or manipulation of the foot-points improves the health of the corresponding organ. Many New Agers hold that this is ancient knowledge that was merely rediscovered in the twentieth century by Fitzgerald and Ingham.

Reiki A healing modality developed in early-twentieth century Japan, which uses a method similar in appearance to the laying on of hands. Reiki practitioners manipulate the Ki intrinsic energy in order to align its flow throughout the body. It can also remove blockages, which lead to poor health and pain.

Reincarnation A common belief in many world religions in which a person's spirit is reborn periodically into new physical bodies, often as part of a longer process of spiritual growth and enlightenment.

Rolfing (also **structural integration)** An alternative healing modality developed by Ida P. Rolf (1896–1979), which uses a variety of methods (deep tissue massage, alignment, and so on) to restore balance to all of the joints from neck to toes.

Saint Germain A mysterious figure who (allegedly) died in 1784, but who many New Agers believe is an immortal ascended master who has never died. During the eighteenth century, the Count of St. Germain was an adventurer, courtier, inventor, mystic, and alchemist. Historians believe that St. Germain was likely the son of Prince Francis II Rákóczi, an exiled Transylvanian nobleman, or possibly the illegitimate son of Maria Anna of Pfalz-Neuburg, the widow of Charles II of Spain. In either case, a number of folks in the twentieth century have either claimed to be St. Germain reborn or the mystic himself.

Samadhi A term found in both Hindu and Buddhist religious practices. It describes a state in which the spiritual practitioner has become one with the object of his meditations.

Samsara A Buddhist term for that which is the opposite of Nirvana. The current physical world is samsara.

Satsang A gathering for the purpose of meditating, chanting, and discussing spiritual matters. The satsang is core event in the guru/disciple dynamic.

Secularism A system of belief that neither depends upon specific faith or rejects it.

Self-Realization The awareness of one's connection with spiritual matters, a process that often provides lucid personal insights.

Seth A nonphysical entity channeled by Jane Roberts (1929–1984) from 1963 until her death. While Roberts was in a trance state, Seth would speak through her. The messages were later transcribed into what are known as the *Seth Material.* Seth dictated a number of larger works that were published in nine volumes: *Seth Speaks; The Nature of Personal Reality; The Nature of the Psyche, Its Human Expression; The Individual and the Nature of Mass Events; The Unknown Reality;* and *Dreams, Evolution, and Value Fulfillment.* The Seth books became enormously popular, selling millions of copies. Topics include dreams, out-of-body travel, life after death, space travel, interdimensional travel, and much more. Manifestation of desires was a frequent theme, often summed up by Seth as, "You create your own reality."

Seven Rays A series of teachings from ascended masters channeled by Alice A. Bailey (1880–1949), Helena P. Blavatsky (1831–1888), and Helena Roerich (1879–1955). According to the channels, the seven rays were part of an ancient belief system, which argued that there were seven essential energy frequencies controlling the spiritual universe. Each human soul was part of one of these rays, and repeated incarnations were necessary to refine that soul.

Shaman A mystic and healer who is generally part of an indigenous religion. A shaman blends healing techniques with spiritual practices.

Shamanic Therapy An approach to healing in which psychic and spiritual skills are used, sometimes in conjunction with herbal and natural reme-

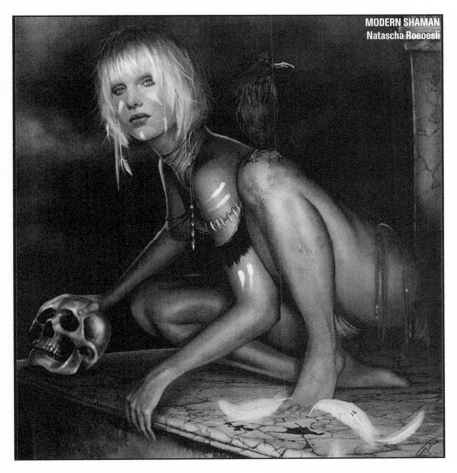

MODERN SHAMAN
Natascha Roeoesli

dies. Shamanistic therapies are used to cure mental, physical, psychic, and spiritual maladies.

Shiatsu An ancient Chinese healing method (purportedly developed in 3000 B.C.E.) that relies on a combination of applied pressure and assisted stretching.

Siddha In Hinduism, a Siddha is a spiritualist possessing psychic abilities.

Silva Method Originally called Silva Mind Control, the method, developed by José Silva, teaches how to increase intelligence, cultivate clairvoyance, and develop skills for self-healing.

Soul   The nonphysical aspect of a person that is indestructible and immortal. Though the soul itself is perfect and immutable, when incarnated the personality that manifests is purely based on organic chemistry and is therefore influenced by hormones, blood sugar, trauma and other purely physical phenomena.

Soulmates   Two souls whose energy vibrations are either perfectly matched or, when combined, create a perfect new frequency. In various new-age beliefs, there is a perfect soul match for everyone. Finding one's soulmate is a positive event that allows both souls to advance down the path to enlightenment. Some New Agers take a somewhat less grand view of soulmates and argue that they are merely two persons who were married (or romantically involved) in a previous life.

Sound Therapy   Also called toning, this is a healing method using various kinds of sounds (tones, chants, musical notes, and so on). It matches the frequencies of healing, so that a person's natural energy waves will match and vibrate at the same healthy frequency. Sound therapy is also used as part of the practice of cultivating and energizing psychic ability.

Spirit Guide   A nonphysical entity that makes contact with a living person in order to positively influence his or her life. The methods of approach, contact, and action vary greatly throughout world cultures, but the concept is found in nearly every religious and spiritual belief.

Spiritual Healing   Using psychic or spiritual energy to increase wellness or effect cures.

Spiritualist   A person who acts upon the firm belief that the spirit world exists and that humans can interact with it. Spiritualists do not necessarily possess paranormal abilities.

Sufi   A Muslim who seeks direct experience with Allah and whose practices approach Islam from a more spiritual rather than doctrinal direction. Though spread throughout Islam, Sufism originated in Persia (now Iran).

Sweat Lodge   A ceremonial sauna used as a purification ritual in many Native-American cultures. Many new-age followers have adopted the practice of taking a "sweat" as part of their journey to spiritual purity.

Synchronicity   A term coined by Carl Jung to describe the phenomena of two events occurring at once.

Synergy   Synergy is a cooperative interaction between two or more agents or forces, so that their combined effect is greater than the sum of their individual effects. The harmonic convergence was an attempt to use synergy to effect a positive global change.

Tantra   The word tantra derives from the root word *tan,* which variously translates as extending, expanding, spreading, continuing, weaving, or manifesting. Humans are part of the continuing creative action of the universe, and can tap into this limitless creative power. Tantra appears in both Hindu and Buddhist scriptures, and these writings describe practices, meditative techniques, and rituals. Tantra also has a strong sexual component, which has been popularized by celebrities (such as Sting) who lauded its enhancement of the bond between sexuality and spirituality.

Taoism   A Chinese spiritual movement based on the Tao Te Ching ("The Way of Life"), written by the great philosopher Laozi (Lao-tzu) (c. sixth century B.C.E.) more than two thousand years ago. Taoism resists definition, but in essence it deals with finding the correct path in life, which is generally balanced between extremes. This middle path is understood by contemplating the nature of opposites. For example, night cannot exist with day, otherwise there is no context in which to define night *as* night. This concept is called the yin and yang.

Theosophy   A branch of philosophy whose name means, "knowledge of the divine." It help lay significant groundwork for the launching of the new age. Theosophy was founded by Helena Petrovna Blavatsky (1831–1891).[44] Among the movement's goals was to know God through spiritual ecstasy, direct intuition, or special individual relations. Theosophy incorporated many practices from Buddhism and Hinduism, which can be seen as one of the reasons why those religions are so heavily represented in modern new-age practices. In 1875 Blavatsky, along with Henry Steel Olcott (1832–1907) and William Quan Judge (1851–1896), founded the Theosophical Society.

Therapeutic Touch   (1) Healing practice developed by nurse Dolores Kriger. (2) General name for any of the healing modalities involving massage and similar practices.

Third Eye   A spot on the forehead, also known as the "brow chakra," which is believed to be the center of psychic ability.

Torah (also the **Pentateuch)**   The five books of Moses are the heart of Judaism and contain all of the laws, traditions, and rituals that bind this ancient faith together.

Trance   A state, resembling sleep, where a person is receptive to a variety of spiritual or psychic experiences, from channeling to astral projection.

Trance Channeler   A modern name for trance medium.

Trager Approach   A healing modality developed by Milton Trager that utilizes gentle, non-intrusive, natural rocking movements to release deep-seated pain and facilitate relaxation, increase physical mobility, and stimulate mental clarity.

Transactional Analysis   Familiarly referred to as TA, a form of psycho-analysis developed in the late 1950s by psychiatrist Eric Berne, which takes a

---

44. See listings for *Book of Dyzan and Seven Rays.*

different view of Freud's concept of the Superego, the Ego and the Id. Berne labeled them the Parent, Adult and Child states, and postulated that our psychological makeup is shaped through our childhood experiences, and a serious study of those experiences will lead to an understanding of healing pathways.

Transformation Any major spiritual change in which self-realization and/or a degree of universal enlightenment elevates a person to a higher level of understanding and acceptance.

Transformation Therapy A form of New Age counseling intended to help a person make serious and permanent changes in their views of their own potential and in their understanding of the universal All.

Universality The belief that God is all and therefore every religion and spiritual path leads to the same source. In this belief everyone is right, and differences are simply a matter of choice or a manifestation of the way in which a person (or group of people) are capable of grasping the concept of the universal All.

Vedic See Ayurvedic.

Vision Quest A spiritual practice common to most Native-American cultures where the spiritual world opens up to a seeker and reveals secrets, life directions, and other wisdom. Many vision quests involve fasting and other purification rituals (in order to prepare the body and mind for the event).

Visualization See Creative Visualization.

Walk-In A term coined by psychic Ruth Montgomery (1912–2001). It explains the ancient Hindu concept of a soul occupying a body whose original soul has departed. Many believe that this happens (at times) during near-death experiences. Depending on the viewpoint, walk-ins may be benign or hostile.

Wet Rebirthing   A form of guided rebirthing experience practiced in water. This is done as a way to simulate the feel of the original birth. The neutral balance of the warm water aids in diffusing negative energy.

Whirling Dervish   Properly known as the Mevlevi Order, or the Mevleviye. These are members of a Sufi order founded by the followers of Jalal al-Din Muhammad Rumi in 1273.[45] Whirling dervishes participate in a ceremony called a "sema" during which they use music, chanting, and a spinning dance to enter religious trance states.

Whitelighter   Originally a derogatory nickname for New Agers. The term is based on the spiritual quest to reach the white light (especially for those who experience out-of-body or near-death experiences). Nowadays, some New Agers have accepted the description, albeit in a tongue-in-cheek manner.

Wu   A Chinese term,[46] which appears in both Taoism and Buddhism that means "void" or "nonbeing." Rather than stating whether something "is" or "is not," the concept of "wu" allows it to be understood without quantification.

Wu Wei   A Chinese concept meaning "not have" but which refers to action without action, a philosophic view of perfect equilibrium.

Xenoglossia (also glossolalia)   Popularly known as "speaking in tongues," glossolalia is the apparently patternless speech uttered during trance states. Within certain religious communities there is a belief that this is the language of the angels.

Yin and Yang   A Taoist concept for mutually inclusive opposites, meaning aspects of a thing that cannot exist without containing some element of its opposite. The opposite provides context for which each element can be under-

45. A thirteenth-century Persian poet, jurist, theologian, and teacher of Sufism. Rumi's poetry is still popular today and is extraordinarily beautiful and poignant.
46. Called "Mu" in Japanese Zen Buddhism.

stood. Yin represents negative forces and is exemplified as passive, feminine, downward, night, etc.; where Yang is the positive force and is correspondingly active, masculine, upward, day. Everything in the universe, both physical and spiritual, and can be understood in terms of its yin and yang properties.

Yoga   A general name for a vast number of spiritual and/or physical practices based on methods first developed in India. The name means, "discipline," and the various yoga methods require strict attention to proper form as well as to diet, proper attitude, and diligence. Most forms of yoga teach meditation as well, and many of them are proven to increase health and fitness.

Yogi   (1) A practitioner of yoga; (2) a person who has attained perfection through the practice of yoga.

Zen   The Japanese name for the form of Mahayana Buddhism developed in India (600 B.C.E.) by Buddhist master, Bodhidharma. Practitioners seek satori, a sudden flowering of blissful illumination, which cannot be explained but only experienced.

— Chapter Ten —
SUPERSTITIONS

⊰ WHAT IS SUPERSTITION? ⊱

Superstitions are not rational, everyone says so. Tossing salt over one's shoulder has no verifiable scientific basis. There are no published financial records proving that the finding of a heads-up penny leads directly to good fortune. Few mother's backs were broken as a direct result of a kid stepping on a crack.

We all know better. It's all nonsense.

Isn't it?

So why is it that so many professional athletes perform little rituals before their games? Why don't actors throw caution to the wind and say "Macbeth" in the theater? Why do so many people touch wood when someone has said something unfortunate? It's because, deep down, beneath the veneer of civilized and scientific cynicism to which we all willingly subscribe, there is an older and more primitive part of each of us that believes that there is magic in the world.

Superstitions are the beliefs, however openly scoffed, in the existence of magic in the world. For most people, superstitions are embarrassments, something they laugh off if someone sees them tossing salt over their shoulder or rubbing their lucky rabbit's foot; but laughing it off doesn't change the actual belief. Every night, millions of people will look up into the twilit sky and make a wish on the first star. Businessmen—captains of industry—will wear their lucky ties to a presentation. Soldiers in battle will pat their pockets to make sure their good luck charms are still there. It's a primitive thing, we all have it whether we admit to it or not.

To believe in a superstition is actually a demonstration of faith, because there is generally nothing to support the sustained belief. There is no evidence. It is the unspoken belief that our world is ruled by forces that deliberately work their will for good or ill. Superstitions, by their nature, insist that the scientific foundations of "cause and effect" are subject to spiritual influence.

Superstitions are a belief in the supernatural, and even those folks who will swear that they hold not the slightest flicker of belief in anything supernatural often have some practice that relies on superstition . . . even if it's reading their horoscope in the morning paper. They may scoff at the content, but they'll still read it time and time again. These same people will buy lottery tickets and use birthdays, street addresses, or other personal codes instead of having a machine randomly pick the number. They may not admit that they believe their personal numbers are lucky, but not admitting is not the same as not believing it. Superstitions prevail.

In this chapter you'll read about superstitions concerning everything from acorns to black cats; from baseball to birthdays. How many of them do you believe?

Acorn   Perhaps one of the simplest and most enduring symbols of life—an acorn carried on a person can bring good luck and ensure a long and happy life. An acorn kept by the window during a storm will keep thunder and lightning outside.

Air Travel   It's good luck to "touch wood" of a living tree before taking off and to keep a lucky charm handy. It also couldn't hurt to cross the seatbelts of vacant seats around you to appease potentially dangerous spirits. However, having live flowers on an airplane is never a good idea from a superstitious standpoint. No one knows why, but like all superstitions, it persists.

SUPERSTITIONS
Jonathan Maberry

Amber This stone has always been a potent good-luck charm. An amber necklace can protect against colds and other common maladies when regularly worn.

Ambulance Watching an ambulance go by is more than just a subtle reminder of how fragile life is—it's also very bad luck. Catholics will often cross themselves after an ambulance passes to discharge the omen. Others might hold their breath until they see a dog that is either black or brown.

Apple   While the adage of "an apple a day keeps the doctor away" is common to most, there are other superstitions associated with the forbidden fruit. Young lovers can predict who they might marry if they utter the names of potential pairings while twisting the stem of an apple. In a game much like "she loves me, she loves me not" with the petals of a flower, the name spoken when the stem of an apple twists free will be your future mate. Some also believe that if you cut an apple in half, the amount of seeds inside will predict how many children you will have.

Automobiles   It's bad luck to buy a car on the thirteenth day of the month, or to buy a new car when nothing is mechanically wrong with your old one. Cars that are green are considered bad luck because the color "interferes" with that of nature. Conversely, buying a car from someone richer than oneself could mean a windfall in the near future. It's also always a good idea to transfer "lucky" items from your old car into a new one.

Axe   Bringing an axe into the home portends the death of a family member.

Babies   Predicting the sex of your baby can be done with a simple pendulum—even a string tied around a coin will do. Simply allow the pendulum to swing over the baby to be and if it travels in a straight line, the baby will be a boy; round or oval movement indicates a girl.

• A baby born with a *caul*—a thin, amniotic membrane covering its head or body—is purported to have "second sight" or some form of extrasensory perception. Other beliefs say such a child will have good luck and wealth throughout his or her life.

• Babies born in the breech position (feet first) are also said to have various mystic abilities.

• If a baby's first tooth appears in the lower jaw, it will have a long and happy life.

Baseball   Professional athletes are perhaps the last holdouts of superstition. Folks who might laugh at a black cat crossing their path can easily accept the idea of a "home-field curse," a lucky bat, or even the unsavory prospect of a pair of socks that should never be washed lest their good luck be tainted. Here are some common myths associated with America's favorite pastime.

•Spitting into your hands before picking up a bat is good luck.

•If a dog is seen walking across a baseball diamond before a game it is bad luck.

•It's bad luck to lend your bat to another player.

•When taking and leaving the field between innings, it is bad luck to tread on the baselines.

•Conversely, some players believe that it's good luck to step on a base when taking and leaving the field between innings.

•If a player is pitching a no-hitter, or is on some hitting streak, it's bad luck to even mention it until after the game, if it all.

•Sleeping with bats or gloves is a common method of keeping batting or pitching streaks alive.

Bats   A bat loose in the home can herald a coming death in the household. It is also regarded as bad luck to see a bat in the daytime, to harm one, or to find one flying around a wedding ceremony. A bat that hits or falls on you is actually a sign of good luck.

Beds   For knitters, it's considered bad luck to start a bedspread or quilt and not complete it. Placing your hat on your bed will also bring bad luck. The phrase "got up on the wrong side of the bed" indicates it's best to get out of bed on the same side in which you got into it.

Bees   If a bee should find its way into your home, you're likely to soon have a visitor. If you should kill a bee, or one should die in your home it can bring bad luck. A colony of bees that collect on the roof of a structure is a sign that there will soon be a fire.

Bells   In many religions, the tolling of a bell can purify the area and keep away demonic forces and bad influences. Also, it is believed that each time a bell rings, an angel gets his or her wings.

Birds   While a bird flying straight for you is a symbol of good fortune, most other superstitions associated with them are much more dire. A bird circling over one's house, tapping upon the window or worse yet, flying into a home itself are all omens of death. Crows and other black birds are generally seen as harbingers of bad luck.

⊰ SUPERSTITIONS ABOUT ⊱ CROWS, RAVENS, AND MAGPIES

- Roadkill as good luck? Apparently, finding a dead crow on the road is considered so.
- Churchyards aren't considered safe havens for those who find a raven there. It's considered bad luck.
- One crow over a house is considered a bad omen, perhaps intimating a death to come. *A crow on the thatch, soon death lifts the latch.*
- In Wales, the black cat superstition is replaced by a single crow crossing your path leading to bad luck. However if a second crow joins his pal, it becomes good luck. *Two crows I see, good luck to me.*
- In New England, however, two crows flying from left to right across your path is considered bad luck.

(continued)

•In the darker ages, European peasants believed a quiet molting season meant that crows were gearing up to pay tribute to the devil with their discarded feathers.

•Although more often seen with pairs of doves, pairs of crows have been released at weddings. If the pair fly off as a duo, it is expected that the couple will have a long happy marriage. If the two birds fly away from each other, the newlyweds may soon part.

•In Chinese mythology, the number three is the number of goodness and light. A three-legged crow is believed to represent the sun, the ultimate embodiment of these characteristics.

•The size of a group of crows or magpies is thought to represent what is to come, as in the following:

One for sorrow, two for mirth,
Three for a wedding, four for a birth,
Five for silver, six for gold,
Seven for a secret not to be told.
Eight for heaven, nine for hell,
And ten for the devil's own sel'.

•If you aren't fond of a magpie counting fortunes, you can cast a spell of protection by making the sign of the cross, raising your hat to the bird, or spitting three times over your right shoulder, saying, "devil, devil, I defy thee."

•Because magpies didn't wear black to the crucifixion of Jesus, it is assumed that God has since cursed them.

•In Scotland, magpies were considered so evil that they

must have a drop of the devil's blood under their tongues.

- In Somerset, England, people would carry an onion with them for protection against magpies and crows.
- Also in Somerset, they took hat-tipping to ravens quite seriously, so as to appease the birds.
- Instead of the Bogeyman, Yorkshire children who were bad were scared with threats of the "great black bird" coming to take them away.
- Never steal a raven's eggs: it is thought to cause the death of a baby.
- King Arthur was supposed to have turned into a raven, clearing the birds of some bad press and giving them a royal air.
- Alexander the Great had two ravens sent from heaven to guide him out of the desert.
- "A House Divided Shall Not Stand." Not in England anyway. The Tower of London, home to ravens for a millennium, represents the crown of England. If the ravens ever leave the tower, then it will fall, and in turn, so goes the crown and country.
- In Wales, a raven perched on your house means prosperity to come.
- In Scotland, if a raven circles above the house, someone in the house will die.
- Rain can be predicted by rooks feeding close to their nests or on the streets in the morning. If they feed far from their nest, however, it should be a nice day.

(continued)

- When the old one died, a new landowner was to stand beneath the rookery and announce the news to the birds. The promise would be added that only he or his friends would be allowed to shoot the birds. However, if the new landowner did not perform this ceremony, the rooks would leave their home. This was considered a bad omen of financial downfall to come.

- In France, a priest gone bad is thought to become a crow, while an evil nun is thought to become a magpie.

- Greeks say "Go to the crows" as we say "Go to hell."

- For something thought impossible to do, the Romans say "to pierce a crow's eye."

- An Irish expression, "You'll follow the crows for it" means a person will miss something once it's gone.

- "I have a bone to pick with you" used to actually be "I have a crow to pick with you."

- Shooting crows seems to be a popular protection racket:

  To protect seed one should shoot rooks and carrion crows.

  To protect baby birds, shoot crows and magpies.

  And for protection for young lambs, ravens should be shot.

Birthday

- How important is the day of the week you were born? Most superstitious folks fall back on this telling nursery rhyme:

  Monday's child is fair of face;

  Tuesday's child is full of grace;

  Wednesday's child is full of woe;

  Thursday's child has far to go;

  Friday's child is loving and giving;

Saturday's child works hard for a living;
But the child born on the Sabbath day
is lucky, bonny, wise, and gay.

•It is believed that in order for a birthday wish to come true, all of the candles must be blown out on the first breath. Clearly, this is a task that gets more difficult as the years pass.

Blue   A blue bead kept on one's person can dispel the evil eye. Also, there is the old adage, "touch blue, your wish will come true"—although that's probably more in the "wishful thinking" category.

Bread   Both the breadmaker and the bread taker should be aware of these superstitions. It's unlucky to sing while baking bread, or to set a loaf on the table upside down after it's been prepared. It's more than just bad manners to leave a piece of bread uneaten on your plate; it can also bring bad luck, in addition to the ire of the cook. It's also best to choose one end from which to slice, as it's bad fortune to cut from both ends. Some might also make the sign of the cross on a loaf of bread before cutting into it the first time.

Brooms   A thoughtful housewarming gift, as a broom brought into a new dwelling means good luck. It's said to be bad luck to bring an old one when you move. When it comes to sweeping, however, neither a borrower nor a lender be—both practices bring bad luck. It's also bad luck to leave a broom standing on its bristles. A quick sweeping of the room of an unwanted guest, after he or she leaves, will ensure that they never return.

Butterfly   If the first butterfly of the season you see is all white, you will have good luck throughout the year.

Calendar   Both hanging up a calendar for the new year, or turning to a new month before the current month has passed is considered unlucky. Calendars should be hung on New Years day, or no later than January 7 (a lucky date), and calendar pages should be turned on the new date. (Don't pull off Oct. 31 unless it's now Nov. 1!)

Calf In some rural cultures it is believed that if the firstborn calf of the season is pure white, the winter will be harsh.

⊰ CAT SUPERSTITIONS ⊱

American:

- Seeing a white cat at night is bad luck.
- Seeing a white cat on the road is considered lucky.
- Good luck will come to you if you dream of a white cat.
- When you see a one-eyed cat, you can make a wish come true. Just spit on your thumb, stamp it in the palm of your hand, and make a wish.
- When moving into a new home, have the cat enter through the window instead of the door—so that it will never leave.
- A black cat crossing your path is considered bad luck.
- A cat washing itself on your doorstep means that clergy will come calling.

English:

- If a cat washes behind its ears, expect rain.
- If a cat is sleeping with all four paws tucked under his body, expect cold weather to come.
- When a cat's pupils get bigger, it will soon rain.
- Seeing a white cat on the way to school is considered bad luck. To prevent the bad luck, a person

must spit or turn away and make the sign of the cross.

- A cat sitting atop a tombstone means that the person buried below has been possessed by the devil.
- Two cats in a fight near a dying person, or over the grave of a recently deceased person, are supposedly the devil and an angel fighting for soul possession.
- Illness will never leave a house if a cat deserts it.
- In the early sixteenth century, a visitor had to kiss the family cat for good luck.

Scottish:

- A strange black cat on your porch leads to wealth.

Italian:

- If you hear a cat sneezing, it means good luck.
- In sixteenth century Italy, a sick man who had a black cat lying on his bed would shortly die.
- If the family cat refuses to stay inside the house, it's considered a bad omen. It is believed cats won't stay where there is illness.

Irish:

- If a black cat crosses a person's path by the light of the moon, a deadly epidemic will soon follow.
- Seventeen years bad luck is granted to a person who kills a cat.

French:

- It is considered bad luck to cross a stream while holding a cat.
- Accidental death follows after seeing a tortoiseshell cat.

(continued)

Dutch:

- In the Netherlands, cats are believed to be gossips, and so aren't allowed in rooms where private conversations are occurring.

Egyptian:

- In Egyptian mythology, cats are sacred to the goddess Isis. In honor of her, if a person killed a cat, he was put to death.

- Archaeologists have found cat cemeteries in Egypt.

Unknown or Multicultural Origins:

- In the seventeenth century, if a cat was washing its face, a storm was brewing.

- If the cat washed its face in front of a group of people, then the first person the cat looked at would soon get married.

- A black cat crossing one's path is good luck, not bad as thought in many other countries, including the United States.

- You can tell what direction a storm is coming from if you note what direction a cat's paw is pointing as it cleans its face.

- Seeing a white cat at night is not just bad luck, it's a harbinger of death.

- Cats are thought to suck the breath from newborns.

- A cat's pupils dilate when the tide is low and contract when it's high tide.

- When a cat lies on its ear, it's a sign of rain.

- A kitten born in May is thought to become a witch's cat.

•A cat that has been bought with money (instead of adopted) will never be a good mouser.

•If a cat sneezes once, it's going to rain.

•If a cat sneezes three times, the family will catch cold.

•Kicking a cat will cause you to develop rheumatism.

•Killing a cat is equal to sacrificing your soul to the devil.

Chimney Sweep   Fans of the 1964 Walt Disney film *Mary Poppins* know very well that it's good luck to shake hands with a chimney sweep.

Cigarette   It is considered unlucky to light three people's cigarettes with the same match.

Circle   The circle has long been regarded as a symbol of good luck and protection. Magick rituals are often done while the conjurer stands in a circle, which will protect him or her from evil influence.

Clock   If a clock that is broken should suddenly chime, it portends a coming death in the household.

Clover   Since four-leafed clovers are less common than other varieties, it is considered good luck to find and possess one. Even the symbol itself (living plant or otherwise) is considered a good-luck charm.

Coins   A coin with a hole in it is a potent good-luck charm and can be worn as an anklet, bracelet, or necklace. Other good luck charms are bent coins, or coins cast into wishing fountains. While finding money is a good omen to almost everyone, finding a coin face up, or from the year you were born is particularly lucky. It's lucky to keep a jar of pennies in your kitchen; and the turning of a silver coin in your pocket, at the sight of the full moon, can make a wish come true.

Bad omens associated with coins include keeping them in more than one pocket and picking up a coin that's *not* heads-up. If you're giving a wallet or a pocketbook as a gift, it's best to throw in a coin to prevent bad luck.

Cough   Some believe that a cough can be cured by taking a hair from the head of the afflicted and placing it between two slices of buttered bread. The sandwich is then fed to a dog while speaking the following: *Eat well you hound, may you be sick and I be sound.*

Clothing   While putting one's clothes on inside out is usually a signal of too little sleep or too much partying, should you happen to do so, it's good luck to wear the item that way for the rest of the day.

Corpse   While touching a corpse is considered lucky, removing a corpse from a home feet first, or by the back door, is a sure sign of misfortune to come.

Crickets   In the damned if you do, damned if you don't category is the humble cricket. Should a cricket find its way into your home, it is bad luck. However, killing the cricket would also lead to misfortune.

Crying   It is said that children who cry loud and long are destined to have long and fulfilling lives, which is probably of little comfort to the caregivers that have to listen. It's also lucky to cry at happy occasions like baby christenings and weddings. However, the tears of a mourner shed on a fresh grave, during a funeral ceremony, ensures that the spirit of the dead will never rest in peace.

Cutlery   It is considered bad luck to drop a knife on the floor, but this bad energy can be dispersed if someone else picks it up. An old nursery rhyme contends: *Knife falls, gentleman calls; fork falls, lady calls; spoon falls, baby squalls.*

⊰ DOG SUPERSTITIONS ⊱

- A howling dog at night means bad luck.

- A black dog is considered unlucky in some parts of the world.

- If a dog licks a newborn, the baby will always be a fast healer.

- Dogs are thought to be guides to the afterlife in both Egyptian and Eskimo cultures.

- Romans used "healer" dogs to lick the diseases out of people.

- If a dog howls by an open door, it is considered a death omen.

- A dog howling at the birth of a baby is supposed to signal an unhappy life for the child.

- Some believed that dogs were witches that took animal form; they howled when other witches were nearby.

- A dog howling three times in a row and then stopping is supposed to signal the moment of a death.

- A dog heard barking first thing in the morning is thought to be a sign of misfortune.

- In Ireland, a strange dog digging up your garden means illness or death is on the way.

- If a dog sleeps with its tail straight out and its paws turned up, bad news is on its way. The direction the tail is pointing indicates the direction the bad news will come from.

- A sure sign of good luck in England is to have a strange dog follow you.

(continued)

- A black-and-white dog crossing your path on the way to a meeting means good luck at the meeting.
- Newlyweds who have a dog run in between them is an indication of many fights to come.
- If a dog runs between a woman's legs, the husband should have reason to doubt her fidelity.
- If a dog runs and hides under a table, expect a strong thunderstorm to develop.
- If a dog eats grass, it is supposed to rain.
- A dog scratching for a long period also means rain to come.
- A dog rolling on the ground is yet another reason to expect rain.
- A person bitten by a wild dog should eat a sandwich consisting of hairs from the dog and rosemary.
- A hangover cure: "Eat the hair of the dog that bit you."
- Black poodles are used on gravestones of German clergy who didn't follow their religion too closely.
- The Roman goddess of the hunt, Diana, was thought to ride with spectral hounds who would find lost souls.
- Greeks thought dogs could foresee evil.
- Sometimes black dogs are thought to be embodiments of unquiet souls; but others are thought to be protective guides to travelers.
- Britain has tales of packs of ghost hounds running over the countryside. These hounds foretell death or disaster. To avoid spotting them, a person should

drop face down on the ground when they hear them coming.

- The black spectral dog of Britain is called the "barghest," and is considered to be a harbinger of death.
- In Scotland, a new friendship will follow a strange dog coming to your house.
- Seeing three white dogs together is considered good luck.
- A black dog that follows a person and refuses to be chased away is considered bad luck.
- Fishermen usually regard dogs as unlucky, so much so that they won't even mention the word "dog" while out at sea.
- Meeting a new dog, especially a Dalmatian, is thought to be good luck.
- A greyhound with a white spot on its forehead is considered good luck.
- A dog howling for no reason is thought to be howling at ghosts.

Doors   It is always advised to leave a place from the same door in which you entered.

Ears   If your right ear should itch it means that someone, somewhere is speaking well of you. Conversely, if your left ear itches, it could mean that someone, somewhere is speaking ill of you.

Easter   It is considered good luck to buy new clothes for the Easter holiday.

Elephants   The elephant has always been an adored symbol of good fortune. Trinkets and other statuary should face a doorway for the maximum release of good vibes and luck.

Fences   It is considered bad luck to shake hands across one. It's also unlucky to have one's fence blown down by the wind or have to crawl through one.

Fly   A single fly finding its way into your home is lucky, as is the dubious honor of one falling into your food or drink.

Friday, the 13th   There are many proposed theories as to why Friday, the 13th is considered unlucky, and there's a kernel of truth to them all. The number 13 is considered unlucky in many cultures. Some say the belief comes from Judas's betrayal of Christ, since he was the 13th guest at the Last Supper, still others refer to an older Norse myth of the death of the god Balder, when 12 gods met for a dinner party and the 13th was the trickster god Loki. Other bad associations with 13 include the gathering of a coven of 12 witches, the 13th member is said to be the devil.

⊰ FRIDAY, THE 13TH ⊱

Friday, the 13th is not a modern superstition. Dim views of the date can be found all through history. For example:

- Christians widely believe that there were only thirteen people present at the Last Supper (Christ and his twelve disciples), and that the thirteenth person, Judas, then betrayed Jesus.
- On Friday, the 13th of October 1307, Philip IV of France ordered the Knights Templar to be arrested and executed. This was done so Philip could confiscate the vast fortune of the Templars.

• The first Passover took place on Friday, the 13th, during which the angel of death descended to earth, though it was on the evening of Shabbat on the 14th of Nisan that the firstborn of Egypt were killed. Bear in mind that the Jewish calendar counts its days from sunset to sunset, so the deaths would technically have occurred on Friday the 13th. *(Exodus 12:6)*

• According to the Mayan calendar, the world will end on Friday, October 13, 4772. Many have miscalculated the Mayan end of days as occurring in 2012. But the writings at Palenque, a Mayan ruin near the Usumacinta River in the Mexican state of Chiapas, are the official record, and they give us a bit more time. According to this more accurate record we won't have to set all our affairs in order until October 13, 4772. Whew!

Gambling   Any sort of lucky charm is a good idea for the gambler; frankly they can use all the good fortune they can get. It's always lucky to play with someone else's cash or while seated on a handkerchief. As one might expect with games of chance, there are many more jinxes than aids. So, picking up cards with one's left hand; having your chips scattered about rather than in even piles; whistling while you play; or even seeing a card fall to the floor can all cause a run of bad luck.

Grasshopper   It is considered good luck to catch a glimpse of a grasshopper, or to find one in the home.

Hats   It's considered unlucky to wear a hat backward, or to place one on a table or bed.

Ham   In some cultures, it's considered good luck to eat ham on New Year's Day.

Hand   There is a belief, mostly among Christians, that Judas Iscariot was left-handed. Therefore left-handed people are believed to be "tainted," and serve as lightning rods for bad luck. On the other *hand*, one of the most common charms against evil, misfortune, and other woes is a hamsa hand.

⊰ HAMSA HAND (ARABIC) ⊱ OR HAMESH HAND (HEBREW)

An ancient amulet used for protection against the evil eye. The words hamsa and hamesh both mean "five" and refer to the digits on the hand. An alternative Islamic name for this charm is the hand of Fatima, a reference to Mohammed's daughter. Another Jewish name for it is the hand of Miriam, a reference to the sister of Moses and Aaron. Many of the commercial hamsa hands include symbols from a number of world religions and spiritual beliefs, apparently going on the assumption that there is no such thing as too much good luck.

Hearse   As with an ambulance, seeing a hearse go by is a reminder that death is near. While it is regarded as good luck to see an empty hearse, it is said to be unlucky to watch a funeral procession or count how many cars are part of it.

Horseshoes   Beliefs on the nature of lucky horseshoes differ throughout the world. In much of Europe, they are hung with the rungs pointing downward. In parts of Ireland and in the United States, they are hung with the rungs pointing upward to ensure the luck doesn't "run out."

Itching   Lucky itches include the right eye and the left palm, meaning that you'll soon come into money. An itchy right palm can mean a debt to come. An itchy nose may mean you're either due for a fight or may kiss a fool—the choice is yours!

Ivy   It is believed that ivy growing on the walls of a building will protect it from bad luck and evil spirits.

Kettle   While the gentle humming of a boiling teakettle can keep evil spirits at bay, it's considered bad luck to have the spout pointed toward a wall.

Knife   Clearly it is bad luck, and dangerous, to hand a knife to another person with the blade facing them. So is finding a knife, or having it stick in the floor after you've dropped it.

Knocking   Hearing a knocking sound can mean there will soon be a death in the household. Of course, it can also mean that there's someone at the door.

Ladders   While it's common knowledge that it's unlucky to walk underneath a ladder, it is also considered bad fortune to pass an item through the rungs of a ladder, or to scale one that has an uneven number of steps.

Ladybug   The humble ladybug is a good omen. One that lands in your hand is a sign of good weather to come. It is considered unlucky to kill one; they're often associated with the Virgin Mary.

Laughing   It is considered unlucky to laugh before breakfast or before praying.

Mirror   While it's commonly known that breaking a mirror will bring seven years of bad luck, breaking one while it's still on the wall is considered an omen of death.

Nail   Both finding a nail and keeping one as a charm are considered lucky. But it is bad luck to lay a new carpet over an old nail in the floor.

⚔ OWL SUPERSTITIONS ⚔

From the tiny elf owl *(Micrathene whitneyi)* to the large and powerful Eurasian eagle-owl *(Bubo bubo)*, owls are part of the mythology and superstitions of nearly every country. The birds live, on average, more than twenty years (some considerably longer), and though they have sometimes been domesticated as pets they are always predators and are always to be respected for their sharp talons, powerful beaks, deep cunning, and eerie call.

Owl superstitions are many and varied.* Here are just a few of the hundreds of different owl beliefs from around the world:

1. According to ancient Afghani legend the owl gave Man flint and iron to make fire—in exchange, Man gave the owl his feathers.

2. In Swahili, East Africa, people believe the owl brings illness to children.

3. Throughout Africa the owl is believed to be the familiar and messenger of sorcerers and witches.

4. In Britain it has long been thought that the owl is the only living creature that can abide a ghost.

5. To the Arabs the owl is a bird of ill omen, the embodiment of evil spirits that carries off children at night.

6. The Aborigines of Australia believe bats represent the souls of men and owls the souls of women.

7. The ancient Babylonians used owl amulets to protect women during childbirth.

*Information on owl superstitions graciously provided by Deane Lewis of owlpages.com.

8. In Brittany seeing an owl on the way to the harvest is a sign of a good yield.

9. In China the owl is associated with lightning (because it brightens the night) and with the drum (because it breaks the silence). Placing owl effigies in each corner of the home protect it against lightning.

10. Hearing an owl hooting near your house also foretells death, according to countless cultures around the world.

11. A European belief of the late Middle Ages held that if an owl hoots during a burial service, the deceased is bound to rise from the grave and haunt the living. Likewise if an owl lands on the roof of an abandoned house then it's proof that a ghost dwells there.

12. In India it is believed that seizures in children can be cured with a broth made from owl eyes.

13. In Ireland if an owl enters the house must be killed at once, for if it flies away it will take the luck of the house with it.

14. In Hebrew lore the owl represents blindness, desolation and is unclean.

15. In Russia: Hunters carry owl claws so that, if they are killed, their souls can use them to climb up to Heaven.

Penny   It's considered good luck to pick up a penny from the street. However, the penny must be heads-up for this to apply.

Pig   A lucky animal. Any symbol or ornaments of it are also considered lucky. However, some fishermen will never utter the word "pig" while on a voyage—it would spoil the catch.

Pigeon   The appearance of a single pigeon on the roof or chimney of a home is sometimes considered to be a harbinger of death.

Pins   If you find a pin it's considered lucky; more so if the pin is bent. As the old adage states: *See a pin and pick it up, all the day you'll have good luck. See a pin, let it lay, and your luck will pass away.*

Praying Mantis   It's good luck to find a praying mantis, but very bad luck to harm or injure one. Any gardener can attest to the validity of this superstition, killing these insects can spell bad luck for your garden as well as yourself.

Rabbit's Foot   It is a commonly held belief that a rabbit's foot is a potent symbol of good luck—for the rabbit, not so much.

Sailing   For ships at sea, it's considered unlucky to change the name of a vessel, not break the wine bottle when it's christened, begin a voyage on a Friday, and stepping on board the first time with your left foot first.

Sailors   Many sailors believe that having tattoos will bring them good luck. In the days when corporal punishment was more common, sailors often covered their backs with religious symbols such as the cross, which they hoped would avert the lash.

Salt   It is considered bad luck to spill salt. Bad fortune can only be dispersed by immediately throwing a bit over one's left shoulder. While some believe the root of this belief stems from Judas' spilling of the salt during the Last Supper, there is little evidence to confirm it. In ancient times, salt was a very expensive commodity and spilling any was simply a matter of bad economics, as well as bad luck.

Sneezing   Long ago it was believed that all bodily functions ceased when you sneezed, so this was a fine opportunity for the devil to enter a waiting body. A "gezunheit" or "god bless you" was given as a wish to protect against evil influence. An old nursery rhyme also states:

> Sneeze on Monday, sneeze for danger;
>
> sneeze on Tuesday, kiss a stranger;
>
> sneeze on Wednesday, get a letter;
>
> sneeze on Thursday, something better;
>
> sneeze on Friday, sneeze for woe;
>
> sneeze on Saturday, a journey to go;
>
> sneeze on Sunday, your safety seek,
>
> for Satan will have you the rest of the week.

Spiders   Despite their fearsome reputation, spiders are recognized as immensely valuable to the ecosystem. If not for the humble spider, we would literally be up to our armpits in flying and crawling insects. An old English rhyme states: *If you wish to live and thrive, let a spider run alive.*

There's also a Creole rhyme about spiders:

> Araignée du matin—chagrin;
>
> araignée du midi—plaisir;
>
> araignée du soir—espoir.

which means *A spider seen in the morning is a sign of grief; a spider seen at noon, of joy; a spider seen in the evening, of hope.* It was also believed that if a spider fell onto your clothes that you would soon come into money.

Umbrella   Opening an umbrella inside is considered a sure way to bring bad luck.

Weddings   Few aspects of life are filled with more superstition than the wedding. The adage of going into marriage with:

something old, something new,

something borrowed, and something blue . . .

actually ends with: *and a silver sixpence in her shoe.* It's also lucky for the bride to wear a borrowed veil, and there are endless associations with the color of the dress the bride might choose.

Some consider it bad luck for a bride to make her own wedding dress, another example of the fates punishing those deemed too confident. Other brides will not wear both their veil and dress until the ceremony itself. Even the *least* superstitious will refuse to see her groom until the ceremony. Some believe the giver of the third present opened at the bridal shower will soon give birth. Some brides gather the ribbons from their shower gifts to use as a makeshift bouquet for the rehearsal. When the bride is ready to leave home for the ceremony, a last look in the mirror is sure to bring her luck. The day of one's wedding also needs careful consideration: *Monday for health, Tuesday for wealth, Wednesday best of all, Thursday for losses, Friday for crosses, Saturday for no luck at all.*

Things to avoid on one's wedding day include open graves, pigs, lizards, a cock's crow, a monk, or a nun. To add to the ignominy of being a bridesmaid, the position's original purpose was to dress like the bride in the hopes of confusing any evil spirits that might come to the wedding as an uninvited guest.

— *Chapter Eleven* —
UFOS AND ALIEN ENCOUNTERS

SINCE PREHISTORIC MAN FIRST RAISED his shaggy head to stare at the sky, there have been strange wonders shining above. Stars and moons, asteroids and comets—and *other* things. Things that, perhaps, are not supposed to be seen in the skies. Objects that follow no natural path set by the mechanics of gravity and planetary rotation. Objects that flash with light and move at speeds no naturally occurring phenomenon can match—and which no man-made object can rival.

Since man was first able to record his observations by painting on cave walls he documented strange lights in the sky, strange craft, and even strange beings. References to bizarre flying craft appear in both historical and holy records of nearly every culture, and in modern times, everyone from NASA astronauts to the man on the street has recorded phenomena of this kind on videotape. Consider this observation found on a piece of papyrus dated to the dynasty of Egypt's Thutmose III (1504–1450 B.C.E.):

> *A circle of fire coming in the sky, noiseless, one rod long with its body and one rod wide. After some days these things became more numerous, shining more than the brightness of the sun. (Translated by Prince Boris de Rachelwiltz (d.1997). Rachelwiltz's translation, though widely distributed, was never officially published.)*

Along the same lines, in the Old Testament Book of Ezekiel, the prophet recounts his encounter with something strange in the skies. He wrote:

> *4. I looked, and behold, a stormy wind came out of the north, a great cloud, with flashing lightning, and a brightness around it, and out of its midst as it were glowing metal, out of the midst of the fire.*
>
> *5. Out of its midst came the likeness of four living creatures. This was their appearance: They had the likeness of a man.*
>
> *6. Everyone had four faces, and each one of them had four wings.*
>
> *7. Their feet were straight feet; and the soles of their feet were like the soles of a calf's foot; and they sparkled like burnished brass.*

And, most significantly:

> *16. The appearance of the wheels and their work was like a beryl: and the four had one likeness; and their appearance and their work was as it were a wheel within a wheel. . . .*
>
> *27. I saw as it were glowing metal, as the appearance of fire within it all around, from the appearance of his waist and upward; and from the appearance of his waist and downward I saw as it were the appearance of fire, and there was brightness around him.*

Biblical scholars argue that these "wheels" are not spinning saucers but rather a metaphor for the continuous cycle of life in God's universe. Others have suggested that Ezekiel was merely dreaming. But the images he describes are compelling and familiar to anyone studying the matter of UFOs.

Accounts of this kind pop up in every culture, all throughout history.

Who are they? What are they? Where do they come from? Why are they visiting Earth? What do they want?

Every time an unknown object is seen in the skies these same questions are raised, often to be immediately countered by attempts at logical explanations from supposed authorities. We are told that the objects are weather balloons; they're clouds reflecting the lights of distant cities; they're normal terrestrial aircraft; they're swamp gas. They are, according to the government, the military, NASA, the weather bureau, and scholarly skeptics, just about anything *except* visitors from beyond. And to be fair, a goodly number of sightings probably are swamp gas, satellites, or something boringly normal. Probably most are.

Not all, however, can be so easily explained. Especially when presidents and astronauts also report sightings. Former Soviet President Mikhail Gorbachev made this dramatic statement: "The phenomenon of UFOs does exist, and it must be treated seriously."[47]

At a speech at the University of Toronto,[48] Paul Hellyer, Canada's Defense Minister from 1963–67, made his country's position very clear: "UFOs are as real as the airplanes that fly over your head."

Closer to home, former President Jimmy Carter (and five-time Nobel Peace Prize nominee) said, "I don't laugh at people anymore when they say they've seen UFOs. It was the darndest thing I've ever seen. It was big, it was very bright, it changed colors, and it was about the size of the moon." He added, "I am convinced that UFOs exist because I have seen one."[49]

That's a hard comment to shake off, especially when Mercury astronaut L. Gordon Cooper included this statement in his open letter to the United Nations: "I believe that these extraterrestrial vehicles and their crews are visiting this planet from other planets, which are a little more technically advanced than we are on Earth."[50]

If notables of this caliber believe in UFOs, why is the government mum on the subject? Perhaps the simplest answer was given by former U.S. Senator Richard B. Russell, Jr. after he sighted a UFO while on a train in Russia on October 4, 1955.[51] When a flood of requests came via mail from newsmen and journalists around the world asking him to comment on his experiences, he said, "Permit me to acknowledge your letters relative to reports that have come to you regarding aerial objects seen in Europe last year. . . . I have discussed this matter with the affected agencies of the government, and they are of the

---

47. *Soviet Youth Magazine,* May 4, 1990.
48. September 25, 2005.
49. A remark made at the Southern Governors Conference while campaigning in 1976.
50. The letter was presented to a U.N. panel discussion on UFOs and E.T.s in New York, in 1985, which was chaired by then U.N. Secretary General Kurt Waldheim.
51. At the time he was a U.S. Senator and Head of Senate Armed Services Committee

opinion that it is not wise to publicize this matter at this time. I regret very much that I am unable to be of assistance to you."

When not outright denying the existence of UFOs, the government typically relies on the stance that some information is not appropriate for sharing with the public. They hint that these objects are top-secret test craft; they float the phrase "national security." They say, ultimately, nothing.

What they have never been able to do, however, is disprove UFOs. In fact their devotion to secrecy, misinformation, and disinformation have just fueled the fires of curiosity.

That UFOs exist is not in question—not if you understand that the key word here is *unidentified*. Those objects whose natures have not been satisfactorily explained away remain unidentified, unknown, and compellingly mysterious. There are hundreds of objects seen in the skies all over the world whose exact nature, origin, and purpose has never been clearly explained away. That much is irrefutable. There are plenty of photographs, plenty of bits of film and video showing strange objects or balls of light moving in ways inconsistent with aerodynamics as we know it. The real problem is that everyone has a theory, and just taking into account the theories of those who believe that these are indeed alien craft, the believed nature of these craft ranges from your standard E.T. visitors to interdimensional explorers, and even time travelers. Many hundreds of persons have stepped forward to claim that they have been abducted by aliens. Some claim to have been implanted with microscopic devices of alien technology—perhaps tracking devices of some kind. The weight of circumstantial and eyewitness evidence is monumental and certainly too substantial to dismiss as swamp gas. Hard evidence is more difficult to find but there are a lot of eyes on the ground (well, on the skies) and many within the UFO community feel that it's only a matter of time before irrefutable proof is had.

Debate over the nature of UFOs is not just confined to whether they are real or not, but there is layer upon layer of theory about government cover-ups, alien-human collaboration, races living in hiding within our society, and much more. There are, in fact, so many theories, that no one theory has a chance to shine out as the leading contender as the most plausible explanation. To this is added the complication that many folks—especially over the last twenty-odd years—have changed their opinions from a belief in alien visitation to a belief that shadowy departments within our own government are experimenting with radical new technologies (which may or may not be retro-engineered from crashed UFOs).

No single volume (let alone a single chapter) can gather together every bit of UFO theory, fact, and speculation, but *Cryptopedia* has collected the most significant talking points and need-to-know terms.

Abductee   Any human or animal taken by an alien.

Abductions   The act of taking humans or animals for the purpose of study. This is a key phrase in Ufology as many hundreds of persons claimed to have been taken by aliens (or something they perceive as them) and been subjected to a variety of tests including ova harvesting, sperm collection, tissue sampling, probes, and a variety of surgical procedures, such as the implantation of minute devices.

◄ ABDUCTION EXPERIENCE ► CLASSIFICATION

In an attempt to provide a useful model for general research, Dr. Richard Butler, a noted researcher in the field of UFO abductions, classified the experiences of his subjects into five primary categories:

- •AE-1: Lucid Dream: These are dream experiences deliberately generated into a subject's unconscious by some means other than abduction.

(continued)

ALIEN AT MY WINDOW
Shareen Knight

•AE-2: Techno/Telepathic Lucid Dream: These dreams are believed to be generated by some external force such as alien science. In these dreams the subjects find that normal dreams collapse and are intruded upon by very specific images. Upon waking, subjects often report having seen a glowing circle on the ceiling of their bedrooms (2–3 feet in diameter) and/or a shaft of cohesive energy leading from the ceiling to their beds. As they watch the beam retracts and the circle vanishes.

•AE-3: Psi/Bio Energy Field Extraction: This is an experience similar to out-of-body experience (OOBE) but is forcibly initiated by some external power. As with the Telepathic Lucid Dreaming the subjects are aware of a beam of cohesive light, and it is along this that they travel. It is during this kind of event that abductees experience memory loss and, quite often, missing segments of time.

- •AE-4: Physical Abduction: The actual removal of a person (body and spirit) to another location using alien technology. In some cases false memories are implanted in order to account for the loss of time.

- •AE-5: Past Life Recall: These are the rarest of the abduction experiences and are often recalled only through regression hypnotherapy. In these cases the abductees often recall being taken to another place, such as aboard a spacecraft or to a secret base on another planet (the moon and Mars are common) or even to an underground military facility on earth.

Adamski, George (1891–1965)   Controversial abductee who claims that during the 1950s he was taken aboard a spacecraft where he met humans from other planets of our solar system (Mars, Saturn, Venus, and so on). He claims to be an eyewitness to cities on the dark side of the moon. Though he produced pieces of a large number of photographic documentation, much of it has been discredited.

Agharians (also **Aghartians)**   One of several races of humanoids that may be related to alien species. These Agharians, variously described as being essentially Nordic or Asian, are supposed to have established an underground kingdom beneath the Gobi desert some thousands of years ago. The Agharians maintain contact with alien races on other planets. After moving there they began interacting with alien races and have possibly interbred.

Agriglyphs (see CROP CIRCLES)

Alf Alien Life Forms.

Alien Bases Locations where aliens are believed to have established permanent landing sites. There are rumors of such bases in Colorado, Nevada, New Mexico, and Utah.

Alien Races The collective name given to the various presumed races of beings from other planets and/or other dimensions believed to have visited earth.

Alpha-Draconians One of the many reptilian races presumed to originally have come from earth and settled in the Alpha Draconis star system. Having come from earth, they maintain a proprietary claim on the planet and will do whatever is required to regain dominance.

Altairians A reptilian race from Altair. Altairians are believed to interact with Grays and the human military.

Amphibians A hybrid race of humans and Reptilians, the Amphibians are semi-aquatic, perhaps less evolved, and more openly hostile (even predatory) than most other alien races. (See also Saurians and Reptilians.)

Anakim, the (see **Elds**).

Andreasson, Betty An early abductee, Betty Andreasson (b.1937) claims to have been taken repeatedly by robotic Grays who are controlled by humanoid higher beings. She is a conference speaker and author of the books *The Andreasson Affair* (1979), *The Watchers* (1990), and *The Watchers II* (1995).

Apro   Aerial Phenomena Research Organization, one of the oldest established UFO groups. It was founded in 1952 by Jim Lorenzen (1922–1986) and Corel Lorenzen (1928–1988); located in Tucson, Arizona.

Area 33   A research area of Los Alamos National Laboratories. Originally used for explosives testing, it has since been converted to lower security scientific activities, including radiotelescopes. Though generally not considered to be a hotspot in the world of UFO studies, an Internet rumor kicked up some years ago claiming that alien artifacts were being stored underground at the site.

Area 51   Also called Dreamland (Data, Repository, Establishment, and Maintenance Land) is a highly classified military installation situation that has been one of the hotspots of the UFO controversy for decades. Located in a corner of the Nevada Test Site, spy planes and stealth aircraft were engineered there, as well as technology for the Strategic Defense Initiative ("Star Wars"). In 1985, residents began hearing heavy rumbling sounds similar to earthquakes and spotted unusual triangle-shaped aircraft flying at unbelievable speeds. As the story was digested in the press, a back-check found an unusual and otherwise unexplained item on the defense budget next which simply read: "Aurora." UFO theorists believe that the government was building supersonic aircraft based on alien technology. Whether this technology was retro-engineered from recovered wreckage or was somehow obtained from aliens is in some debate.

Arnold, Kenneth (1915–1984)   A native of Washington state who observed nine disc-shaped objects flying over the Cascade Mountains on June 25, 1947. As a direct result of his description, the term "flying saucer" was coined. Four days later he saw a second batch of saucers over the La Grande Valley in Oregon, and this time there were approximately 20–25 of them.

Aryans   Nordic humans, or humanoids, who were reportedly abducted by reptilian aliens (Reptoids), genetically altered, given implants, and returned to earth.

Astral Ship   A craft created through mental power and force of will in which an astral body can travel through the astral plane.

ATIC   The Air Technical Intelligence Center at Wright-Patterson Air Force Base located in Dayton, Ohio, which oversaw Project Blue Book. In its 1948 top-secret assessment of the matter, ATIC concluded that UFOs were very likely alien spacecraft. This has since been strenuously denied.

Atlans   A group or race of generally benevolent humans believed by some Ufologists to inhabit a gigantic set of caverns beneath Brazil and surrounding areas. Atlans are believed to be the same race as the founders, and former inhabitants, of Atlantis (the Atlanteans). Other theories hold that though the present occupants of these caves are called Atlans, they are not genetic relations to the more celebrated Atlantean race and are merely descendants of other humans who found and occupied these caves.

Bedroom Visitors   Aliens that are sighted at night while invading human households.

Bell, Art (b.1945)   Former host of the "Dreamland" radio show on UFOs and the paranormal (now hosted by Whitley Strieber). Bell has often been labeled a "conspiracy theorist," but is well-regarded throughout the community of UFO researchers.

Bellatrax   The star system believed to be the home of the smallest race of Grays (see Grays), whose average height is about three to four feet.

Bender, Albert K. L.   The former editor of a UFO periodical called *Space Review,* which ceased publication following threats from "men in dark suits."

Bender went on to write about these intimidators in his book: *Flying Saucers and the Three Men in Black* (1963).

Berlitz, Charles (1914–2003)   Noted author of *The Philadelphia Experiment* (1979) and other significant writings on strange phenomena. For more on the Philadelphia Experiment see THE RAINBOW PROJECT in this chapter.

Bernarians   One of the lesser-known alien races, originating from the region of Bernard's Star. (See the ORANGE.)

Black Projects   A term used by governments to classify ultrasensitive projects essential to national security. Knowledge of project details are on a severely restricted need-to-know basis, and the general release of these details would result in catastrophic harm to governments or security. Among the UFO community, it is believed that the government is aware of them but considers all information, experimentation, contact, and product development to be top secret. A companion theory is that the government either believes (or claims to believe) that revealing knowledge of UFOs would cause hysteria, despite a number of national Harris Polls (among others) indicating that the majority of the population already believes in UFOs *and* believes that the government is covering it up.

Blanchard, William (1916–1966)   The colonel at the Roswell base who gave the go-ahead for the press release stating that the government had recovered debris from a downed UFO. This was almost instantly recanted and later obstinately refuted.

Blue Book, Project   Launched in early 1952, Project Blue Book was the last "official" investigation into UFO activity. It was dedicated to assessing reports of UFOs and determining if they existed, and if so, whether they presented a threat. It is generally believed in the UFO community that Blue Book was also interested in determining whether alien technology could be adapted for use by the U.S. military. Blue Book was closed in 1969 after reaching findings in the now infamous Condon Report that UFOs did not exist, or so the official story goes. However, a rumor persists that one of its members personally sighted a UFO and filed a report. Mysteriously, his report vanished from government records. In 1973, one of the Blue Book investigators, Dr. J. Allen Hynek, continued his research as part of the private sector and founded the Center for UFO Studies. Hynek is also notable for the creation of the numbered levels of alien encounters, one of which became the inspiration for the film *Close Encounters of the Third Kind*.

Blues (also **Star Warriors**)   An alien race similar in many respects to the Grays (large heads, almond-shaped eyes, and so on) who are apparently nonviolent and benevolent. Among the Hopi Indians of northern New Mexico they are known as "Star warriors." Much of the information about the Blues comes from the writings and teaching of the Hopi/Apache dancer Robert Morningsky, who claims to have made repeated contact with them. Morningsky claims that the Blues arrived shortly after the Grays. They came to warn the U.S. Government not to enter into dealings with the other race. The Blues were ignored, and the Grays, apparently, took offense at this attempted interference. Thereafter, the Blues went into hiding.

Blue Paper, Project   The government's more covert post-Blue Book investigations into UFO activity.

Booteans   A potentially destructive and hostile Reptilian race from the Bootes system, which is believed to be involved in the infiltration of human society with implant devices.

Boylan, Richard (b.1939)   A resident of Sacramento, California, who reported UFO sightings over Groom Lake.

Bronk, Detlev (1897–1975)   One of the men believed to have been part of the MJ-12 project. Bronk, a physiologist and biophysicist was chairman of the

National Research Council, a member of the Medical Advisory Board of the Atomic Energy Commission, and along with Vannevar Bush, a scientific advisor to President Truman. Bronk is often credited as being the doctor who performed the autopsies on the four small, human-like beings recovered from the Roswell crash.

Brown, Thomas Townsend (1905–1985)   A scientist actively working on methods of making saucer-shaped objects fly, using a variety of means other than nuclear or fossil fuels.

Bullard, Thomas E. (b.1949)   A well-known scholarly archivist of UFO incidents and findings. His compilation of abduction case histories, *The Sympathic Ear* (1995, The Fund for UFO Research), is regarded as a landmark book.

Burrowers   A mutant offshoot of the Saurians who live like moles beneath the earth in tunnels they've burrowed with their own bodies. Though generally not hostile, the Burrowers will attack intruders who enter their caves.

Bush, Dr. Vannevar (1890–1974)   Another alleged member of the MJ-12, who was also President Truman's scientific advisor during World War II and into the 1940s.

Byrd, Admiral Richard E. (1888–1957)   One of history's greatest naval pilots and early transatlantic fliers, Byrd was the first person to fly over the North Pole (in 1926). Some Ufologists believe that Byrd found an entrance to the hollow inner core of the earth while exploring the South Pole as part of the secret government mission called Operation Highjump. Debate still rages about the veracity or spuriousness of the "hollow earth theory."

Carswell Air Force Base   A Texas base where a very well-documented sighting took place on February 4, 1954. Control-tower personnel reported seeing a craft with elliptical wings, a long fuselage, and a stabilizer with no visible engines.

Capenter, John (b.1948) A Ufologist specializing in reports of alien abductions.

Cash, Betty A self-declared abductee who filed suit, unsuccessfully, against the U.S. Government, claiming that the UFO was actually a U.S. secret military craft. Cash was one of three people involved in the Cash-Landrum case in 1980.

Cash-Landrum Case In late 1980 in Huffman, Texas, Betty Cash (1930–1998), Vickie Landrum (b.1923), and her grandson Colby Landrum (b. 1973), were abducted by a diamond-shaped craft. It laid down a barrier of fire, forcing them to stop their car. They got out to observe the craft, with Betty Cash walking ahead to take a closer look. After watching for several minutes, a fleet of unmarked black helicopters arrived and chased the object out of sight. Shortly after, the three witnesses returned home and began to suffer severe nausea, diarrhea, and vomiting; all received sunburns. Cash maintained that the craft itself was a government device and filed suit for damages, but ultimately lost the case. (See Project Snowbird.)

Cathie, Bruce (b.1930) A pilot for New Zealand Air who claims to have discovered a worldwide system of grids—similar in ways to the longitude and latitude lines—used by UFOs for navigation. Cathie wrote about his theories in his books, *Anti-Gravity and the World Grid, Energy Grid,* and recently published software allowing anyone to plot these WORLDGRIDS™ on a map of any area in the world.

Cattle Mutilations Throughout the world there have been reports (well-documented by photos and examinations) of cattle that have been killed and strangely mutilated, left on the farms where they were raised. The bodies had been exsanguinated (drained of blood), and, despite the savagery of the wounds, there was no incidental blood surrounding their corpses. The wounds inflicted appear to have been made by some unusual method, possibly surgical lasers.

As the mutilations predate the development of surgical lasers of sufficient potency and portability, theorists have suggested that aliens are the culprits. There have been scores of theories as to why aliens would conduct such experiments.

CAUS (Citizens Against UFO Secrecy)   A nonprofit organization set up to urge governments to open their files and share their knowledge and information about UFOs and alien contact. CAUS cites the Freedom of Information Act (FOIA) in their cases. So far Citizens Against UFO Secrecy has met with little real success.

Cetians (Tau Cetians)   A race of extraterrestrial humans (or humanoids) from the Tau Ceti star system similar in appearance to medieval Mediterraneans, but with slightly pointed ears, broader noses, and an average height of about 5.5 feet.

Chameleon   Reptilian aliens with theriomorphic abilities (meaning that they can deliberately change their physical appearance). This shapeshifter ability is believed to be the result of deliberate genetic alteration and breeding programs. This theriomorphy is accomplished by technosis (the shifting of molecules to form new patterns). Some theorists, however, contend that the apparent change in appearance is not an actual physical change, but merely a holographic projection.

Chupacabra   El Chupacabra translates as "sucker of goats." It is a bizarre being that has three powerful claws on each hand, a ruff of tall spines running from skull to tailbone, mottled skin, and a voracious appetite. Throughout Latin America there have been countless reports of a strange creature—or race of creatures—that viciously attacks livestock and drinks their blood and other vital fluids. Because goats were among the first known victims of this beast, the monster earned its nickname.

The Chupacabra sightings began shortly after a series of UFO sightings mostly over Mexico. Some fringe groups insist that aliens have—intentionally or accidentally—released an extraterrestrial predator animal, which is now breeding and attacking terrestrial animals. This idea was explored briefly in an episode of the TV series, *The X-Files*, and in a few direct-to-video horror films. In UFO circles such creatures are referred to as Anomalous Biological Entities (UBEs). The earliest sightings of the Chupacabra were in Puerto Rico, beginning in the early 1990s. From 2000 to 2004 there have been nearly 4,000 cases of unexplained animal mutilations in that small island territory.

Close Encounters (CE rating)   (See HYNEK CLASSIFICATION SYSTEM and VALLEE CLASSIFICATION SYSTEM.)

Communion   A book by noted horror author Whitley Strieber in which he recounts his real-life abduction by unknown beings. In Strieber's earlier writings he seems certain that the abductions were perpetrated by aliens; but, more recently, he leans toward a more terrestrial and *governmental* explanation. The book was followed by a number of very well-written best-selling sequels. A movie, *Communion*, starring Christopher Walken, was released in 1989. Strieber maintains the Web site *Unknown Country* (www.unknowncountry. com), which openly discusses abduction and other related phenomena, and he has a Webcast radio show, *Dreamland*, every Saturday.

Condon, Edward   Author of the 1969 report, *Scientific Study of Unidentified Flying Objects*, which was biased against UFO belief. It contributed to the USAF's goal of shutting down Project Bluebook and, thereby, closed the public out of further government-sponsored research into the subject.

Cooper, Leroy Gordon   One of the original seven Mercury astronauts, and a major supporter of UFO beliefs.[52] Cooper claims to have seen and photographed a UFO and openly criticized the U.S. government for maintaining a coverup.

---

52. His comments are quoted from his obituary on CNN.com Monday, October 4, 2004.

Crop Circles   Crop circles, or agriglyphs, are strange, and often rather beautiful patterns that appear in fields around the world. Their nature, purpose, and origin are unknown. The UFO community generally believes them to be the work of aliens, though why they would be leaving such symbols is anyone's guess.

The first modern agriglyphs appeared in Warminster, England, on August 12, 1972. The event was reported by Bryce Bond and Arthur Shuttlewood. The circle was approximately 30 feet in diameter. Since then there have been approximately 10,000 such marks left in twenty-nine countries around the world. Some circles are just that, while others depict mathematical symbols, patterns, illustrations, and more. They range in size from fairly small (a few meters across) to massive (.75 mile).

Some recent crop circles have clearly been the work of industrious pranksters; but many agriglyphs are too geometrically perfect, and appeared in too short a time, to be the work of jokers. Also, circles made by pranksters always show marks of boards and other tools used to bend down the plants; whereas those made by the unknown "circlemakers" leave no traces as to how they're made.

In recent years strange small balls of light have been seen at the sites similar to the will o' the wisp from folklore; they have been spotted by eyewitnesses as well as video cameras. Also, a sound similar to a cricket's warble has been recorded in and around these areas. When analyzed by NASA's Jet Propulsion Laboratory, the sound was measured as 100 bpm (beats per minute) and valued at a frequency of 5.2 kHz; the upshot being that the sound was mechanical in nature.

CUFOS   The Center for UFO Studies, established by Dr. Allen Hynek and based in Evanson, Illinois. CUFOS was set up after NICAP was dissolved.

Dark Side Hypothesis   A collection of theories formed by John Lear, a Lockheed L-1011 captain, famous for his revelations about aerial phenomena and UFOs. The major claims of the Dark Side Hypothesis are:

•The U.S. Government has collected wreckage from dozens of UFO crashes.

•In 1962 the U.S. government launched Project Redlight, whose mission is to retro-engineer alien technology and/or learn how to fly recovered craft. These experiments were carried out at Area 51.

•Area 51 has since fallen under alien control.

•The U.S. government was complicit in the abduction of a set number of humans, but once the aliens exceeded that number there was a violent conflict during which forty-four top human scientists were killed. A Delta Force team sent in to rescue those scientists was nearly wiped out.

•During the 1980s a truce was worked out between the aliens and the U.S. Government and the two parties are once more working together.

A secret group within the U.S. government is overseeing the ongoing program of abductions, and abductees are being implanted with devices that, when triggered, will bring them under total control.

Disinformation   A strategy used by many governments to deliberately place false information into the hands of the opposition and weaken the credibility of those persons or groups trying to investigate secrets or present findings. Considering the many contradictory stories and theories regarding UFOs, it seems likely that a campaign of disinformation has been in force for some time.

Dracos (also Mothmen)   The ruling elite of the Reptilians whose nickname, "the Mothmen" comes from the fact that they have leathery wings, similar to dragon wings. Not surprisingly, they're also known as the dragon race (and in fact, *dracul* is the Romanian word for dragon). Some believe that this race of aliens inspired all of human cultures' many myths and legends of dragons.

Draco-Borgs   Alien Reptilians enhanced with cybernetic equipment.

Drake-Equation This is a statistical evaluation, which supports the likelihood that intelligent life may exist in the universe.

Dwarfs These are humanoid creatures—possibly aliens or alien-human hybrids—believed to live in underground caverns throughout the Midwest and Southwest United States. Some reports suggest that these are Grays.

EBE Extraterrestrial Biological Entities. Within the UFO community this is the most common acronym used to describe an alien being.

Edom Electronic Dissolution of Memory, a term used to describe the UFO-related phenomenon of "missing time."

Element 115 An as-yet unknown element that Robert Lazer allegedly examined while working on UFO wreckage at Area 51 in Nevada. The element is apparently crucial to anti-gravity technology.

Els Els (short for Elder Races) are a race of alien giants presumed to have originated in the Orion group. Many believe that the Els are destined to fight an apocalyptic battle against the Reptilian races. A race of giants, Els are believed to have helped build the pyramids.

E.T. Acronym for extraterrestrial entity, or alien.

Fire in the Sky A motion picture based on the Travis Walton abduction case that was criticized by many Ufologists for deviating too far from the true account given in the book.

Flying Discs An early nickname given to some UFOs because of their round and mostly flat shape.

Flying Saucer A term coined by newspapers in 1947 following Kenneth Arnold's famous daytime sighting of nine UFOs in the Northwest. Arnold had described their movements through the sky by comparing them to the movements of a saucer skipping across the surface of a lake. Interestingly, the

UFO OVER LAKE David Croston

crafts seen by Arnold were not saucer shaped; they more closely resembled boomerangs. However, the image as described was compelling, and the name stuck.

Foo Fighters During World War II pilots of fighters and bombers occasionally reported strange objects in the skies, which often paralleled the flight paths of their planes. Beginning in 1941, pilots on all sides of the conflict reported these craft, using terms such as disc-like, circular, wedge-shaped, and metallic to describe them. These "bogies" often flashed or glowed, emitted or reflected light. These "foo fighters" were able to maneuver in ways no known aircraft could match, and they could travel at incredible speeds. The objects were able to make right-angle turns, accelerate—and decelerate with astonishing rapidity—and even hover. The one thing the foo fighters did not do, however, was attack.

⊰ FOO FIGHTERS: ⊱ A FIRSTHAND ACCOUNT

"Anything else?" Captain Lawson, Intelligence Officer of the 873rd Bomb Squadron was addressing the crew of "Homer's roamers" as he finished up his interrogation after their return from a night mission to Tokyo on May 24, 1945.

First Lt. Homer B. Wall, the airplane commander, spoke up. "Sergeant Whalen, tell Captain Lawson about the incident that happened off the coast of Japan on our way home."

Right gunner Dave Whelan said, "Yes sir, here's what happened. We had left the target area and were probably about twenty miles out to sea, just east of Tokyo, when I noticed a disturbance off our right wing tip. There appeared a display of lights, which pulsated and changed color while I watched. It was following our flight path, although erratically, with a hovering attitude. I called in to Lieutenant Wall on the intercom to alert him of this event."

Alerted by Whalen's call, Lt. John Arata quickly put his radar antenna in an "up" position to scan the area. He found that it would not raise high enough, being designed to give "ground" return to locate targets for bombing runs. His position in the aircraft was just aft of Whelan's, and he could easily move to the viewing area. Arata did so after informing Wall of his intention to take a look. Wall had ordered that all lights be extinguished, and the crew complied with this order. Arata made the transition with some difficulty in the dark, but finally arrived at a place where he could see the "lights." Whelan had accurately de-

(continued)

scribed the phenomena. He told Captain Lawson that he corrob-orated Whelan's story.

After going about 200 miles in a southerly direction, as they flew a course to return to Saipan, Whelan reported that the object had disappeared.

Captain Lawson asked questions but did not seem to be too concerned. Some conversation ensued including the possibility that what they had seen was a "baka" bomb, the Japanese equiv-alent of Germany's V2 missile, although the bomb was supposed to be piloted. St. Elmo's fire was also discussed. The session ended without a conclusion as to what they had seen.

Several years went by and Arata was attending a movie when a newsreel item showing "flying saucers" appeared on the screen. In newspaper accounts of this event, reference was made to the fact that flying saucers were first seen by B-29 crews as they left target areas in Japan.

This was just one of many UFO reports filed by US military prior to the Roswell incident of 1947. These reports establish an ongoing awareness of UFOs that contradict the government's later denials.

Fort, Charles (1874–1932)   A writer of some note, Fort was one of the first official Ufologists who unearthed a pattern of odd reports regarding unex-plained aerial phenomena. He began researching the literature and news re-ports of UFOs and wrote a number of significant books on the subject, including *Lo!* and *The Book of the Damned*.

Fortean Times   A very influential magazine based in England that pub-lishes, among other things, accounts of UFOs. *The Fortean Times* also sponsors a number of symposia throughout the United States.

Fowler, Raymond   A UFO researcher, formerly of the U.S. Air Force Security Service. He is widely respected on both sides of the UFO debate for his honesty and attention to meticulous detail when recording information. He is also the author of several influential books on the subject, including *The Andreasson Affair* (1979), *The Watchers* (1990), and *The MUFON Field Investigator's Manual* (1975).

Ghost Rockets   A nickname given to objects seen in the skies over Scandinavia in 1946. Over two thousand were seen, and though they resembled conventional rockets, they did not exhibit flames or any other kind of exhaust. Unlike missiles they traveled at variable speeds and demonstrated remarkable aerial agility, doing turns and movements that neither rockets nor missiles, of any known manufacture, could match.

Grails   A subspecies of the Grays who are taller, much thinner, and have sticklike limbs, which are nevertheless extremely strong. A Grail was shown in the film *Close Encounters of the Third Kind* shortly before the Grays appeared.

Grays   The most commonly reported type of alien, the Grays are generally short (2 to 5 feet in height), humanoid (a head, two arms, a torso, and two legs), and have unusually large eyes. They have little or no nose, and a thin, lipless mouth. The Grays are believed to be behind most abductions, alien experiments, and more devious plots against humanity. Many Ufologists believe that the Grays are working in an uneasy alliance with a shadow sector of the U.S. government as part of a plan to eventually dominate all life on earth. The exact motive and specifics of this alliance vary in the telling.

Grays are often believed to be Saurian aliens and, largely because of the Betty and Barney Hill abduction incident, are believed to have come from the Zeta Reticuli system.

Greens   An alien race of humanoids with greenish or olive skin who live in vast underground caverns located beneath Europe.

Hangar 18   An aircraft hangar at Area 51 in which crashed alien craft were supposedly stored.

Hill Abduction Case   The most famous of all UFO abduction cases, the Betty Hill (1919–2004) and Barney Hill (1922–1969) incident took place in September 1961. The couple was driving along a road in New Hampshire when they saw a strange light in the sky. They stopped to take a better look, and, as they did so, the light reversed direction and approached them. They saw a circular aircraft with windows from which blue lights shone. As the craft approached, they could see figures through the window. The couple got spooked and left. When they got home, however, they realized that they were missing two hours from their evening, an occurrence for which they had no explanation.

Over the next few days, Betty Hill began having vivid and disturbing dreams about alien abduction. Distressed and confused, particularly about the missing time, the couple agreed to undergo hypnotic regression. They underwent this separately, and the stories they recounted matched perfectly.

In the story they told that their car had been stalled, and that men (presumably aliens) helped them out of their car. Inside the ship, they were separated and subjected to thorough physical examinations, including the taking of tissue and fluid samples from different parts of their bodies. During the regression therapy Betty was able to sketch a likeness of a 3D star map she had been shown while aboard the craft. An amateur researcher ultimately identified the star configuration as that of zeta reticuli, and the aliens themselves are widely believed to have been Grays.

Hoagland, Richard (b.1945)   A controversial but popular figure in the UFO world, Hoagland is a major proponent of the belief that NASA and the U.S. government are managing a huge cover-up of UFO knowledge. Over the years Hoagland has presented a number of fascinating theories, including:

•The face on Mars is an alien construct and shows a human/feline hybrid.

•Some of the rocks surrounding the landing sites of the Mars exploration rovers are actually pieces of Martian machinery.

•Rocks on Mars that contained biological fossils were deliberately destroyed by NASA's rover.

•Iapetus, a moon of Saturn, is an artificial world inhabited by aliens.

•NASA is suppressing knowledge of an alien civilization on the moon.

Hopkins, Budd (b.1931)   A major, albeit controversial, figure in alien abduction research, Hopkins used regression hypnosis to uncover his own abduction experiences. He's since authored several important books, including *Missing Time* (1981).

Hybrids   Any of the purported genetic crossbreeds of aliens and humans. Various stories have floated around for years that the creation of an alien-human hybrid is something of a holy grail—either in order to establish interspecies harmony or, conversely, to pave the way for a smooth and total takeover of earth.

Hynek, J. Allen (1910–1986)   One of the most respected and influential UFO researchers of the twentieth century, Dr. Hynek was an astronomer and astrophysicist who worked in early satellite development and tracking. In 1952, Hynek was asked to serve as an advisor for Project Sign (which became Project Grudge and later Project Blue Book). He was also asked to consult on the government's investigation into the nature of UFOs.

Hynek began his UFO involvement as a skeptic and a very harsh critic of any reports of alien craft. He worked very hard to dismiss or explain such reports as ordinary phenomena (or bad reportage). Over time, and faced with the sheer volume of UFO reports, Hynek became far less skeptical. In his article, *"Unusual Aerial Phenomena,"* for the April, 1953, issue of *The Journal of the Optical Society of America,* Hynek made one of his most profound statements:

"Ridicule is not part of the scientific method, and people should not be taught that it is. The steady flow of reports, often made in concert by reliable observers, raises questions of scientific obligation and responsibility."

Over time, Hynek developed the legendary scale to measure the significance of *close encounters* with alien beings. First presented in his landmark 1972 book, *The UFO Experience: A Scientific Study,* the scale runs as follows:

1. **Nocturnal Light:** Any anomalous light(s) seen in the night sky whose description rules out the possibilities of aircraft lights, stars, meteors, and the like.

2. **Daylight Disk:** UFOs seen in the distant daytime sky. The UFOs classed in this category can be other shapes as well, like cigars, eggs, and ovals.

3. **Radar-Visuals:** Where UFOs are tracked on radar and can be seen at the place illustrated at the same time.

4. **Close Encounters:**

   – of the First Kind (CEI)—A UFO in close proximity (within approximately 500 feet) of the witness.

   – of the Second Kind (CEII)—A UFO that leaves markings on the ground, causes burns or paralysis to humans, frightens animals, and interferes with car engines or TV and radio reception.

   – of the Third Kind (CEIII)—A CEI or CEII, which have visible occupants.

Iguanoids   Another Reptilian alien race, this one bearing a superficial resemblance to iguanas. The Iguanoids stand about 5 feet tall, have long tails, tapered snouts, and are sometimes seen wearing black clothing that resembles hooded cloaks.

Implants   Any of a variety of alien devices surgically deposited inside human beings, often in the sinus areas (though there are stories of implants in nearly every part of the body). These implants are generally belived to either be tracking devices or mind-control tools. Attempts to remove implants are frequently fatal.

Jacobs, Dr. David (b.1942)   A famous UFO abduction researcher from Temple University who has interviewed more than three hundred abductees and witnesses, including BUDD HOPKINS.

Keel, John A. (b.1930)   A Ufologist and author who postulated that aliens are not extraterrestrials but *ultraterrestrials*, or beings from other dimensions. In his view these beings are no more favorably disposed toward humans than we are to lab rats. His books include *The Mothman Prophecies, Disneyland of the Gods, The Complete Guide to Mysterious Beings*, and *Our Haunted Planet*.

Keyhoe, Donald (1897–1988)   One of the most significant figures in UFO research. Major Keyhoe, a former U.S. Marine fighter pilot, was very vocal in his pleas that the U.S. government take the matter of UFOs seriously and conduct proper and thorough research. His article "Flying Saucers Are Real" appeared in the January 1950 issue of *True Magazine*. It caused such a flap and garnered so much attention that Keyhoe expanded it into a book of the same name, which went on to sell a half million copies. His most powerful book, 1953's *Flying Saucers from Outer Space,* is filled with official reports and interviews with Air Force and other military personnel.

In 1956, Keyhoe became a director for NICAP (National Investigations Committee on Aerial Phenomena). The organization suffered from financial mismanagement and disinformation infiltration, but nevertheless heightened UFO awareness for decades. Even former President Jimmy Carter filed a NICAP report following his sighting. When NICAP folded its archives of UFO sightings the case files were purchased by the Center for UFO Studies (CUFOS).

Klarer, Elizebeth (1910–1994)   A highly controversial figure in UFO history. Klarer, a native of South Africa, made a number of astounding claims over the years, including that she was a UFO observer for the South African Air Force during World War II. Her most eye-popping claim is that she had sex with a humanoid alien, and was actually taken to his home planet in the Alpha-Centauri star system. The sexual union resulted in a pregnancy, and she delivered a son who, she said, remained on that planet even though she was returned to earth.

LaPaz, Lincoln (1897–1985)   A professor of mathematics and an astronomer from the University of New Mexico who served as a consultant to the Air Force's Project Twinkle in 1949 while they were investigating reports of "green fireballs." In his report, LaPaz concluded that they were neither meteorites nor conventional fireballs and were not of explainable origin.

Lazar, Robert (b.1959)   An electronics and physics scientist who worked at Los Alamos in the polarized proton section, focusing on (among other things) particle accelerators. In early 1989, Lazar was a guest on KLAS-TV in Las Vegas and claimed to have worked in S-4, a top-secret division ten miles south of Area 51. He claimed to have been employed there between December 1988 and April 1989 for the purpose of reverse engineering the propulsion systems of a crashed alien saucer.

Lazar said that he saw nine different alien craft at S-4, and that the crafts used some form of gravity draft. He had entry into the craft, and was also present when a test crew flew the ship, doing a few simple turns and passes. Lazar also observed a mysterious material called "element 115," which was not a terrestrial element.[53] It was Lazar's contention that a mere kilogram of element 115 would release approximately the energy of forty-seven 10-megaton hydrogen bombs.

After Lazar resigned from the project he claimed that there was an attempt on his life, ostensibly to silence him. As a result, he went public to use celebrity as a shield.

Lindemann, Michael (b.1949)   A celebrated American Ufologist who lectures on the connection between UFOs and U.S. military covert weapons development based on alien technology. He is the cofounder of the Institute for

---

53. Only 114 elements are currently known to science.

the Study of Contact with Nonhuman Intelligence (ISCNI, Inc.). Lindemann is the author of a number of influential books including *UFOs and the Alien Presence: Six Viewpoints* (1990) and *UFOs and the New World Order* (1992).

Los Alamos   One of the locations where debris and corpses from alien crashes are (or were) presumed to be kept. The original Roswell crash debris is believed to have been taken to Los Alamos in 1947.

Los Angeles Air Raid of 1942   U.S. military fired on unknown aircraft above Los Angeles on February 25, 1942, believing them to be enemy fighter bombers. However, when response aircraft were launched, the pilots reported seeing fifteen to twenty unidentifiable airships flying in an erratic manner. In an odd coincidence, one of the National Guardsmen present during this "air raid" was a very young DeForest Kelley (1920–1999), who would later take on the role of planet-hopping physician Dr. Leonard "Bones" McCoy on the original 1960s *Star Trek*.

Luna   Name given in Ufology to a presumed alien base on the dark side of the moon. Some believers claim that Apollo astronauts took film footage of this base, which showed habitats and spacecraft, but that the military and the U.S. government have suppressed the documentation. No film clips or stills have, sadly, leaked out.

Majestic   The highest known level of U.S. government security, purported to be thirty-eight levels higher than "top secret."

Majestic-12   An alleged group formed in 1953 on special orders from the White House to study UFOs, acquire information, decide on UFO-related policy, and essentially begin the whole U.S. government cover up on the subject. In 1987, a set of briefing documents for MJ-12 was discovered that listed the members of the group: Dr. Lloyd Berkner, Dr. Detlev Bronk, Dr. Vannevar Bush, James Forrestal, Gordon Gray, Vice Admiral Roscoe Hillenkoetter, Dr.

Jerome Hunsaker, Dr. Donald Menzel, General Robert Montague, Rear Admiral Sidney Souers, General Nathan Twining, and General Hoyt Vandenberg.

Some years later, however, these documents were revealed to be fakes, and the "signature" of then-President Harry Truman was discovered to have been lifted from a 1947 memo. Despite this, many UFO followers hold to their belief that MJ-12 existed, and they contend that the signature issue was actually a piece of modern governmental disinformation.

Marcel, Jesse (1917–1986)   Marcel was an experienced combat officer at the 509th Bomb Group Intelligence Office at the Army Air Force base at Roswell Field. He was the first military officer to observe the legendary crash, which was scattered across the fields of Mac Brazel's ranch. Marcel collected some of the debris and carted it back to the base in order to show it to his superiors.

Colonel William Blanchard, Marcel's direct superior, gave him authority to release the statement to the press that the military had, indeed, recovered a downed alien craft. This claim was very quickly recanted by General Roger Ramey, who told the press that the debris was the wreckage of a failed weather balloon. Marcel was ordered to sit through a press conference and insist that he had made a mistake when identifying the materials found.

Some years later, when he was no longer a serving officer, Marcel recanted again, switching back to his original story. His later statements include this description: "There was all kinds of stuff—small beams about three eighths or half inch square with some sort of hieroglyphics on them that nobody could decipher. These looked something like balsa wood, and were of about the same weight, except that they were not wood at all. They were very hard, although flexible, and would not burn. There was a great deal of unusual parchment-like substance, which was brown in color and extremely strong, and a great number of small pieces of a metal-like tinfoil, except that it wasn't tinfoil."

Because of Marcel's outstanding combat experience and service record, his statements stand as one of the most solid and difficult to knock. And, he was in a position to know, and tell, the truth.

Marcel Jr., Jesse (b.1936)   The son of Major Jesse Marcel who speaks on UFOs. He draws heavily on what his father told him, and what he remembers from the actual crash (when his father brought alien artifacts home to show the family).

⊰ THE FACE ON MARS ⊱

In July of 1976, the Viking Orbiter 1 was taking low-altitude images of the Cydonia region of Mars as part of the search for likely touchdown sites for the Viking Lander 2. While taking photos of mesas and buttes along an escarpment that separates the heavily cratered south from the lower-lying and less pitted northern planes, one shot (taken on July 25) showed a rocky formation that resembled a face.

Because the image—especially when taken from certain angles—was so striking, many Ufologists have taken the stance that it is artificial and, as such, is proof of extraterrestrial life.

When photographed from other angles, including directly above the object, the resemblance to a face becomes far less distinct. This fact has not diminished the arguments that the Face on Mars is a deliberate construct. Outspoken UFOlogists such as Richard Hoagland have not backed down at all from this belief.

It will be interesting to see what happens when the next Mars mission touches down.

Martians   An as-yet unproven race of beings who some believe still live somewhere beneath the surface of the red planet. Hardcore UFOlogists maintain that Mars is currently under the control of the hostile Grays.

Martin, Jorge   One of the top UFO investigators in Puerto Rico, Jorge Martin has investigated hundreds of incidents throughout that island since 1975.

McDonald, James   Dr. McDonald was a senior physicist at the Institute of Atmospheric Physics and a professor in the Department of Meteorology at the University of Arizona. He was also a very outspoken critic of NASA and its refusal to take UFOs seriously. During the late 1960s, Dr. McDonald repeatedly challenged NASA to take an active role in researching UFOs. Before he was able to make any significant inroads into his cause, he committed suicide under extremely suspicious circumstances. His death has, naturally, fueled conspiracy speculation for decades.

Meier, Eduard (b.1937)   A Swiss farmer who has shared hundreds of color photos of UFOs. His claims that the crafts come from the Pleiades (500 light years distant) has fueled some truly fiery debates within the UFO community, as to whether his assertions are real or totally fabricated. Meier, who also has video footage of these aliens and their crafts, claims to have been taken on trips in both space and time.

Men in Black   Since the late 1950s there have been hundreds of reports of mysterious men dressed in plain black suits who have shown up at the homes of people who have made reports of alien encounters. Unlike the characters played by Will Smith and Tommy Lee Jones, these men in black are hostile, dangerous, and do not seem to be protecting earth from the scum of the universe. Rather the reverse, as many believe the men in black are either in league with aliens, are government agents shutting down anyone who speaks too much on the subject, or even possibly aliens themselves.

When the MIB show up, they strongly caution against further disclosure of UFO-related events. Many sources report that these men always walk with a limp, that they speak in uninflected voices (or in some cases grating sing-song tones), and drive unmarked black cars.

Michalak, Stephen (1916–1999)   The UFO encounter incident involving Stephen Michalak endures as one of the most remarkable events of Ufology, and certainly one of the most heavily documented cases. Michalak, a resident of Winnipeg, was prospecting near Falcon Lake, Manitoba, when he saw a UFO land on a large flat rock. Michalak crept close to investigate and while he was standing close to what looked like an exhaust vent a shot of hot gas erupted from it, igniting his shirt and leaving a grid-shaped burn mark on his abdomen. Before the injury Michalak made detailed sketches of the craft.

Missing Time   A UFO-related phenomenon in which some people who have had encounters, ranging from abductions to sightings, claim they lost a significant chunk of time for which they cannot account. In some cases the "missing time" is only a few minutes, but some folks have reported missing hours and even days.

Moon-Eyes   An alleged race of giants (seven to nine feet in height) who have black eyes that wrap around their heads (like sunglasses) and pale blue skin. In the few sightings of these Moon-Eyes, the creatures appear to be nonhostile.

Mothmen   A race of winged subterranean alien creatures with horns and bodies similar to gargoyles or devils and who are believed to be the inspirations for both. The "mothmen" are smart, devious, and malicious. Also known as ciakars, pteroids, birdmen, and winged draco, these creatures are believed to live in underground caverns located variously in places such as Dule, New Mexico; Montauk Point, Long Island; and Point Pleasant, West Virginia.

Nagas   An alleged race of reptilian aliens that some believe have visited earth for many thousands of years. They are also the basis for the beliefs in serpent men, which can be found in various cultures. The name, Nagas, comes from the Sanskrit word *Naga,* meaning "serpent"—particularly the cobra. In Buddhist sutras the word may refer to "elephant" as easily as it does to "snake," largely due to the elephant's prehensile trunk.

In Ufology, the Nagas are also known as Reptilians, Reptiloids, Reptoids, Homesaurus, and by the more generic name of "lizard men." These creatures are believed to live primarily in huge caves beneath the Himalayas.

NICAP   The National Investigations Committee on Aerial Phenomena. This was one of the most important civilian UFO organizations of the 50s and 60s. It took a firm stand to oppose any kind of governmental secrecy. The group was founded in 1956 by Thomas Townsend Brown, and later governed by Major Donald Keyhoe. Though good natured and well-intentioned, NICAP was poorly managed and eventually folded. Its files were obtained by CUFOS.

Nonphysical Entities   Invisible entities that exist in our world. Some Nonphysical Entities can manifest images and even, at times, physical bodies, but they do not have actual physical forms. Some Ufologists speculate that both ghosts and aliens are actually different aspects of these interdimensional beings and that neither are actually alien to this planet—just to our normal human perceptions.

Nordic   A presumed race of aliens with humanoid bodies and blond hair, which gives them the appearance of normal humans of Nordic or Scandinavian descent.

NAICCR   The North American Institute for Crop Circle Research is a group formed in 1990 to study crop circles in North America.

Oeschler, Bob   A former Air Force officer who is frequently at the center of controversy. On the one hand he was praised by serious UFO researchers for his analysis of photographic and recorded evidence. On the other he has made claims that precisely mirror ones made previously by others.

Operation Highjump The code name[54] given to a massive expedition launched by the U.S. Navy in late 1946 into early 1947. A dozen ships and several thousand men were to make their way to the Antarctic rim to train personnel and test materials in the frigid zones; extend American sovereignty over much of the Antarctic continent; determine the feasibility of establishing bases in the Antarctic; and perform various scientific testing. Highjump was launched under the direct command of Admiral Richard E. Byrd, and the mission resulted in great scientific advances, tragic losses of men and material, and the birth of an ongoing debate about the nature of our planet and its inhabitants.

Some Ufologists maintain that Byrd discovered the entrance to a cavern system leading to the hollow center of the Earth. In this story, Byrd's forces were attacked by aircraft capable of unbelievable speeds and maneuverability. Despite overwhelming evidence to the contrary, including satellite photography, radar, and first-hand accounts of the nature of the southern icecap, many Ufologists hold to the belief that what Byrd found is there, and that only a government coverup prevents it from becoming general knowledge.

Orange An alien race whose origins and nature seem to be in some dispute among Ufologists. Some contend that the creatures are alien-human hybrids whose skin color has an orange cast to it; others hold that they are an entirely alien race with bristling hair that has been variously described as red, yellow, or orange; still others hold that they are Grays wearing atmosphere suits with orange filaments sprouting from them (perhaps sensors). The majority of Orange sightings have been in the southwestern United States and in northwestern Mexico.

Orion A star system known as "the great hunter" whose component stars include Belelgeuse, Rigel, Bellatrix, Mintaka, and others. Orion is believed by many Ufologists to be the home of the alien Grays.

---

54. Given by Chester W. Nimitz, Chief of Naval Operations.

Palmer, Ray   Ray Palmer, the editor for *Amazing Stories* science fiction magazine, was one of the first persons to make the claims that Admiral Byrd's mission to the Antarctic resulted in the discovery of an underground civilization and a hollow earth.

Pine Gap   A U.S.-owned military base located in the Australian outback (twelve miles from Alice Springs) that has earned the nickname "Australia's Area 51." A number of people have stepped forward with claims that they saw nonterrestrial craft and aliens on and around the base. There have even been reports of "white disks" flying near the base. In an interesting twist, many of the witnesses claim that these saucer-shaped aircraft bore USAF insignia, leading to speculation that the base is being used to test craft retro-engineered from alien technology.

Pleiadians   An alien race from the Pleiades star cluster that many Ufologists believe seeded the galaxy with their DNA. By this belief, nearly all life in the galaxy, including homosapiens, are descended from this population project.

The Pleiadians are believed to be compassionate and elevated beings who have left behind all negative emotions. Many channelers[55] claim to receive messages from these beings. The messages of the Pleiadians is one of peace and love, but they also send warnings of a coming stellar war and tyranny.

Pope, Nick (b.1965)   A former British Ministry of Defense member whose job was to handle all information related to UFOs. Once he left that position, he stepped forward to state that there was definitely a coverup of UFO knowledge being maintained by all world governments. He is one of only a few highly placed persons to make such statements, and his former position lends great credence to his claims.

Quintero, Liberato Anibel   A Colombian farmer who claimed that in November 1976 he was abducted by three female aliens who then had sex with

55. See listing for channeling in chapter 4

him repeatedly. He said that whenever he would tire they would make him drink a yellowish liquid that would restore his sexual vigor. Afterward he was given an injection that knocked him out, and he was returned to earth. This is one of a handful of alien abduction stories in which sexual intercourse is a factor. There is a far greater body of testimony about aliens harvesting eggs and sperm, but without the benefit of good old-fashioned earth-type sex.

Quazgaa The name of the leader of a group of alien beings (possibly Grays) who reportedly abducted Betty Andreasson on January 25, 1967.

Rainbow, Project The code name for an alleged test during World War II in which the military used radical technology to make the USS *Eldridge* (DE-173) invisible to all forms of enemy detection, including direct observation with the naked eye. Known as the "Philadelphia experiment" (the ship was based there), the trial was reported by some to have gone horribly wrong, and the ship was thrown into an alternate dimension.

The Navy denies this and willingly presents records, crew manifests, and other documentation to show that the ship was in active service until 1951, when she was decommissioned and sold to the Greek Navy and renamed the *Leon*. Those persons who maintain that the experiment was real claim that another ship was renamed and sold to Greece as part of an elaborate coverup.

Ramey, Roger (1903–1963) The officer who took operational control of the escalating Roswell incident following the news release to the press that claimed "U.S. captures flying disk." It was General Ramey who concocted the weather-balloon story and had it issued as the "official story."

Randle, Kevin (b.1949) An Air Force captain and outspoken expert on UFOs, Kevin Randle has written a number of significant books on the subject, including *Faces of the Visitors: An Illustrated Reference to Alien Contact; The Abduction Enigma: The Truth Behind the Mass Alien Abductions of the Late 20th Century* (with William P. Cone and Russ Estes); *Project Moon Dust: Beyond Roswell—Ex-*

posing the Government's Continuing Covert UFO Investigations and Cover-Ups; and many others, including exposés on Roswell and Blue Book.

Reptoids (also Reptilians, Draconians)   The alien race from the Draco star system, and the extraterrestrials who have the nastiest reputations. The Reptoids are known for using mind control, implants, probes, and all of the other less pleasant forms of experimentation. Some Ufologists claim that the Reptoids are carnivores that favor human flesh. Charming.

The Robertson Panel   A government panel that met at the Pentagon in early 1953 to discuss the issue of UFOs and establish military policy for all encounters, which included a process of debunking and disinformation. Their findings were released as a top-secret document called the Durant Report.

Roswell Autopsy Film   A legendary piece of film footage that supposedly shows an autopsy of one of the Grays recovered from the Roswell crash.

Roswell Crash   The most famous UFO incident of all time, in which an object crashed on a farm near Corona, New Mexico, during a thunderstorm in 1947. The next morning a farmer, Mac Brazel, found wreckage on his property (the debris was strewn across half a mile of ground). None of the wreckage was identifiable to him as having come from any known aircraft.

A few days later, he brought some of the debris into town and showed it to the sheriff, George Wilcox. He immediately contacted the authorities at the Roswell Army Air Field. At the base, Major Jesse Marcel immediately organized a trip to inspect the wreckage. He reported his findings to his commanding officer, William Blanchard. Marcel and Sheridan Cavitt (from the counterintelligence department) went back to the ranch and loaded as much of the wreckage as they could onto two vehicles, which were taken to the base. It was then flown to Washington D.C. for study.

Cavitt returned to the site to continue collecting debris while Marcel took a sidetrip home to show some artifacts to his family. The materials were unlike anything any of them had ever seen, including something that looked like tin-foil, but which returned to an unmarked state no matter how severely it was crumpled.

The Army issued a press release stating that they had recovered a flying saucer, but, almost immediately, this was recanted and replaced by a story about the recovery of material from a wrecked weather balloon. The military suddenly intensified security and Mac Brazel was placed under house arrest for a week while teams of investigators scoured his ranch for every scrap of debris. Brazel was sternly warned not to tell anyone about what he had found.

The government has stuck by its story ever since, and UFO researchers have worked diligently to uncover proof that the crash actually happened. Over the years rumors have leaked out that alien bodies were also recovered at the site.

Ruppelt, Edward (1922–1960) Author of one of the most important early books on UFOs, *The Report On Unidentified Flying Objects* (1956). In it Captain Ruppelt discusses his involvement with the "flying saucer group" as part of Project Grudge earlier in that decade.

Santilli, Ray A British film producer claiming to have discovered a piece of video that showed the autopsy of an alien being from the original Roswell crash. This *Alien Autopsy* video was released in May of 1995 and became the center of a storm of controversy. Although many people initially believed in it, the voices of skeptics became louder and clearer as time went on. Pathologists and surgeons who viewed the film expressed doubts about the accuracy of the techniques and procedures used. The suspicion was raised that the alien was nothing more than an elaborate dummy. Objects that appeared onscreen were cast into doubt when it became clear that they were not available to medicine at the time of the Roswell crash, such as a type of warning sign that experts from OSHA claim were not used until 1967.

Fox TV aired two specials on the alien autopsy, the first more or less trying to establish that it was real; and then a later one that debunked it. Santilli later amended his claims saying that only *some* of the footage was real; he and his partner, Gary Schoefield, faked the rest to fill in gaps left by the partial actual footage.

Saucer, Project   The unofficial name given to the first investigation conducted by the Air Force.

Scully, Frank (1892–1964)   Scully was the author of the book, *Behind the Flying Saucers,* which was published in 1950. It kicked off the belief that the government had recovered extraterrestrial spacecraft and alien beings.

SETI: The Search for Extraterrestrial Intelligence   A government-funded project that monitors electromagnetic wave emissions from outer space. It does this in the hopes of discovered signals or patterns that would indicate extraterrestrial intelligence.

In an era of conspiracy theories and fears about the government actually doing what it claims to be doing, many Ufologists have expressed doubts that SETI is searching for anything and is, in fact, designed to offer proof that intelligent life does not exist beyond our planet.

Sign, Project   The first of the Air Force's official investigations into UFOs. Started in January, 1948, Project Sign probed hundreds of reported sightings before concluding a year later that only 20 percent of these sightings were unexplainable.

Snowbird, Project   One of several alleged military projects intended to retro-engineer alien technology from crashed UFOs and adapt it for human use.

Steiger, Brad (b.1936)   An influential and respected author of a number of books related to Ufology, including: *Mysteries of Time and Space* (1974); *Other Worlds, Other Universes; Playing The Reality Game* (1975); *Philadelphia Experiment and Other UFO Conspiracies* (1990); and *Project Bluebook (1976).*

Strieber, Whitley (b.1945)   A best-selling author on a variety of subjects, including horror: *The Hunger* (1981), *Cat Magic* (1986); speculative fiction: *War Day* (1984); science fiction: *The Grays* (2006); and an extensive amount of non-fiction stemming from personal experience as an abductee: *Communion: A True Story* (1987), *Transformation* (1988), *The Breakthrough* (1995), and *The Secret School* (1996).

Stringfield, Leonard (1920–1994)   An early giant of the UFO world, Stringfield coined the phrase "UFO retrievals," and brought much of Ufology into mainstream credibility—separating it from science fiction and hysteria. Stringfield is the author of several seminal UFO books, including *The UFO Crash-Retrieval Syndrome: Status Report II: New Sources* (1980) and *The UFO Crash/Retrievals: Amassing The Evidence* (1982).

Swamp Gas   A naturally occurring chemical event in which methane gas released from decaying animal and plant matter in swamps spontaneously ignites in the air. These sudden bursts of fiery light are the root of some badly reported UFO sightings.

Taos Hum   In Taos, New Mexico, a number of local residents have reported hearing a strange humming sound that has no apparent origin. The reports of this sound seem to coincide with the presence of black helicopters and cattle mutilations.

Tectonic Strain Theory (TST)   A theory that all paranormal events—everything from UFOs to ghosts—can be explained by seismic activity, which generates electromagnetic radiation and temporarily warps perception.

Telosian   Tall fair-haired aliens who live in a network of ancient caverns beneath the Western United States, particularly in the region of Mount Shasta.

Teros (Telos)   A general term for any of the groups of aliens, humans, or alien-human hybrids who live in the alleged cavern system inside the hollow earth.

Tunguska Event At 7:17 a.m. on June 30, 1908, there was a tremendous explosion near the Podkamennaya (Stony) Tunguska River in what is now Evenkia, Siberia. The blast devastated over 2100 kilometers of dense forest, destroying an estimated sixty million trees. Although many scientists believe that it was the result of a meteorite striking the earth, there was very little evidence of a crater, and certainly not one as large as would be expected by the intensity of the explosion. This led to a modified view that perhaps the meteorite exploded before it struck the ground.

Researchers have found traces of nickel and iridium, elements frequently found in meteorites, and that has strengthened the belief that this was a naturally-occurring event. The blast pattern, however, is strikingly similar to that of atomic weapons blasts, creating a butterfly pattern of destruction on the ground.

The most recent theories from the scientific community argue that the object was an asteroid, a claim supported by the reported angle of trajectory, which would have brought it in from the asteroid belt that exists between Mars and Jupiter. The downside to this theory is that asteroids typically leave very large craters and this one exploded in the air. There is even a theory being floated that the blast was caused by a very small black hole.

So, what was it? Ufologists have long argued that the blast was caused by an explosion of the engines of an alien spacecraft. A competing theory was that benign aliens used a powerful weapon to utterly destroy an incoming threat from a more malign alien race.

Twinkle Project A secret project launched by the military to investigate the strange green fireballs sighted in various spots around the United States in the late 1940s and early 1950s.

UFO Unidentified Flying Object, a term used for any item seen in the sky that hasn't yet been identified and which does not necessarily refer to alien spacecraft.

Ufology   The study—formal or informal—of anything related to UFOs, aliens, and similar topics.

Unusual Ground Markings (UGM)   A Ufology term referring to any of a number of measurable phenomena on the ground, which includes: landing burns, crop circles, footprints, UFO lander strut indentations, and so on.

Vallee, Jacques (b.1939)   French-born UFO astrophysicist who worked with Dr. J. Allen Hynek at Northwestern University in the 1960s. Vallee was the author of many articles on UFOs and related subjects, always taking a scientific point of view.

Vegans   An alien race believed to have originated in the Vega star system and who bear a resemblance to darker-skinned Asians or Indians.

Walton, Travis (b.1953)   A famous alien abductee and author of the books, *Fire in the Sky: Based on a True Story* (1978) and *The Walton Affair*. Hollywood did a film version of *Fire in the Sky* (1993), based on Walton's experiences, which starred Robert Patrick, who went on to play the role of Doggit in the last seasons of *The X-Files*.

Xenomorph   A general term for an alien being.

Xenophobe   A condition in which someone is afraid of the unknown. Many UFO skeptics have claimed that xenophobia—and not rational thought— is behind the widespread belief in alien life.

X-Files   A successful and long-running TV show, which ran from 1993 until 2002. It concerned two FBI agents investigating cases that have an element of the unknown—an "X" factor—which separates them from conventional crimes. The lead investigator was Fox Mulder (played by David Duchovny) who was the believer of the pair, and was on a personal crusade to find his missing sister (who he believed was abducted by aliens). His partner, Dana

Scully (Gillian Anderson) was a total skeptic for most of the run of the show, but whose attitude took a 180-degree turn in the last couple of seasons.

The show found a tremendous following and gave a strong boost to Ufology and other areas of the paranormal. It also made cultural icons of Scully and Mulder.

Zamora, Lonnie   Sergeant Lonnie Zamora, a member of the Socorro police department in New Mexico, claimed to have witnessed an alien landing on April 24, 1964. The report was later investigated by Project Blue Book and stands as one of the best-documented cases of alien encounters.

Zeta Reticuli   A binary star system approximately 37 light years away from earth, which is the presumed origin of the aliens that abducted Betty and Barney Hill.

— Chapter Twelve —
VODOUN

THROUGHOUT THE WORLD there are many enemies of evil. In the case of the religion of Vodoun in Benin and Haiti, the enemies of evil are the houngan (male priest) or mambo (female priestess). Their temple, the *hounfour* (or *humfort*), is the center of their religious practice. It's also the sacred and protected workshop where these priests prepare their rituals, charms, and magicks for their ongoing battle with the various demons, spirits, and monsters who plague them and their native peoples.

Vodoun (also called Vodun, Voudou, or Sevi Lwa) is a religion buried under centuries of misunderstanding, propaganda, and slander by nonpractitioners. Most popularly known as Voodoo by the general public, this faith has earned a very bad and undeserved reputation, mostly by Christian communities who labeled it as devil worship. Pop culture—films, novels, and so on—have done a great deal of damage to the reputation of what is, quite truthfully, an organized, positive religion.

The name "Vodoun" is traceable to an ancient African word for "spirit" in the language of the Yoruba people of West African who lived in eighteenth- and nineteenth-century Dahomey; but the religion itself has roots going back hundreds, if not thousands, of years. At one time Dahomey was a vast kingdom that occupied parts of today's Togo, Benin, and Nigeria.

When Africa was plundered for its human cargoes, the slaves brought Vodoun with them to Haiti and other islands in the West Indies, and even to the United States. The religion was, of course, changed by the clash of cultures and interruptions due to the frequent deaths of those houngans who died as slaves before passing on the complete set of rites and practices. Nonetheless, it survived. Worldwide there are about sixty million followers of Vodoun.

When Christians from Europe and America tried to forcibly stamp out Vodoun, the priests went underground, hiding their religion by using the names of Christian saints to disguise their own spirits ("loa").

Vodoun was again attacked and suppressed during the time of Marxist regimes in Africa. When Benin established a democratic government in 1989, however, the religion emerged from hiding. In 1996 it became that country's official religion.

Religions similar to Vodoun have emerged in various places around the world, particularly in South America under the names *Umbanda*, *Quimbanda* or *Candomble*.

The darker "Voodoo" of movies, fiction, and church propaganda bears little or no resemblance to true Vodoun beyond a purely superficial similarity. Anyone taking a moment to look an inch deeper than the fiction will see the true religion.

However, within Vodoun—as within all religions—there is a constant battle of good and evil. Indeed one of the truest marks of a religion is an acceptance of the duality of universal forces: one that seeks to harm or corrupt humanity, and one that seeks to protect and redeem.

When confronted by the evil Baka[56] it is only a Houngan or Mambo who can stop it because ordinary persons do not possess the power to overcome this dreadful evil. Houngans are required to make the complex and powerful charms needed to thwart the Baka or even destroy them.

One of the great tasks facing the houngan is the balancing of appeal and appeasement that entices the great loa spirits to help humankind. The loa often take sides against one another, often at the behest of someone who has

---

56. A shapeshifting reanimated spirit of a bokor, or dark priest of Vodoun

made a particularly powerful prayer and offering. If this appeal leads to the kind of imbalance which results in harm, sickness, or other ill, then a different houngan is called in to cajole the loa to relent; or to bring a second loa in to protect the oppressed person and restore him to health. It is delicate work and every detail of each ritual must be followed with strict reverence, respect for all of the loas—no matter which side they are taking—and a deep, abiding faith.

The cosmology of Vodoun is very complex, with hundreds of gods and spirits. The chief god is Olorun, but he is very remote and seldom bothers with human affairs. He appointed a somewhat lesser god, Obatala, to create the earth and all life forms. After this was done there was a conflict between the two gods, and the lesser god was temporarily banished.

Among the lesser spirits there are those originated from dahomey (called the rada) and those who came into being after the people had been taken to America and Haiti. These were called the Petro.

In Vodoun it is believed that each person has a soul that is composed of two separate spiritual entities. There is the *ti bon ange* or "little guardian angel" and the *a gros bon ange* or "big guardian angel." It is the little spirit that is the conscious and active part of the soul, and the part that leaves the body during sleep or when a loa possesses a person during a ritual. While the ti bon ange is absent from the body, it is vulnerable, and evil spirits love to attack it. Following are key terms of spirits, practitioners and practices of Vodoun.

Agau   A violent loa associated with tremors of the earth and storms. His possessions can be so violent as to cause death. It is said that when the earth shakes, Agau is angry.

Ago   A ritual exclamation similar to the Judeo-Christian expression, "amen."

Agwé   The loa of the seas, and patron to fishermen and sailors. His symbol is the boat. Sacrifices made to Agwé are set on small rafts and set adrift. If the craft sinks, the sacrifice has been accepted. He is also called the "shell of the sea," "the eel," and the "tadpole of the pond."

Aizan   The loa of the marketplace, Aizan also serves as a guardian of the hounfor. In rituals, mounds of earth surrounded by palm leaves symbolize Aizan. She is one of the oldest loa, and she prefers a sacrifice of black or white goats, or russet-colored oxen.

Asson   A rattle made of a hollowed calabash gourd, which serves as the symbol of the houngan or mambo, the two highest initiates in a voodoo temple. The gourd is filled with a mixture of snake vertebrae and stones, which represent the bones of long dead African ancestors.

Azaca   The loa of agriculture and protector of crops, Azaca is most often depicted as a pipe-smoking peasant carrying a sack and wearing a straw hat. Sacrifices to him are most often of cakes and cornmeal. Once he receives his sacrifice, he takes his offering into the corner to devour in secret.

Badé   The loa of the wind and companion to Sogbo, the loa of lightning, and Agau, the loa of the storm.

Bagi   Any of the separate chambers inside of a honfour. Smaller places of worship may have just a few bagi, larger temples may contain many more.

Bakulu   A loa so terrible that he is rarely invoked. He lives in the woods and drags great chains behind him. Since no one wants to be possessed by him, his sacrifices are taken out to the woods and simply left there.

Baptême   Voodoo ritual objects that are "baptized" or consecrated for use.

Baron Samedi (also **Baron Cimetière** and **Baron-la-Croix)**   The most powerful of the loa of death, Baron Samedi controls the passageway between life and death. He is often portrayed smoking a cigarette with a black top hat and dark glasses. His symbols are the cross, the coffin, and the phallus. When his followers are possessed by him, they often tell lewd jokes, make obscene gestures and acquire a taste for rum in which twenty-one hot peppers have been added.

Barque d'Agoué   A raft onto which offerings to Agau, the loa of the sea, are prepared and then set adrift. If the craft sinks, the sacrifice has been accepted.

Barriè   The gateway between the material world and the world of the loa.

Bassin   A pool or tank of water found in a temple where voodoo is practiced. A bassin may be small enough for ritual cleansing or large enough for followers to be immersed (in a rite similar to baptism).

Battérie   The four components of ritual music in voodoo, consisting of three drums and an ogan, a flat iron bell. The music has a hypnotic effect on the followers and heightens the experience of worship.

Baton   A length of stick, cane, or crutch used by a legba during rituals.

Battérie Maconnique   A rhythm produced by clapping hands and drums. The tapping cadence symbolizes rapping on the door to the loa realm.

Bizango   A secret society that supposedly practices zombification and other dark voodoo rituals.

Bokor   A houngan who practices what would be considered to be "black magic." It is said that they "serve the loa with both hands." Bokors generally are not associated with a temple, but work in secret, willing to sell their services to the highest bidder.

Bosou Koblamin   Popular during times of strife and war, this violent petro loa is said to be a man with three horns, symbolizing strength, wildness, and violence. Ceremonies to him are popular, as he is given a prized offering of a pig. Such events give all gathered a chance to feast when food for the masses might not be readily available.

Boucan   A ritual bonfire.

BOKOR Ken Meyer, Jr.

Boula   The smallest drum used in voodoo rituals.

Boule Zen   A ceremony where a govi, or clay pot containing the soul of the dead is burned, releasing it to the land of the dead.

Brigette   The loa of money and ill-gotten fortunes, she is the wife of Baron Samedi. Brigette dresses in purple and resides in a tree in a cemetery. Her preferred sacrifice is a black chicken, and she is comparable to Catholicism's St. Brigid of Ireland (patron of dairy workers, nuns, and scholars).

Brise   Despite his fearsome appearance, this loa of the hills and wood is gentle and loves children. He can take the form of an owl, and demands speckled hens for his sacrifice.

Brulé-Zin   Performed after the canzo, this is the final initiation into the voodoo cult. Literally, a "trial by fire," the ritual involves handling boiling cornmeal and walking across hot coals.

Canzo   The first level of initiation into the voodoo cult, this grueling ritual can take a week to complete. It involves intense study, fasting, purification of the soul and spirit, and the ingestion of various substances—the effects of which range from the sedative to the manic.

Carrefour   The most powerful of the petro loa, he represents the dark of night. By his will, bad luck and misfortune are permitted to enter the living world. His color is black, and his symbol is a crossroad.

Cheval   While this term literally means "horse," it is used to refer to a person who has been possessed, or mounted (hence the metaphor) by a loa.

Clairin   A white Haitian rum, and a favored drink of the petro loa.

Congo   A handsome (but unfeeling) loa, he enjoys sacrifices of spicy foods and mixed drinks.

Congo Savanne   Perhaps the fiercest and most powerful petro loa, Congo Savanne does not require sacrifices but chooses to devour humans instead, grinding them up like wheat.

Connaissance   Refers to the entire body of knowledge of the loa, voodoo rites, and herbal remedies. Generally, this knowledge is passed down from generation to generation, but other aspects are revealed by supernatural forces to a houngan or mambo over the course of their service and training.

Corps Cadavre   The aspects of the physical form that rot away after death, as opposed to the soul, which is everlasting.

Coucher   Meaning "to be put to bed," this is the point of canzo when initiates are sealed away in the temple for a lengthy period of reflection and study.

Creole   In voodoo, this term describes practices, rituals, language, and loa that originate in Haiti rather than Africa.

Dahomey   Now comprised of Togo, Benin, and Nigeria, this west African region is the birthplace of many voodoo rites, practices, and rituals. The term is also synonymous with the loa that originate there, such as *Erzulie Fréda Dahomey.*

Damballah-Wedo   The father of all the loa, Damballah represents ancient knowledge and the foundations of voodoo. He is also called "the rainbow serpent" and is purported to hold the very earth between his coils. His color is white, and only white food and drink items may be sacrificed to him. Ironically, despite his reptilian origins, he is comparable to Catholicism's St. Patrick.

Danh-Hwe   Literally, a "serpent house" used as refuge and shelter for pythons and other reptiles. The term also refers to a region of Dahomey, Africa, which serves as a cultural center for the serpent cult.

Débâtement   The violent movements and struggles a person undergoes while being possessed by a loa. Once these motions cease, the person is fully under the loa's control.

Dessounin   A ritual that separates the life force from the body after death.

Djévo   A ritual chamber of isolation where voodoo initiates may be interred during the canzo initiation. The experience is to represent the grave, where the subjects "die" and are reborn.

Dossa   The first child born after the birth of twins. He or she is believed to be gifted with supernatural powers.

Drapeaux   Brightly colored flags used during rituals.

Engagement   Akin to a "deal with the devil," this is a pact between a bokor and a petro loa, where a huge price is paid for the execution of some dark deed or desire.

Erzulie   The loa of beauty, love, and the moon, Erzulie is said to represent the female ideal. She is the wife of Ogoun, Legba, and Agoue, and sacrifices to her are in the form of fresh flowers, rich desserts, champagne, perfumes, candles, and white doves.

Erzulie Dantor   The dark half of Erzulie embodies jealousy and vengeance, and she is unfeeling toward females. Her symbol is a heart pierced with a dagger and her preferred sacrifice is a black pig.

Erzuile Fréda Dahomey   The conception of Erzuile as a white woman who lives in luxury.

Espirit   A raised spirit of the dead.

Fon   The language and the people of the Dahomey and Yoruba regions of West Africa. Today, it is the language primarily spoken in Benin and Togo.

Garde   A charm used to ward off curses and black magic.

Ghede   A loa of the dead, this term also describes the family of gods associated with him. He is wise, as he has accumulated the knowledge of all who have ever died. Ghede is represented as an undertaker figure dressed entirely in black, and his followers often dress as corpses or other skeletal figures.

Ginen   Pertaining to Africa, or a loa who is African in origin.

Given the Asson   When a houngan or mambo is granted the level of priest, he or she is said to have been "given the asson."

Govi   Clay pots that hold the souls of dead ancestors. These pots are burned in a ritual, which releases the souls to the land of the dead.

Grand Bois   The elusive loa of the forests and the protector of wildlife. He must be invoked before an initiate can enter the priesthood.

Grand Maître   The voodoo belief in a supreme being who created the world and is comparable to Judeo-Christian monotheistic ideas.

Gros-Bon-Ange   While this term literally means "great good angel," it represents the moment during conception where the life force enters the soul. This energy is shared by all living things. Upon death, it leaves the body and returns to the cosmos.

Hoholi   Sesame seeds which are placed in a coffin before it is buried to prevent the corpse from being tampered with by a bokor.

Hounfor   The "mystery house," sanctuary, or inner sanctum in which voodoo rituals are practiced; a voodoo temple.

Houngan   A fully initiated male priest of voodoo. One who has "received the asson" or sacred rattle used in rituals. The term is a combination of the African "Nganga" meaning "chief priest" with the prefix *houn*, a Fon term meaning "spirit."

Hounsi   A temple worker who has not yet achieved the level of houngan or mambo, generally responsible for mundane tasks. Also termed *hounsis bossale* (from *"bossale,"* meaning wild or uncultivated).

Houngenikon   A ritual assistant to a houngan or mambo.

Loa   The loa are the deities of voodoo. The term is used in both singular and plural forms. There are loa for most facets of life, as well as ones devoted to the

HOUNGAN Ken Meyer, Jr.

afterlife. The term comes from the Yoruba word for "mystery," and the collective deities are sometimes referred to as "the mysteries."

Legba The most powerful of all the loa, legba guards the barrier between the material and spiritual worlds. Because no loa can pass through this barrier without legba's permission, all ritual practices begin by invoking his spirit. His color is black, and his symbol is the cross.

Macoute   A sack made of straw carried by peasant folk and associated with Azaca, the loa of agriculture.

Mambo   A fully initiated female priestess of voodoo. One who has received the asson, or sacred rattle.

Mami Wata   Goddess of the sea, mami wata is most often represented as a beautiful woman or mermaid. She is very concerned with the health and material possessions of her followers. Those who ignore her many demands may be afflicted by barrenness or venereal disease.

Mangé Loa   In this, the most frequently performed ritual in voodoo, food or animal sacrifices are offered up to the loa. Literally, this is a "feeding of the gods." Each loa has a taste for a particular food or drink, all the better to summon the loa to the living world. When rituals are held outside, food and other offerings might be left at a crossroad or other place of significance.

Mangé Morts   This ritual is held upon the death of a houngan, mambo, or hounsi; a feast of the dead.

Mangé Sec   A ritual where only food, and not living animal sacrifices, are offered up to the loa.

Maman   The largest of the three drums used in voodoo rituals.

Mounting   The act of possession in voodoo. During rituals, a loa will "mount" the participant, seizing control of his or her body for a time.

Pé   A stone or altar located in the center of each room inside a hounfor that holds ritual items.

Peristyle   An open area where public rituals are held, covered with a simple roof and surrounded by a low wall.

Petro   The "dark loa," the petro are not evil per se, but exist to provide a balance to the loa. Most Petro rituals originated in Haiti rather than Africa. Some

VODOUN PRIESTESS Ken Meyer, Jr.

believe that the petro cult was born of the slave trade, when gods of action and aggression became necessary evils.

Sogbo   The loa of lightning and the protector of banners and flags often used in voodoo rituals. He is always accompanied by Bade, the loa of the winds. Those possessed by him throw polished stones to the ground, which are later collected and held in reverence.

Sorcière   A female bokor or sorceror.

Socle   A cement structure where offering to the various loa are placed.

Taureau-Trois-Graines   Literally, the "bull with three testicles." Those possessed by this loa are thrown to the ground in a violent rage and can only be placated by feeding them a handful of grass.

Ti-Bon-Ange   The alternate aspect to *the gros-bon-age,* this "little good angel" half of the soul is the source of one's personality, and a storehouse of all the knowledge and experiences of life.

Ti-Jean-Petro   A petro loa often depicted as a one footed dwarf. He is the protector of dark rituals, and is often called upon by those who would practice black magic.

Tonelle   A simple, makeshift peristyle held up by poles.

Traitement   An herbal cure created and administered by a houngan or mambo.

Twins   Twins are said to hold special powers because of their duality, and are recognized during every voodoo ceremony.

Verser   The act of pouring liquid on the ground as an offering to a loa.

Vodouisant   A member of a voodoo cult who has yet to be initiated, but who is permitted to participate in rituals and other activities.

Wedo   Relating to the African city of Ouhdeh in Dahomey, this term describes any loa specific to that region.

Yemaya   A goddess normally associated with Santeria rather than Voodoo, this "mother of the sea" or "mother of the fishes" is said to dress in seven blue and white skirts. She is considered to be the fountain of life, and is often depicted as a mermaid.

Zen   A pot used to prepare food as an offering to a loa.

Ze Rouge   Literally "with red eyes," this term is used to describe the actions of the petro loa.

Zétoile   The forces guiding a person's destiny that reside in the heavens.

— Chapter Thirteen —
WICCA (WITCHCRAFT, OLDE AND NEW)

WICCA IS INDEED A RELIGION filled with mystery and misinformation. In some respects unimaginably ancient in depth and scope; in others, barely thirty years old. It was only in 1974 that the American Counsel of Witches put their stamp on what would come to be known as the *Wiccan Rede*. This main Wiccan tenet is composed of eight simple words, which succinctly govern all conduct: "An it harm none, do what thou wilt." It's only a pity that those who would persecute these gentle souls couldn't take the simple sentiment to heart.

It would be doing a disservice to Wiccans to analyze their modern rites without at least a nod back to the time of the very birth of witchcraft. The Hollywood machine and religious paranoia might suggest tripping back just a few hundred years to the Middle Ages, or to imagine oneself lost in the religious fervor—and madness—of the Salem witch trials.

However, the way to the beginning is much further. The roots of witchcraft were borne of the crude social structures of the Paleolithic age—when people lived in caves and hunted and gathered their food on the open plains.

In those times many gods governed the lives of men. The appearance of the sun in the morning was the act of one god, and another caused the winds to blow. Still another god made the water flow down from the mountains to the streams nearby.

Perhaps the most important of these early deities was the god of the hunt.

For without the good graces of this divinity, there would be starvation, despite the best intentions of all other gods combined.

The fervent wishes for a successful hunt gave birth to the first religious rituals. Today we would refer to these as a type of "sympathetic magic"—the play-acting and repetition of an event in the hopes of bringing about a similar outcome in reality.

A group of hunters might test their spears on a clay mass sculpted to resemble an elusive bison. Perhaps a tribal chieftain might don an animal skin and bind branches to his head to mimic the appearance of horns. By becoming part of the hunt, the goal was easier to visualize, and in the end, hopefully, easier to obtain.

As religious crusaders of all types later made their way to the far corners of their world, it's not difficult to imagine a group of these "civilized" men stumbling upon one of these hunting rituals. It's not difficult to imagine the mixture of fear, hate, and pity this might instill. It's also not too far a stretch to imagine why Judeo-Christian demons have usually had horns.

Despite the naïveté of the worldview at the time of its conception, Wicca is sensibly polytheistic. Both a fertile maternal goddess figure and her consort, the "horned god," are acknowledged as a creation aspect, and spiritual values were assigned to inanimate objects and the elements—a practice known as animism.

This "horned god" took many forms throughout history. To the Greeks, he was Pan; the Saxons called him Woden; the Scots prayed to Dev'la. He is also known by the Celtic name of Cernunnos (or horned one) in many different manifestations of the craft.

Wiccan meetings and rituals are as much social gatherings as a chance to worship. They're also closely linked to a lunar calendar, which can be illustrated as a wheel. The eight main holidays are equidistant from one another in this circle—three of them are in the "dark half" of the year (from November to May), and three reside in the "light half" (from May to November). The remaining two holidays lie on opposite cusps between the dark and the light.

Some groups of witches, or covens, will meet weekly, others try to meet at least once monthly on the night of the full moon—for a minimum of 13 gatherings each year. These lesser gatherings are called esbats. The major holidays are called Sabbats (from the French *s'ebattre,* meaning to revel or celebrate). There are four Greater Sabbats.

Samhain, observed October 31, is traditionally a time of year to shed weaknesses and bad habits. In more agrarian times, these days were when cattle least likely to make it through the coming winter were marked for slaughter. As part of the rituals, congregants jot down unwanted personal traits onto scraps of paper, which are later consumed by flame in the hopes of purging them.

Imbolc, observed February 2, is the "festival of lights." The concept of witches flying upon brooms likely springs from an Imbolc ritual where all of those gathered "sweep" the ritual circle of that which is no longer needed.

Beltane, observed April 30, is a celebration of spring. Celebrants dance around a maypole and may drive their cattle between two columns of fire to ensure a healthy yield of milk for the coming season.

Lughnasadh, observed August 1, is a celebration of summer and all the season's bounties. There are also four lesser Sabbats: spring and autumn equinox (also called Ostara and Mabon); and summer and winter solstice (or Midsummer and Yule).

There are Wiccan versions of nearly every familiar Western religious practice. Should two witches wish to marry, there is a ceremony called "handfasting." The practice is a bit more understated than its cousins, as couples are not joined "till death do us part," but rather "for so long as love shall last."

When this love wanes, the ritual of "handparting" dissolves the relationship with far less acrimony than a traditional divorce. It allows for an agreed-upon division of property and care for any children this relationship may have produced.

Newly born witches are brought into the fold through "Wiccaning," a ritual in which a child is anointed with salt water and ceremonially passed through incense smoke. A "crossing of the bridge" may be performed upon the death of a witch.

As most Wiccans see the flesh as a vessel for the spirit and little else, there are few rules governing the disposal of remains after death. Some prefer cremation, others choose burial, and still others may even leave their body to medical research—all are equally accepted.

Wicca is closely tied with both the spiritual and natural worlds. It's no surprise then that time not spent in ritual or prayer is spent in both arcane and natural studies.

A Wiccan might practice the creation of spells and charms; meditation; the interpretation of dreams; channeling; tarot card-reading; divination; scrying (crystal-ball gazing); chiromancy (palmistry); tasseography (tea-leaf reading); reading runes; numerology; astrology; gem therapy; herbalism; botany; color magick; candle magick; love magick; sex magick; binding; protection magick; healing magick; and making wines, meads, and ale.

Sadly, it was this dedication and proficiency in their craft that first led to the persecution of witches. When prayer and skill led to a large bounty of crops while other farmers didn't enjoy similar luck, it was thought that witches caused the crops *not* to grow.

It is worthy to note that two favorite pejorative terms for "a witch" really aren't so bad at all. The term "pagan" comes from the Latin for "a denizen of the country," and "heathen" means one who dwells on the heath (an even tract of uncultivated land). These two terms might describe someone not quite urbane, but hardly evil.

Hardly evil, but hardly understood, witches were persecuted for centuries, and the bias and hatred continues on many levels to this day. King James I enacted the Witchcraft Act in 1604. While the initial act was revamped in 1736, the last laws against the practice of witchcraft were not repealed until 1951.

The following is a glossary of some important Wiccan terms and practices:

Altar   A flat surface or table where rituals are performed.

Amulet   An object charged with energies used to ward off various bad influences and spirits.

Aura   The energy field that surrounds all living things. To some, auras are visual in the form of colors that denote aspects of one's personality, emotional condition and spirituality.

Auric Healing   A healing ritual that involves the visualization of a specific color of light around the afflicted person. The choice of color depends upon the ailment. Violet and lavender have a calming effect; green, yellow, and orange are used to invigorate the subject; and dark blues soothe diseases of the blood and bodily organs.

Asperger   A device used to sprinkle water for purification in a ritual. This may be crafted of metal, or more natural materials, such as branches, may be used.

Athame   A ritual knife that serves as the main tool for creating Wiccan charms and spells. A very personal item, many practitioners choose to create their own from steel or iron rather than purchasing one. The blade is further personalized by being carved with runes or other symbols meaningful to the owner.

Bell   The sounding of a bell signifies the beginning and end of a ritual.

Beltane   From the Old Irish for "bright fire," this pagan holiday is observed April 30. The festival is a celebration of fertility and features events such as maypole dancing and bonfires.

Besom   Another term for a broomstick.

Book of Shadows   Also known as "the black book" or grimoire—this is where all the rituals, beliefs, and rules of a coven are kept. In some cases, these books are written in runic form, so that only members of the coven might read them. The item is held dear and may be passed down through generations.

Censer   An incense burner.

Constructive Magick   Magic rituals, spells, or charms that are intended for good or spiritual growth.

❧ DAUGHTERS OF ❧ THE WOLF

Prior to the sixteenth century, the Benandanti of Italy were predominantly men, though these fellows claimed that they were also werewolves. Not your mad supernatural killer werewolves, but beings of great power who fought on the side of heaven against all manner of evil. The name means "good walkers," though they were also called the "Hounds of God," and at night they would enter a trance state, adopt their werewolf forms, and descend into hell to fight the forces of evil. A number of these werewolves were tried by the Inquisition, but at least one of them, a Livonian man named Theiss, was freed after his trial because the court could not prove that he was not fighting on the right side.

From the seventeenth century on, the Benandanti went through a substantial change and nowadays most of them are female and are Italy's equivalent to the Wiccans of Ireland and Scotland. This change began in the

Friuli district of northern Italy when women who followed the "natural way" used their knowledge and powers to drive away negative energies. This battle was altered somewhat in folktales, so that it appeared to be a battle of good witches and bad witches, but that's not the case. The Benandanti were, in essence, a fertility cult who worked to protect all life from an unnatural harm.

Coven   A small group of witches, generally numbering twelve or less. The term possibly derives from "to convene."

Covenstead   A ritual chamber or any place the coven regularly meets to hold rituals.

WICCAN POWER Michael Bateson

Covendom   The area around a coven, which traditionally extends one league (about three terrestrial miles) in all directions from the covenstead.

Cowan   A term used in the Wiccan community to describe someone outside of the religion. May be considered derogatory.

Cross-Quarter Days   See MAJOR SABBATS

Deosil   A ritual movement or dancing "with the sun" (clockwise). The opposite motion is termed "widdershins."

Destructive Magick   Spells done for purposes of "evil" or personal gain, such as binding, elimination, or extermination.

Dianic Wicca   A system of Wiccan beliefs and practices centered around women.

Dowsing Rod   More commonly known as a divining rod, these forked sticks are purported to reveal sources of water or oil

Eclectic Wicca   Any Wiccan-related practices that do not follow the older wiccan traditions and are generally comprised of practices drawn from various cultures and religious and/or spiritual paths.

Equinox   The two times each year when the length of day and night is the most equal.

Esbat   Regular meetings of a coven, which is not one of the holidays. Some covens meet on the full moon, others on the new moon, and still other groups meet weekly.

Familiar   A spiritual companion of a witch. This spirit may manifest itself as a holy object or animal, such as a cat.

Gem Therapy   A ritual of healing that involves the placing of various precious and semi-precious stones upon affected areas. The stones are chosen by color.

WICCAN
Abranda Icle Sisson

Handfasting   A Wiccan marriage ceremony. Rather than being joined "till death do us part," the Handfasting ceremony joins together a bride and groom "for so long as love shall last." During this ceremony, the couple might jump over a broomstick for good luck. In modern times, this pagan ritual is often followed by a traditional wedding ceremony.

Handparting   The Wiccan ceremony of divorce. Ironically, this ritual differs little from its Western counterpart, and begins with an agreement on the division of mutual property as well as child support.

Imbolc   This pagan holiday is observed February 2. Its name comes from the Irish for "in the belly," alluding to the time of the year when sheep have their young. This festival is also called Oimelc, meaning "ewe's milk." The rite is celebrated as a festival of lights, marking the lengthening of daylight and the coming of spring. In modern Ireland, this holiday still marks the first day of spring.

Low Magick   Historically, this refers to magick and rituals performed by the lower classes of society.

Lughnasadh   Falling at the mid point between the Summer Solstice and Autumnal Equinox, this pagan holiday is observed on or around the 1st of August. It symbolizes the beginning of the harvest.

Malleus Malleficarum   Written in 1486 by Heinrich Kramer and James Springer, the "Witch's Hammer" served as a guidebook for the Inquisitors of the Middle Ages, offering methods and information on how to identify and dispatch witches. The effects of this inflammatory tome were felt for centuries after its publication.

WICCAN WITH ATHAME
Katerina Koukiotis

Moon (Waxing) The time period between the new moon through the appearance of the first quarter, ending when the moon is full. Certain spells or charms must be completed during the proper phasing of the moon.

Moon (Waning) The time period from the full moon through to the last quarter, ending with the appearance of a new moon. Certain spells or charms must be completed during the proper phasing of the moon.

Mojo Bag A small pouch or sack worn around the neck and filled with various fetish items, charms, stones, or herbs used to ward off evil or attain a certain goal.

Pentacle A five-pointed star surrounded by a circle. The points represent Spirit, Air, Water, Fire, and Earth. It is perhaps the most recognized symbol of Wicca and is often used as a theme in jewelry, t-shirts, flags, and other Wiccan memorabilia.

Pentagram Officially, this is a five-pointed star not surrounded by a circle, but often the terms pentacle and pentagram are used interchangeably.

Pranic Healing A ritual of healing that involves the transfer of "prana" (the body's vital forces) from the healer to the afflicted.

Runes Pieces of bone, stone, clay or other materials, marked with symbols, which are used for divination.

Sabbat (greater) One of the four major Wiccan holidays (See SAMHAIN, IM-BOLC, BELTANE, and LUGHNASADH).

Sabbath (lesser) Any one of the four lesser Wiccan holidays (spring and autumn equinoxes, and summer and winter solstices).

Salt Salt is used in many rituals and practices for purification

Samhain Taken from the Celtic for "summer's end," Samhain is a pagan celebration of the last harvest, observed October 31 through November 1. Traditionally at this time of year, the livestock were brought down from their summer grazing pasture, and a portion of them were marked for slaughter.

Scourge   A ritual whip sometimes employed for self-flagellation or stimulation of the chakras.

Scrying   The practice of gazing into any reflective surface for visions of the future. Crystal-ball gazing is one method of scrying, but mirrors or polished metal are also used in the practice.

Skyclad   Those who practice rituals naked, "clad" only by the sky.

Smudge Sticks   Bundles of various herbs and greens that, when burned, release a blanket of smoke, thus purifying a ritual area.

Solitary Practitioner   A witch who practices alone, without adherence to a coven. This situation might be out of choice or of necessity.

Strega   Italian witchcraft; also used as Italian for witch.

Talisman   A manmade object with magical powers, most often used to avert evil and bring good fortune to one who wears it. Talismans made by individuals for their own use are historically more powerful than those crafted by others. They may be composed of any material and gain their power by inscription or consecration.

Tarot   A deck of cards used for divination.

Warlock   Actually *not* the term for a male witch, the literal translation is "oath breaker." It is not used in Wicca.

Witchcraft Act   Passed by King James I in 1604. The declaration associated any witchcraft with the workings of the devil, and made any such acts punishable by hanging. Before this statute was enacted, such crimes were punishable by one year's imprisonment. The act was repealed in 1736. It is worthy of note, however, that laws against the practice of witchcraft in England weren't fully repealed until 1951.

Woden   The term for "god" in Saxon witchcraft

Wicanning   A pagan birth rite that welcomes newly born witches into the fold.

Widdershins   A ritual movement or dance "away from the sun" (counter-clockwise). Movement is the opposite direction is called *deosil.*

Wild Magic   A nonstandard term for wiccan-style magic used by nonwic-cans. The name is derived from role playing games (RPG) but is now often associated with real-world practices.

Witches Ladder   In destructive magic, a ritual involving the tying of forty knots into a rope to cause the death of an enemy. The rope is then hidden, and the only way to reverse the spell is to find the rope and undo all of the knots. This term also applies to a cord strung with forty beads or tied into forty knots. This then acts as an aid to counting, so the witch can concentrate on the casting of a spell.

— *Artist Index* —

MICHAEL IAN BATESON is an award-winning Web designer, artist, and illustrator. He currently resides in Denver, Colorado. Additional works can be viewed at www.michaelianbateson.com.

JASON BEAM is a story-telling illustrator of classic macabre tales. He has earned worldwide popularity, and he stands among some of the most unique artists of digital contemporary art. His frenetic attention to detail and creepy combination of sensual imagery and evocative settings give his work a graceful elegance bordering on the cryptically surreal. Jason Beam's work has been featured in numerous publications, displayed at noted galleries in Chicago, Philadelphia, Salem, and in the permanent collection in the Centre Jeanne D'Arc Museum in Orleans, France. His Web site is www.jasonbeamstudios.com.

ALAN F. BECK has been an artist, designer, and illustrator for over thirty years, doing work for many major corporations including book covers and magazine illustrations. His award-winning work has been exhibited in shows and Science Fiction/Fantasy conventions all across the U.S. and has won numerous awards and honors. Alan is a member of the Association of Science Fiction Artists and the Brooklyn Artists Coalition.

LILIAN BROCA is a Canadian visual artist. For thirteen years she was a Fine Arts Faculty member at Kwantlen College, teaching Painting and Drawing. Her art career spans thirty-four years, during which she has had more than 65 exhibitions in many parts of Canada, the U.S., and Europe. Her work is included in important private and public collections around the world. Broca received the Lorenzo Il Magnifico gold medal in the 2003 Florence Biennale International Exhibition. Visit her Web site: www.lilianbroca.com.

BILL CHANCELLOR has been doing covers for *Cult Movies Magazine* for years, specializing in classic monsters from the Universal Pictures era, as well as photo-real paintings of Vincent Price as Dr. Phibes, *Star Wars,* and even the Three Stooges. He has also done DVD covers for cult horror films such as *The Asphyx,* and the legendary black vampire movie *Ganja and Hess.* E-mail: bchance104@aol.com; Website: members.tripod.com/~chancellor35.

DAVID CROSTON says, "Even though I have mainly done pencil portraits throughout my life, what I love to produce is science-fiction art due to my belief in possible life elsewhere in the universe."

DOUGLAS EGOLF is a self-taught artist from Columbia City, Indiana. Doug enjoys creating covers and logos for bands and painting wall murals. He is also fascinated with all things paranormal. Egolf is a field investigator for MUFON Indiana. The basis for his art is to shine a light on subjects that often remain hidden from the minds of the average person. He can be contacted at Projekt_e2001@yahoo.com or through his Web site at projektegolf. freehosting.net.

HERVÉ SCOTT FLAMENT is the grandson of the clown John Scott who traveled throughout Europe with the Australian Circus in the early part of the twentieth century. Hervé was born in Paris on February 1, 1959. He began studies in the natural sciences intending to become either a paleontologist or a zoologist, but he changed paths in 1977 when the punk movement unfurled in the Western world. He started playing guitar a few months before and dedicated the next ten years of his life to music. He played with several French punk bands and set up the group Ici Paris who recorded one LP and four singles. New interests carried him into uncharted directions, and he began to paint. He immediately sold his first paintings, which inspired him to devote more of his time towards his new endeavor. Hervé taught himself to paint and brought back an ancient painting technique that no present art school could have taught him. Visit his Web site: www.scottflament.com.

ADAM GARLAND lives in British Columbia where he teaches in the digital animation field. His abiding interest in fantasy and the gothic side of art is reflected in his artwork. E-mail: cowsmanaut@hotmail.com.

KATHY GOLD is a science-fiction and fantasy digital artist and storyteller. Her art, created using computer software, is designed to tell a story, whether it's part of a series or a single work. Kathy was born in Budapest, Hungary and immigrated to the United States at age six. Being a shy, only child, she turned to her imagination and creativity as an outlet to express her feelings. Besides writing, acting, and singing, Kathy also paints with oils, mainly landscapes. Kathy's graphic novels can be downloaded from centaurgirl.com.

MORBIDEUS W. GOODELL is an artist and illustrator living in Maine with his wife and two children. Morbideus and wife, Dee, also own and run Postmortem Productions of Maine: www.Postmortem-Prod.com. They sell T-shirts, prints of Morbideus's artwork and Dee's photography. E-mail: Morbideus@Postmortem-Prod.com or Morbideus@MorbideusGallery.com; Web site: www.Morbideus Gallery.com.

ANDY JONES was born in England and currently lives in North Wales. Andy is a wildlife artist and recently expanded into digital art. He produces fantasy/horror illustrations, including concept art for movies. E-mail: agj71@hotmail .com; Web site: andy—jones.gfxartist.com/artworks.

FRAN KIRSCH is an art therapist and photographer from Pennsylvania.

SHAREEN KNIGHT is a painter, writer, and landscape photographer who, after an earlier life in California, now lives in a remote part of British Columbia.

With her dog and two cats, she is renovating a 1910 farmhouse, enjoying organic gardening, and keeping the bears out of her orchard.

KATERNINA KOUKIOTIS is a self taught traditional artist from Queens, N.Y. who has always believed that fantasy art is a way to escape from reality and bring the magic of dreams into the waking world. Visit her Web site: katerina art.com or contact her at katerinaart@aol.com.

JONATHAN MABERRY is a professional writer and writing teacher. He has contributed artwork to a number of books and magazines over the last thirty years. Limited editions of his pencil work are available on his Web sites: ghostroadblues.com and www.vampireuniverse.com.

KEN MEYER, JR. has worked as an illustrator for twenty years, working in comics, paper, and online games, educational media, books, magazines, and more. He has appeared in seven volumes of *Spectrum,* the best SF/Fantasy art of the year, *Heavy Metal Magazine* and more. He produces the Tori Amos calendar each year for the RAINN organization. Commissions are available and freelance work is encouraged. E-mail: kenmeyerjr@comcast.net; Web site: www.kenmeyerjr.com/portfolio.

LEE MOYER is an award-winning artist who has been featured in *Spectrum 12, D'Artiste-Digital Painting, Design Graphics Magazine,* and in the Smithsonian Institution's Natural History Museum. Clients include: Paramount Pictures, 20th Century-Fox, Sony Pictures, The Discovery Channel, Electronic Arts, Hasbro, Pharmacopeia, Career Builder, BET, McGraw-Hill, Philips Media, Dark Horse Entertainment, and the National Zoo. He lives in Portland, Oregon, with his talented photographer wife, Annaliese, and their dog, Lego.

LEO PLAW is a self-taught artist who has worked in many artistic fields, from video production and computer games to ceramic designs and oil paintings. His work has also been exhibited in Sydney and Brisbane and published internationally. Additionally, he has sold his artwork at countless markets and festivals. Leo has worked with local and international bands, creating swirls of light and color with video art. Leo has worked with the likes of George, Full Fathom Five, On Inc. Salmonella Dub (NZ), and the Mad Professor (UK). His psychedelic lights shows have also been featured in a number of dance parties. Leo left for Europe in 2003 and began a studio in Berlin. He also had the chance to meet with artists affiliated with the Vienna School of Fantastic Realism. He recently relocated to London.

NATASCHA ROEOESLI was born and raised in Switzerland, the daughter of two photographers. She currently lives in Greece, working as a freelance illustrator and concept artist for gaming companies as well as for private clients and authors and publishers. Her award-winning art has been published in several books and magazines and is seen on popular trading cards. She has been featured in Ballistic Publishing's *Exotique* and 3Dtotal's *Digital Art Masters*. Her Web site is www.tascha.ch; E-Mail: n@tascha.ch; projects@tascha.ch.

RITA ISABEL SANCHO is from Portugal and lives in a calm city known as Viseu. Currently she's living with her parents and finishing high school, studying multimedia. She is known as Acida through art sites such as GFXartist.com, Shadowness.com, deviantART.com. She has had a passion for art for many years since she was very little. Besides photo manipulation, Rita is exploring the world of photography and painting. Actually she's working for .psdmag, a Polish magazine.

JENNIFER SINGLETON is a fantasy artist from Australia who was drawn to the world of faery at an early age and still spends her spare time painting and drawing elves, faeries, witches, vampires, and any wonderful creature of dark, otherworldly beauty. Her Web site is www.twilightwhispers.com

ABRANDA ICLE SISSON is an illustrator specializing in fantasy and mythical illustration. She draws from her Celtic ancestry to create vibrantly colored works of art in watercolor and acrylic. She has illustrated children's literature, won several art awards, and been a member of the Masters of Fantasy collection. Abranda currently runs her professional art studio, MuddVision at www.muddvision.com in Washington with her beautiful daughter.

SARA JO WEST is a book editor and photographer originally from Long Island. Currently she lives in Pennsylvania. West is a founding partner of Career Doctor for Writers (www.careerdoctorforwriters.com).

SAM WEST-MENSCH is a history major at Northeastern University. His love of the ancient world has led him to take journeys around the world.